UNDECIDED

How to Ditch
the Endless Quest
for Perfect and
Find the Career—
and Life—That's
Right for You

BARBARA KELLEY AND SHANNON KELLEY

SEAL PRESS

UNDECIDED
How to Ditch the Endless Quest for Perfect and
Find the Career—and Life—That's Right for You

Copyright © 2011 by Barbara Kelley and Shannon Kelley

Published by
Seal Press
A Member of the Perseus Books Group
1700 Fourth Street
Berkeley, California

Library of Congress Cataloging-in-Publication Data

Kelley, Barbara Bailey, 1948-
  Undecided : how to ditch the endless quest for perfect and find the career
(and life) that's right for you / by Barbara and Shannon Kelley.
    p. cm.
  ISBN 978-1-58005-341-9
  1. Women—Vocational guidance. 2. Vocational guidance. I. Kelley, Shannon, 1975- II. Title.
  HF5382.6.K45 2011
  650.1—dc22

                                    2010045416

9 8 7 6 5 4 3 2 1

Cover and interior design by Domini Dragoone
Printed in the United States of America
Distributed by Publishers Group West

We dedicate this book to anyone
who's ever made a decision for us.

CONTENTS

The events, facts, and conversations presented in this book are true and based upon our own reporting and personal experiences. To protect the privacy of all the undecided women who so freely shared their stories with us, we have referred to them by fictional first names. In rare cases, we've also altered minor details.

References to "Shannon" and "Barbara" refer to the authors of this book.

UNCHARTED TERRITORY

'Would you tell me, please, which way I ought to go from here?' asked Alice. 'That depends a good deal on where you want to get to,' said the Cat.
—from *Alice in Wonderland*

AS GOOD IDEAS OFTEN ARE, this one was born of sweat and booze.

We began this trek on the Dipsea Trail, a notorious Northern California hike that starts in Mill Valley, a small town just past the Golden Gate Bridge. The trail begins with a wicked climb up 650 steps carved into a hillside and ends a brutal (and lovely) seven miles later (and after a 2,200-foot climb and descent) on the other side of Mount Tamalpais, at the tiny town of Stinson Beach on the coast of the Pacific Ocean.

We'd begun the day talking about a phenomenon we'd noticed again and again in women of the postfeminist generation—a general malaise with symptoms that are a combination of "analysis paralysis," "grass is greener" syndrome, and a sense that there are far too many choices to deal with. It was a mystery, yet it seemed an indisputable touchstone of the zeitgeist: women who, despite apparently having it all (good education, great job, cool place to live), are miserable. And for a reason they seem unable to quite put their finger on.

Sure, it could be easy to dismiss these ladies as spoiled. Here they have everything their mothers had ever dreamed of. And yet, the angst is real. *And* universal. These are women who were bred for success. And seem to be miserable because of it.

By the time we'd come down the mountain and crawled to the nearest bar to grab a beer (it was a sunny day in September, after all; it practically demanded an ice-cold Hefeweizen with a slice of lemon), we knew we wanted to explore this phenomenon. And later that night—as often happens when you combine an exhausting hike, iced knees, and a glass or two (okay, maybe three) of pinot noir—an idea took shape.

This mystery, let's investigate it. Talk to these women. Find the research. What are the causes? Is there a fix? We wanted to connect the dots. Get to the bottom of what seemed to be a generational epidemic of chronic indecision. And invite the reader along for the ride.

As backstory, Barbara had written a short op-ed on "choice overload" for the *Christian Science Monitor* a few months before, noting what she'd noticed in her students, her kids, their friends, and her friends' kids. The op-ed was picked up by her university's alumni magazine, and the response was overwhelming: "That's me!" "That's my daughter!"

But, Shannon insisted during that hike, just documenting the malaise in an eight-hundred-word editorial piece couldn't even scratch the surface. It's so juicy, she said. Let's dig deeper, lots deeper. Let's get to the bottom of it. And thus, *Undecided* was born.

And soon, it took on a life of its own.

And once it began taking shape, Shannon too found the response to be torrential. Her friends, their friends, near-strangers she'd meet at a party, would all pull her aside to confess: This *thing* you're talking about, this book you're writing. That's me!

We'd tapped a universal issue and we knew it. A few months later, we started our blog on the subject, and from day one were rewarded with comments—some funny, some heartfelt, all breathtakingly honest—from women throughout the country, weighing in on the ways in which they felt sabotaged, by everything from the opportunities (and mirages) of a postfeminist society to their own expectations.

Once we started our trip, our investigation took several routes. The first was shared experience: We talked to hundreds of women—Millennials, Gen-Xers, Baby Boomers—across the country and listened to their stories. We dug into the research to understand what goes on in our brains when we try to choose between Door No. 1 and Door No. 2—and why no matter what we choose, we're often dissatisfied. We explored the very nature of happiness, and why it can be so elusive. We explored why it is we sometimes find ourselves caught up in the chase for the symbols of someone else's definition of success. We talked to the experts, both the folks in the trenches and academics, too: men and women who could explain some of the issues—societal and otherwise—that underlie our dissatisfaction, and who could offer insight, perspective, even solutions.

We thought deeply (okay, and argued, too) about the weight of great expectations, the insidious lie of "having it all," and the illusion of unlimited options on women who had not yet learned to deal with them.

What we found were growing pains: It may be great to have options, but until we learn how to deal with them, life can be a bitch.

We also found prescriptives, including the route to the simplest and yet most profound remedy of them all: Know yourself.

Along the way, we came across a couple of media firestorms—an idea that if women were unhappy, well, feminism was to blame. What we found was that if anything, feminism hasn't gone far enough: We're living in an unchanged world whose reality turns out to be a far cry from the messaging we're fed. (We'll go there.)

New research also surfaced, implying that twentysomethings are in the throes of a new stage of development. Dubbed "emerging adulthood," it's marked by a reluctance to commit. While there is some credence to that (we'll go there too), we think the root of all this angst goes way deeper.

We also were asked, more times than we can count, why this dissatisfaction, this indecision, was a *woman's* issue. Weren't young men equally undecided, dissatisfied? Equally stressed out? *Why women?* To which we answered: It's generational. Men have been raised for generations to go, seek and conquer; to succeed in a workplace designed expressly by and for them. For women, there's a layer of newness to it all: We're going forth without either a net or enough role models to pave the way. Sure, men can be equally angsty in the face of choices, and we appreciate that, but for women, this angst, this indecision, this trial and error is a product of less than fifty years of progress. It's uncharted territory. (Don't believe us? Ask your mother. Or your grandmother.) We're hacking our way through a landscape that proves, time and again, that the reality doesn't quite measure up to the rose-colored image we expect.

In fact, because this is a generational issue, we think that our collaboration on this book (with all the discussions, arguments, and attempts to see things through each other's eyes) results in a more complete picture. You, dear reader, are not getting one perspective or the other, but rather a shared perspective that offers a deeper, richer, and more textured analysis than either one of us could have offered on our own.

Which brings us to some questions we've been asked, over and over: "What's it like for a mother and daughter to work together? And who's the boss?"

To which we would have to say, you know, we're undecided.

BARBARA KELLEY
SHANNON KELLEY
AUGUST 2010

Simplicity is making the journey of this life with just
enough baggage.
—Charles Dudley Warner

ONE

YOU ARE HERE

You take your life in your own hands, and what happens?
A terrible thing: No one to blame.
—Erica Jong

WHEN WE FIRST CATCH UP WITH thirty-year-old Hannah—a pint-sized blond with intense eyes and a wide smile—she's at home in her New York City apartment, studying for the GRE, the generic entrance exam for graduate school. This would be unremarkable except for the fact that until a week and a half ago, she was studying for the GMAT, the specific entrance exam for business school. In fact, she went through the entire Kaplan GMAT prep course—which she decided to do after initially signing up for the Kaplan GRE prep course in the hopes of earning a Master of Public Administration (MPA) degree . . . and then, two classes into it, changing her mind.

Confused? So is she.

After this last and hopefully final change of heart, she is now planning, once again, to earn an MPA, and to then parlay that degree into a job in ecotourism, voluntourism, or a cultural exchange program like Unesco because, she says, travel is all she's ever wanted to do—especially after spending her entire junior year of college abroad. But back then, she says, "I didn't think there was any possible way that it could be a career, that I could travel for my whole life. My parents are conservative; me and my sister were raised, like, you find a good job—you have one job after college, and that's all you do."

So, convinced that a career in travel was too pie-in-the-sky, she pursued a career in fashion (itself pretty lofty) with single-minded focus: while still an undergrad at UCLA, she cold-called Hollywood stylists and other industry players and eventually scored internships at Hugo Boss and Saks Fifth Avenue, as well as a job with a stylist for the MTV Movie Awards. After college, she moved to New York; a few years later, she was an assistant market editor at *Vogue*.

She was no doubt living out the very fantasy that countless other girls had deemed too pie-in-the-sky—and the sort of American Dream her parents may have been chasing when they immigrated to the United States from Slovakia when she was six. Yet before long, she found herself a little antsy, a little bored, a little distracted by what she *wasn't* doing. So she took a different position—as associate fashion editor—where she was fulfilled both in terms of creative expression and in terms of travel, producing six-figure photo shoots in far-flung destinations, dressing the likes of George Clooney, Jennifer Aniston, and Kate Hudson. She also found fulfillment in getting her fashion fix—she was granted access to the iconic "clothes closet," where designer duds were hers for the borrowing. (Swoon.) Even her anal-retentive side was fulfilled by the huge amount of organization required to pull off such large-scale spectacles.

It was almost perfect.

So she quit.

Thinking she should maybe explore the business side of the industry, she took a job as a buyer at Bergdorf Goodman. Hated it.

"I lasted six weeks before I quit," she says with a rueful laugh.

But *Elle* was hiring and offered her a market editor position. "So I went back to editorial work, thinking I would like it more because it was a different position than I had at *Vogue*. I thought I would like it, and I kind of did, but the work environment was awful . . . the infrastructure wasn't what I was used to after being at *Vogue*."

Unfortunately—or, to hear her tell it today, fortunately—she became a casualty of a restructuring not long after taking the job.

"I was laid off and I didn't care," she says. "I packed my bags and left for Asia for four months. . . . When I left, I was like, I don't want to go back into fashion, I don't like the industry, I don't like the players, it's not fulfilling enough. I was very much wondering, what's on the other side of the fence? So when I went to Asia, I didn't even think about it. I just knew that I loved traveling more than anything on the planet."

Case closed, right? Hardly.

Immediately upon her return, she started to panic about being unemployed, so she put out her feelers. Not surprisingly, after having spent her entire career in the fashion industry, those feelers snagged her yet another job in the world of high fashion, this time at the label Theory—where she was again laid off, five days shy of her thirtieth birthday.

And that brings us to her plans to take the GRE, apply to grad school, earn an MPA, and, at long last, find a way to make travel a part—a *big* part—of her career.

Yet despite the fact that travel is her passion and she's come up with a coherent vision for a career in the travel industry, she continues to second-guess herself. "I was back and forth between an MPA and an MBA for weeks," Hannah moans.

She started out on the path to the MPA and the life she'd always dreamed about, signing up for Kaplan's GRE prep course. She stuck with it for two classes. And then she panicked.

"I got nervous that I made the wrong decision," she says. "So I emailed a girlfriend of mine who worked in finance and said to her, 'Oh my god, I don't know what to do, MBA or MPA.' And she said MBA. Why I listened to her I have no idea. She's not me; I don't want to be in that world; it's just not my environment. But I went to Kaplan and changed to the GMAT prep course. And then I went all the way through the class and went so far as to sign up for the GMAT. And then, about a week and a half ago, I changed my mind. I thought, what am I doing? I don't want to be doing this. And now I'm taking the GRE; I'm studying for it now."

Hannah talks as quickly as she changes direction. She's clearly smart, motivated, and successful. She's also thoughtful, reflective, and completely convinced that there's something seriously wrong with her. She peppers her story with self-lamentations and analyses: "Why am I like this?" "I don't know what my problem is." "I have a tendency to leap before I look." "I am a walking contradiction."

"The grass is always greener," she says. "Like, do I want to move to San Francisco? Colorado? South America? Will life be any better in any of those places? Probably not. But it might be, so there's that risk that I'm taking by not moving." And something in her tone suggests that she's not simply throwing out random examples. In fact, it sounds as though, just by putting voice to the options, she might be convincing herself that these are other avenues that she needs to explore. Like, right now.

It's that fear of missing out that's the killer. "My biggest problem is I don't want to *not* do something. . . . I need to do everything," she says.

"It's just having so many options, and wanting to do all of them. And feeling like I can and I should and I will do everything that has been afforded to me."

It's a sentiment that's easy to relate to. So much so, in fact, that it's easy to forget that this woman was working at *Vogue,* literally putting clothes on the back of George Clooney. She was living the dream, excelling at the career she'd fought for, the proverbial job a million girls would kill for. Hannah had it all—and it was exactly what she'd always wanted—or what she thought she did. But contentment eluded her. Those doubts, those frustrations—they nagged at her. They still do.

COMMITMENT PHOBIA. ANALYSIS paralysis. Grass-is-greener syndrome. You name it, Hannah's plagued by it. But she's not alone. Far from it. She's a poster girl for the current zeitgeist: Unlike her mother, she was born of a generation blessed with limitless choices—and of a generation that has found that the more choices you have, the harder it is to find happiness. It's a generation that appears to have everything yet can't help feeling that things are just not right.

You might call it an epidemic, a sign of the times for American women. Take Sarah, for example, a twenty-nine-year-old lawyer making well into the six figures only a few years out of law school. She wants only one thing: sweet escape from practicing law. Ask her about it, and she'll claim to have no idea why she ever even applied to law school in the first place—indeed, that she never really wanted to be a lawyer. And yet apply she did, and she found herself at a second-tier law school. She ranked in the top ten of her class, making the law review and ultimately scoring a gig with a big high-end law firm—quite a coup, as very few firms bother recruiting at law schools below the first tier. She's made a huge amount of money from the start but has never liked what she does—has actually pretty thoroughly hated much of the work, spending a significant chunk of her time keeping her fingers crossed that she'll never have to go into court. Raised in California by parents who vacationed at their wine country ranch and vineyard, what Sarah really wants to do is open a wine bar. Her fondest hope is to get laid off—with a severance package, of course.

And then there's Jane, twenty-seven. Worried that only "perfect" will do, she has yet to commit to anything other than a series of uninspiring jobs since graduating from college. This is not for lack of trying, however. Over the years, she's spent lots of time investigating possible careers and grad schools. She took a summer course in the business school at Stanford and conducted countless "informational interviews" with people who seem happy in their careers, gathering information from journalists, lawyers, and entrepreneurs so that she'd be armed to make an informed decision. Perhaps too informed.

As Malcolm Gladwell explained in his book *Blink,* "too much information" isn't just a clever expression—the best decisions are often the ones made before giving yourself too much time to think.[1] And he's not the only one to have found that a clogged mind is a confused mind: The classic 1950s "Magical Number Seven" study showed that the human brain can hold seven bits of information in working memory at any given time.[2] Any more, and things can get dicey.

We'll get deeper into the science of decision making in Chapter 5, but here's a taste: In another study, participants were asked to memorize either seven digits or two; then they were offered their choice of a snack—fruit or "gooey chocolate cake." And guess what happened? Those whose brains were maxed out with seven numbers let the emotional side of their brains do the deciding and overwhelmingly chose cake. But the two-digit folks had some room for reason: They chose fruit.[3] So basically, when the brain is cluttered with too much information, emotions drive our choices. Ergo, the bigger the cognitive load we're carrying at any given time, the less able we are to think rationally.

As for Jane, she continued to bounce. She applied to business school. She applied to law school. She didn't get in on one count; decided not to go on the other. So overwhelmed by the choices that confronted her, she once confided that she wished she had grown up in a culture where everything, from spouse to career, would be chosen for her.

And then there's Melissa, thirty-eight, who took on whatever was asked of her at a string of jobs, ascending into the upper echelons of project management at large companies ranging from HBO to Microsoft. She recently went back to school to pursue her passion, earning a master's in counseling. She splits her time between several different centers and the local hospital, ferociously logging the hours required for her certificate. But once she gets it, she has no idea what she'll do with it. Private practice? Take it back to corporate America? She doesn't know and often worries that this detour into work she clearly loves is steering her away from work society tells her she is supposed to do, thereby knocking her out of competition for anything but mediocrity. "I just feel like I should be more . . . successful," she says. It's as though she fears she can't have both—her passion *and* success—making the choice to change directions in pursuit of her passion all the more terrifying.

WHAT IS THE matter with these women?

They should be stoked. But instead they're stressed. Restless. Stuck in a cycle where they're constantly second-guessing themselves and looking over their shoulders. And they can't quite figure out why.

Their mothers are left scratching their heads, wondering what's with their daughters, who have more options than they ever dreamed possible. Said Sharon, a sixty-something mother who came of age during the opening strains of the women's movement: "When I was your age, women had three options: teacher, secretary, nurse. You don't know how lucky you are!"

Indeed, for the first time for American women, most all of the doors are open. In fact, the landscape of today would be scarcely recognizable to the feminists of the second wave. In a post-postfeminist, post–*Sex & the City*, post-Facebook world, recent years have seen us riding an unprecedented economic rollercoaster against the background of some amazing firsts: The first female presidential candidate. The first female speaker of the house. The first female vice-presidential candidate on the Republican ticket. And, whether it's because of the tanking economy (and the fact that more men than women lost their jobs, a phenomenon dubbed the "mancession") or because of life itself, women now make up more than half of the workforce. And yet what we see is that increased options go hand in hand with increased angst.

Take Lauren—a writer, editor, and reader of our blog—who left this comment: "Yes, I swim in a sea of confusion over my options! Being a woman who feels she is unlimited, I've spent too much time debating my opportunities instead of picking one path and sticking with it. I can't complain; life has been good. I do, however, feel concern that I might be overlooking the one thing that is my 'calling.' From orchestra conductor to herpetologist to cartographer to photographer to writer, I've wanted to do it all. I also know that I can; we all can."

Or this one, from Melissa: "My sister used to tease me that I was on the semester system in life because I was always moving and changing jobs. But really I was just worried that I was missing my 'true calling' or not doing enough to fulfill my parents' expectations after all that schooling. (Come to find out later that their only expectation was that I be happy.) Now I'm almost forty and starting yet another new career (this one will be the *one* . . . I hope). Looking back, I can see how the choices and self-inflicted expectations led to a major paralysis in my midtwenties."

It's like the dirty little secret that nobody's talking about, but everybody's keeping. Call it one big growth spurt, with much of this unspoken angst revolving around the pressure to choose, something old-school feminists might never have predicted.

Slowly, allusions to this syndrome are starting to emerge. There's this commentary on an item from an online installation from the International Museum of Women: "The wide variety of opportunities available to young women today is liberating for some, but for others it can be a source of confusion. . . . With so many different opportunities and life paths to choose from, how do you know which is right for you?"[4] Or this, from a *Salon* post about Rachel Lehmann-Haupt's book *In Her Own Sweet Time*: "The downside of having too many choices, it seems to me, is that it can make it hard to know when the time has come to choose just one."[5] Or this, from the recent best-selling novel *Commencement,* in which one character sums it up tidily: "They were the first generation of women whose struggle with choice had nothing to do with getting it and everything to do with having too much of it—there were so many options that it felt impossible and exhausting to pick the right ones."[6]

And that angst is only magnified because these feelings are so at odds with the conventional wisdom with which today's young women were raised: *All these choices—what a blessing! You can be anything you want! You can do anything you want! You don't know how lucky you are to live in an era marked by the number of open doors you have before you!*

You. Can. Have. It. All.

But, given that mantra, is it any wonder we can't commit? That, as Chloe, a thirty-one-year-old art director at an alt-newsweekly put it, "For our generation, commitment is like a kind of death"? Could this be why the average tenure of college-educated women between the ages of twenty-five and thirty-four in any one job is only 2.6 years, according to the U.S. Bureau of Labor Statistics?[7] Or why a recent Pew Research survey found that 65 percent of women classify themselves as "movers" rather than "stayers," and 45 percent of those who have moved say they will move again?[8]

We've learned not to settle. After all, thanks to feminism's successes, thanks to the women who gave voice to their dissatisfaction and drove the changes of the first and the second waves, women today are free—no, encouraged—no, *expected*—to seek out "better." Which is great . . . mostly. But the lure of "better," the implicit promise of "better"—well, that's where it gets tricky.

Neither does it help that, while we've been stuck in neutral, stunned in the face of so many options—much like the kid cut loose in the candy store—an idea started to gain traction: A job ceased to be just a job; now it had to have meaning, too.

A ho-hum nine-to-fiver that reliably pays the bills? You can do better than that! Find your true calling—only then will you know bliss! Living your truth will bring you success!

Call it the spiritualization of the career world. And the influences driving this frantic search for meaning are everywhere, from President Obama—who has called on youth to engage with the community—to the growing number of university initiatives that encourage (and in many cases, require) students to participate in community-based learning programs and to consider careers in public service after they graduate in order to foster a spirit of "giving back." The message is that they should work to make a difference—and not only after hours, but while they're on the clock. Throw that into the mix, and suddenly a job is more than just a means to put food on the table—a job represents your calling.

Are we so desperate to make meaning from our jobs, to choose something we love, because work—no longer relegated to the nine-to-five routines of generations past—has leaked into our home lives? Is it because we women, newly welcomed into the world of work, have come to believe it is the wellspring of personal meaning, that our newfound entrée into professional life defines us? Or is this all part of the American ethic of individuality, the inalienable right to pursue our own happiness?

Whatever the reason, once you add to the smorgasbord of choices the desire for a heavy side dish of meaning, the decision of which path to choose becomes infinitely more layered, and infinitely more fraught.

SO YEAH, WE are in the midst of a great experiment indeed. The bottom line is that—regardless of age or circumstance, and for all kinds of reasons—women are universally overwhelmed. But can all of this angst also be a catalyst for opportunity? And if so, how do we seize it?

A nice place to start might be in recognizing our shared experience, and considering where we've come from. As *Boston Globe* columnist Ellen Goodman put it, "On college campuses where women take rights for granted, many shy away from the F-word as if it were a dangerous brand. A second narrative has taken hold in many parts of the culture that says one generation's feminism made the next generation unhappy." She goes on to say, "There is talk about too many pressures and too many choices. It's as if the success of feminism was to blame, rather than its unfinished work. Indeed it took Mary Cheney to offer bracing words at a recent Barnard College gathering: 'This notion that women today are overwhelmed with choices, my God, my grandmother would have killed to have these choices.'"[9]

She probably would have. But what grandma didn't realize—couldn't have realized—was how it would feel to have all of these options laid out before her . . . and to have to make up her mind, to pick one. And now, women like Jane—who have reaped the benefits of the feminist movement but who have no personal connection to the struggle that earned those benefits—are experiencing the other side of the same coin, waxing nostalgic for an optionless world whose limits they've never known.

Going back isn't the answer; but that doesn't mean our work here is finished. Just getting access to all these paths was the first step, but while feminism's momentum carried us to this point—with all the open doors women had hoped for—something stalled along the way. And now we're stuck, idling, at a collective crossroads, "suffering some collective growing pains," as feminist icon Germaine Greer put it in a 2009 interview on WBUR.[10] The end of the road isn't behind us—we're in the midst of a movement that's still got some serious work to do.

In the meantime, though, isn't it ironic? We got the options we fought for but ran out of gas before we learned to embrace our right to seize these choices with enthusiasm and confidence. Instead we're angsty. Antsy. And we want to know: Now what? Where do we go from here?

Modern psychology offers some interesting takes. For instance, some of this inability to make a choice—and to be happy with it—may have to do with how we define success, the very nature of contentment, and our ineptitude at predicting our own happiness. Researchers in affective science, such as UC Berkeley psychologist Dacher Keltner, highlight connections between happiness, compassion, and altruism, suggesting that society's conventional definitions of success—you know, the fat bank account, the 2.1 kids, the white picket fence—may be all wrong.[11] And in his book *Stumbling on Happiness,* Harvard psychologist Daniel Gilbert found that the brain is woefully out of its element when it attempts to imagine the future; yes, humans are better at it than any other creature, but our brains are still mightily consumed with the present. Gilbert says that's why decisions based on how we think we'll feel, or what we think we'll want, or what we think will make us happy are all nothing more than blind guesses, guesses that the brain makes based on how we're feeling now. And for that reason, in experiment after experiment, Gilbert found that those decisions were almost always wrong; that, indeed, we humans know very little about the hearts and minds of the people we are about to become.[12]

So how on earth are we supposed to make the kinds of choices that will affect us for years to come? Some advise giving your long-term goals priority and having patience; others challenge that notion, proposing that we mere mortals are categorically incapable of getting beyond the here-and-now, of delaying gratification. In *What Should I Do with My Life?* Po Bronson writes, "Finding what we believe in and what we can do about it is one of life's great dramas. . . . Don't cling to a single scenario, allow yourself many paths. . . . Give it a lifetime to pay off. Things you work hardest for are the things you will most treasure."[13]

Great advice, right?

But here's yet another snag: Behavioral economists, such as Harvard's David Laibson, have found that when making choices, we tend to misimagine the future—to inflate our future-self's powers of organization, time management, and willpower. As he told *Harvard Magazine,* "If you ask people, 'Which do you want now, fruit or chocolate?' they say, 'Chocolate!' But 'Which one a week from now?' they will say, 'Fruit.' Now we want chocolate, cigarettes, and a trashy movie. In the future, we want to eat fruit, quit smoking, and watch Bergman films."[14] (Talk about an inability to accurately imagine ourselves in the future! Have you ever seen a Bergman film? Everyone smokes. Future self would need willpower of epic proportions.)

All of which leaves women like Hannah, Sarah, Jane, and Melissa unhappily idling at crossroads of their own. And what they're feeling is real. It's everywhere. And it's issues large and small.

For Hannah, even shopping is a loaded metaphor. "My friend and I will be in a store, and she'll be like, 'Do you like these jeans?' I'm like, 'Yeah,' and she's like, 'Great, I'll buy them.' And I'm like, 'How could you do that? What about all these other jeans?'"

It's interesting that Hannah brought up shopping—although, given her past life spent in the clothes closet at *Vogue* magazine, not entirely surprising—because shopping for jeans is a favorite metaphor of Swarthmore psychologist Barry Schwartz, who penned the pivotal book *Paradox of Choice*.[15] (Full disclosure: Schwartz was shopping for jeans at the Gap; Hannah . . . not so much.) Schwartz found the experience of standing before a wall of options so overwhelming as to leave him longing for the days when jeans came in only one style—and not an especially flattering style at that. Yes, even a relatively frumpy college professor was stumped by denim-option overload. In his book, Schwartz talks not only about how having so many choices makes picking one a million times harder than it should be, but also about how, in the face of so many options, there's no way *not* to come out of the store worrying that the perfect pair was actually one of the ones he'd discarded on the dressing room floor, or one of the ones he never even got around to trying on. He calls that "opportunity cost." We call it those nagging daydreams about the road not traveled.

Of course, Schwartz thinks some of us are more prone to dissatisfaction than others, which has to do with whether you are a Maximizer—

always in search of the best—or a Satisficer, who looks only for "good enough." One study categorized job-hunting college seniors as either Maximizers or Satisficers and found that the Maximizers found better jobs—but a year later were more worried, overwhelmed, and depressed than their "good enough" peers—and less satisfied.[16] The researchers found that even when Maximizers get what they want, they may not always want what they get, leading many to conclude that, when all is said and done, the choice is ours: We can have either a happy, vanilla life, or an interesting—if perhaps less happy—one where all of the thirty-one flavors are on the menu. If choices are what we're after, we'll probably find them. But, time and again, the women we've spoken to report the same experience: Choices make life hard. So, do difficulty and challenge necessarily equate to unhappiness? And if so, does seeking out lots of choices necessarily make us gluttons for punishment?

Many other psychologists have demonstrated the oh-so inconvenient truth that applies to all of us: When faced with a dizzying array of choices, the result is often stress, regret, paralysis, and dissatisfaction. There was the iconic jam study, out of Stanford and Columbia, which tested two displays of jam in a grocery store. One featured six varieties; the other, twenty-four. More customers flocked to the latter, but ten times as many actually bought jam from the former. Ten times![17] WNYC's *Radiolab* illustrated the choice conundrum by sending two reporters to choose the perfect apple from an overwhelmingly large display at a grocery store—they sweated their decisions and wound up sorely disappointed with their picks.[18] Jonah Lehrer, author of *How We Decide,* told NPR's Terry Gross that the impetus for his book was his struggle to choose which kind of Cheerios to buy in the grocery store one day.[19] (Not which kind of cereal. Which kind of *Cheerios.*)

It's fascinating stuff—and in Chapter 5 we'll take a deeper look at how our brains are wired and at the science of the choice conundrum.

As for all those studies, they make a lot of sense, and we certainly know the feeling . . . but these guys are talking about jam and jeans, apples and Cheerios. And the angst they found is measurable. But now, extrapolate that stress, that overwhelm, that angst to the ultimate question—What am I going to do with my life?—and is it any wonder that today's women are in such a state? Is it any wonder Jane is pining for an arranged marriage, or that Hannah couldn't find happiness, even in the halls of *Vogue* magazine—even, it bears repeating, putting clothes on the back of George Clooney?

For the first time, we women have the world at our fingertips. We've been told "You can do anything you want" since the days when our biggest decision was whether to choose mom's right breast or left breast. But no one's gone before us to blaze this particular trail. The groundbreaking "firsts" have brought us to where we are, but now they're just more potential roads to travel. And there's still plenty of unmarked terrain.

SOME MONTHS LATER, we're back on Hannah's couch. Her personal-choice conundrum has just developed a brand-new wrinkle. She just found out that she has been accepted to New York University's MPA program: Exactly what she thought she wanted. She must be thrilled. Right? Well . . . while she was waiting for her acceptance, she started doing freelance production work. She kinda likes it.

And so she finds herself back at square one. "I did want to go back to school," she says. "But I like the production work. Do I want to go into debt to go to graduate school? And really, after I get my MPA . . . now I'm not really sure what I would do then."

TWO

OH, THE PLACES YOU'LL GO

I became an overachiever to gain approval from the world.
—Madonna

"YOU CAN HAVE IT ALL." Oh, such an empowering message. The promise! The future! The *pressure!* And especially for those of you born anywhere between 1977 and 1994, it all hits home: the weight of the great expectations you've been saddled with since birth. Maybe even before then, when your mom may have fed you a steady diet of Mozart in utero.

At some 76 million strong, this "Millennial Generation," sometimes dubbed "Gen Y," represents one quarter of the American population.[1] This is the generation, Morley Safer once said on *60 Minutes,* that "was raised by doting parents who told them they are special, played in little leagues with no winners or losers, or all winners. They are laden with trophies just for participating."[2] And for the women of this "Baby on Board" generation, it all ratchets up. Like their older sisters, they too are grappling with the illusions of unlimited choices, and the pressure to take advantage of them all. But the difference is in the paralysis. Mostly too young to be aching for the road not traveled, these women are instead paralyzed by the smorgasbord of choices themselves—and the expectation that whatever they choose, they will succeed. And succeed *big*. Raised with the refrain—you can do anything!—they've been overprogrammed, overscheduled, and fed on approval. Because they learned early on that they must (they will!) do something amazing with their lives, choices have become even more fraught. The result? Indecision. Analysis paralysis. A whole lot of angst.

Take Molly, for example. Raised to believe she could, and should, reach for the stars once she closed the book on college, she packed her bags after graduation, swapped one coast for the other, donned the requisite black suit, and, two years later, found herself flailing. The quintessential overachiever, she earned a near 4.0 in college and won awards for her reporting at her college newspaper. And yet at twenty-four, she worried that she was watching the death of what she'd always thought was supposed to be her dream. She wondered if she had set herself up to fail.

"I worked so hard, and my bar was set so high for what kinds of jobs I was going to shoot for," she says. "No one tells you 'Here are the real jobs that are available.' I only thought about the dream jobs." Shortly after graduation, she found herself in New York City at *The Economist*—although not as a journalist. While some people might have seen this as a dream job, for Molly it felt like failure. But so programmed to that good-student cycle—work hard, earn good grades, move up—she mindlessly followed that formula, right into a job she didn't want. "I did everything my boss asked, I did it perfectly, I sucked up. In six months, I got promoted. It was one of the fastest promotions they'd experienced. I tried really hard, and I moved to the next step; I tried really hard, and

I moved to the *next* step. And now I've gotten to the point where I'm like, wait a minute, how did I get this far? I just blindly tried really hard without really thinking, What's the end? Where is this getting me?"

Molly began to question the wisdom of what she'd been chasing. "I put on a suit every day and walk around midtown Manhattan with important people who are predominantly male. I work at an organization where it's mainly white British men, and I get to be someone important there because I'm a young woman. I think I felt this need to prove myself—and the awkward glamour that went along with that—rather than thinking, Do I really want to do this?" She realized a lot of her friends were in the same boat, talking the good talk about their jobs, pumping themselves up, but always ending their spiel with "I know I'm not doing *that,* but . . . Maybe it was idealistic, or maybe it was, you know, trying to be tough cookies and trying to be the best out there. But we all had these really great expectations." For Molly, the expectation was that she would become a reporter, a dream that never materialized.

"Women have been taught we can be whatever we want to be. But I'm so oversaturated with choices that I could make to define myself—which is great, because this isn't an opportunity that women had decades ago, and I definitely feel very empowered to do a lot of good things—but there's also so much pressure to not only make a lot of choices but to really have it all. It's great that we *can* have it all, but I think that everyone now feels that there's this overwhelming *responsibility* to have it all, to really do something profound. Versus just, you know, be happy and get by."

You know what's coming next. Like Hannah, but for different reasons, Molly quit. "It was one of the hardest choices I've ever made, because I knew in my gut that I was unhappy, but on paper it made a lot of sense for me to keep working there. I had good health insurance, I was making a good salary, I had a steady job . . . but I was just unhappy, and to make a choice based on feelings versus what logically made sense was really difficult." Molly aggressively went on the prowl for a new gig and was rewarded with a couple of job offers from media companies (two on the same day), all of which came complete with their own sets of issues. Among them, moving. She turned them both down and ended up at a small start-up (an organic baby-clothes company run out of a loft), something she never envisioned for herself. In analyzing the facts, she realized that it all came down to how she felt.

"Since I've been in my twenties, the biggest choice I made was to move to New York, and since then, I've felt like I was just making very small choices. And this was going to be my first really big, life-changing decision." Her parents, her boyfriend, all wanted to weigh in, but in the end she realized the decision had to be her own. "It's hard to adjust to being a grownup and realizing that the repercussions of your choices mean so much more. My parents were like, 'It's gonna be all right. We'll take care of it for you.' The thing is, I had to figure it out, because at the end of the day, it was me who was going to take care of me, and if I screwed up, I was the one who was going to deal with the repercussions. It all came down to the fact that I was unhappy."

GRANTED, THIS ALL is an issue of privilege—we should be so lucky, right? But the disquiet is no less real, and Molly's story hits on a bunch of things: How relatively new it is for us to be in charge of our own lives. The importance of trusting our gut. What we mean when we use the word "happy." We'll address all of these issues in other chapters of the book, but for right now, let's look at this—the fact that the generation of women that lives by day planners and checklists, that has more choices than their mothers ever dreamed possible, never learned how to make them.

We asked Jenny—an attorney who alternately loves her job and wants to ditch it in favor of arranging flowers—what parents could do to make this whole choice-overload business easier. Her answer? Teach us how to make decisions.

Swarthmore's Barry Schwartz finds that intriguing. "Here's an interesting fact," he says. "There is no research on this. No one has studied how children learn to choose. Which I think is a sign that nobody thought this was a problem. You look at your preferences, and then you choose the one that's highest on your list. End of story. There's no developmental research on choice in five-year-olds, stuff like that. And I think what saves parents from really doing damage is that real life gets in the way. You ask your four-year-old what she would like for lunch, and three hours later, she still hasn't decided. So the next time, you ask, 'What do you want, grilled cheese or peanut butter?' Because you have errands to run, right? And you can't stick around, and eventually you just throw down a grilled-cheese sandwich. So your kids basically teach *you* how to present options to them. At first blush, every parent would think, 'I'm an enlightened parent, living in a free society; I want my kids to have as much choice as possible.'"

Flash-forward to college, and it becomes more dicey than what to have for lunch. Like other universities, Swarthmore does a great job of encouraging students to explore their options, Schwartz says. "We're very good at letting kids keep all the doors open, nurturing whatever they're interested in, whatever they're good at. But the point is finally reached when they have to go through one door and hear the other doors slam shut, and they have a very hard time knowing how to make that decision." And, says Schwartz, the modern world of infinite choices—or the illusion of such—creates Maximizers: "If there are a million different kinds of cereal, well, they must be there for a reason. So your job is to figure out which one is the best one."

All of which often leads to that sinking feeling that no matter what your choice was, you blew it. "This is the great misery of looking for the best," Schwartz says. "Nothing is ever going to be perfect, so whatever you end up choosing, you're going to imagine that something else would have been better. I think that when there is a lot of choice, it is inevitable that our expectations about 'how good the option we choose should be' will go up. So this is a sad tale of people trying to live out the implicit promise of modern America and discovering that it is just not achievable."

It's easy to blame parents who maybe want too much for their kids, but it's more complicated than that, says Schwartz. "I think parents are struggling to make everything possible for their kids, and they don't appreciate that making everything possible is not the right answer to the question. That you need constraints. And it's not just to prevent your kids from doing damage to themselves, it's to enable your kid to make decisions." It all leads to the search for "perfect," he says. "This is one of those great examples of unintended consequences. We want somehow to nurture in our kids the sense that they can overcome any obstacle and do anything. And, you know, it's nice to have that sense, because we imagine they'll persevere when things are hard. But what we don't appreciate is that what comes along for the ride is their sense that the 'anything' they happen to be doing may not be the 'right' thing."

No kidding. Who knew that the flip side of high expectations, the modern woman's birthright, would be constant pressure, not unlike a raging migraine (which are, by the way, more prevalent in women). Then there are the choices. So many. Too many? With the constant backbeat: You're so lucky to have them! In a "My Turn" column for

Newsweek back in 2004, twentysomething writer Jenny Norenberg tracked the vagaries of her college chums' lives in the years since college. She was one of the first to lament the fact that with countless options comes the pressure to find the perfect life. What she found was that the freedom to do anything had resulted in bouncing from town to town, job to grad school—and back again. "It seems that having so many choices has sometimes overwhelmed us," she wrote. "In the seven years since I left home for college, I've had thirteen addresses and lived in six cities. How can I stay with one person, at one job, in one city, when I have the world at my fingertips?"[3]

Sound familiar? Part of this bouncing around is developmental, a symptom of what's been dubbed the Quarterlife Crisis, the first stop on the lifelong trek known as "taking stock." Forbes reporter Hana Alberts describes quarterlifers—a demographic between eighteen and thirty-four that's 60 million strong—as "confused and even paralyzed by too many choices and a lack of direction."[4] Quarterlife is a time, she writes, filled with landmarks like first jobs, first apartments, first loves, first children—and with those landmarks, loads of which-way-should-I-gos: Where do I live? With whom? Work for love or money? Cut my hair or keep it long?

So true, says Abby, a smart twentysomething writer who started out in journalism, left that gig for a job doing PR for a nonprofit, and then traded that one for a job doing PR for *another* nonprofit. "Especially with all the recent layoffs, quarterlifers like myself are stuck answering the age-old question: 'What should I do with my life?' I have a fulltime job I enjoy, and I am *still* struggling." At one point, in fact, she said she, too, struggled with the hair question. "Long or short? Sounds silly, but honestly . . . the best thing about being in your midtwenties is that you can dress and act like a teenager—and get away with it—*and* dress and act like an upwardly mobile junior executive and get away with it. The worst part about being in your midtwenties is trying to decide which of those images accurately reflects *you*."

Ultimately, she solved the hair issue by cutting off eleven inches. And while she initially loved that first PR job, being bright and driven, she soon outgrew it. So she played "guts ball." She'd been shopping around for a new challenge, and interviewed for two great jobs. "One was greater than the other, though. I felt positive about both prospects, and so *done* with my current job, that I put my two weeks' notice in. That same day I was offered the not-as-great-job *and* had an amazing interview with the super-great job. Well, the super-great job was taking their damn time, so I decided to turn down the offer, basically risking everything on the chance that the super-great job would make me an offer. I am not really sure what I want, so I was hoping an offer from the super-great job would make up my mind for me. But the offer didn't come, so I had to make a choice. And the choice was risky." But not, it turns out, terminally so. A few days later, shortly after she packed up her office, she was offered the job she wanted.

Most women might not be so lucky. But they can definitely identify with Abby's quest for the better job (and possibly, the eternal question: long or short hair). On one hand, as the Pew Center study on Millennials found, this is a generation that is "confident, upbeat, and open to change."[5] They are also workers who want to be challenged on the job—or who bail when they are not.[6] (However, for all this jostling to define the Millennials, the *New York Times* recently reported on a controversy over whether it's even possible to characterize a generation. One thing folks on both sides of the argument agreed on, however, was this: Millennial women show increased levels of self-confidence and competence.[7]) But as über-achievers, these are women who've been

reaching for gold stars ever since kindergarten. And, as part of a generation that's been given praise (plastic trophies, too) just for showing up,
they assumed they deserved it. Perfection became the goal. Anything
less? Well, not just "not good," but for some overachieving women, "failure." Meanwhile, there was that other lie foisted upon these unsuspect-
ing girls: *You can have it all!* They heard it so much—often from mothers who wanted their daughters to have all the options they never had
themselves—that they came to believe it.

Which may be one reason that decisions and adult commitments
become so hard: They mean too much.

BUT LET'S BACK up. In a 2010 piece on twentysomething angst, *Washington Post* reporter Lindsay Minnema talked to Jeffrey Jensen Arnett, a
professor of psychology at Clark University in Massachusetts who wrote
*Emerging Adulthood: The Winding Road from Late Teens through the Twen-
ties.* Arnett pointed out that this generation experiences a much longer
transition to adulthood: They're not dependent on their parents, but they
don't have a stable life structure, either. "They go in a lot of directions,
change jobs a lot, change love partners. They go through a long period of
figuring out who they are and how they fit in the world," Arnett said.[8]

In a later piece in the *New York Times Magazine,* writer Robin Marantz Henig explains Arnett's definition of "emerging adulthood" (Arnett
pretty much owns the term) as a time when "young men and women are
more self-focused than at any other time of life, less certain about the
future and yet also more optimistic, no matter what their economic background. This is where the 'sense of possibilities' comes in [Arnett] says;
they have not yet tempered their idealistic visions of what awaits."[9]

That *New York Times* article seemed to imply that these "emerging
adults" could be defined by the fact that they had delayed the traditional

markers of adult life—a thesis that set the interwebs adither in the days to follow. One such debate took shape on Slate.com, where the daughter of the *New York Times Magazine* article's author, Samantha Henig (herself an emerging adult), offered this: "And although plenty has been written about Gen Y twentysomethings hopping from job to job and shirking the family life, I feel like Arnett's positive branding of this phase—not the entitled 'extended adolescence' but the forward-looking 'emerging adulthood'—does something new. If he's right, then it's not that we're lazy or scared of commitment, nor is it as simple as being victims of a bad economy; we're going through a necessary phase of development that will help us take on the grown-up responsibilities coming our way."[10]

According to the MacArthur Foundation Research Network on Transitions to Adulthood, back in 1960, 77 percent of women had reached the traditional grown-up milestones by age thirty: married, kids, job, degree. By 2005, that number had plummeted to 27 percent.[11] All of which might sound kind of cool if those twentysomethings were, you know, running around the world climbing mountains or learning capoeira. But most of them are right here—often paying off student loans, trying to figure out what to do with their lives, wrestling with decisions large and small. Jane confesses that she struggles with any decision. "I've been trying to decide on a car to purchase for five years. Five years!" she says. "Hybrid? Four-wheel drive? Fun? Practical? Lease? Buy? Red? Leather? Floormats? Cupholders? It's embarrassing, frankly. Although, should I be embarrassed or embrace it? Share it or hide it? Fake it or own it? I digress."

Funny. But then again, not, when the decision involves more than wheels. Add the Millennial zeitgeist to the mix *(a job isn't just a job; it must be a calling, and it better be spectacular),* and what you've got is a recipe for disappointment.

Nicole was the editor of her college newspaper and is a year out of college. Raised in the Midwest, she was taught she could do whatever she wanted in life—so long as she tried hard and didn't give up. She believed it. Until—*reality check!*—she realized she'd have to trade her lifelong dreams of journalism for a job in retail, just to pay the rent. It was hard to swallow, especially for a success-oriented woman who had always measured herself by her achievements.

"I had tried a lot of things—but I decided on journalism. That's what I wanted. And yet that's what I can't get," she said a few months after graduation, when she was doing time at a local Banana Republic. The fact that she was folding sweaters instead of writing leads did not compute. "I graduated at the top of my class, ready to face the world with that shiny I-can-beat-the-recession drive for success, just like I had achieved in the classroom. Things suddenly went dark when I realized the real world isn't really like school. I've struggled, agonized, over why I can't make my dream of getting a job in journalism happen. In a world with boundless opportunities, what do you do when you realize the one thing you've been waiting for isn't available? Or worse: It was, but you just didn't get it?"

Her stint at Banana Republic gave way to an internship at a national PR firm, which led her, a year later, to a crossroads: A good chance of being hired on full-time at the PR firm, an internship at a digital journalism start-up, or a part-time job at her local newspaper along with a move back to her high-school bedroom. It left her in a tizzy.

"I guess it will all play out soon and I'll go from there," she said. "But look at my life right now. Completely undecided. And I am annoyingly fearful of making the final decision. My dad does not believe I could ruminate this much over decisions about jobs and said he'd never thought so much about one in his whole life. When I told him that I would have to think about the offer at the PR firm, he about died. It's fun and exciting to have different options, but it's stressful watching them all unfold without any real say." Just a week later, the PR prospect had dissolved, and she found the digital journalism gig brought its own issues—not the least of which was money—and so she's back home with mom and pop.

"It feels like, if I am going to ever get my crack at being a journalist, it's probably going to be on my own terms. I mean, we'll see how working in the newsroom at the Omaha World Herald goes—and maybe I'll get some freelance work. But ultimately, that will probably be one step on the road to something else. Anyway, in the midst of all this indecision, I've started to put some effort into studying for the LSAT. We'll see."

THE IRONY IS that for all this torment over career decisions, very few of us consider them permanent. A survey conducted by international staffing company Adecco during the height of the 2009 recession shows that when it comes to work, most of us are constantly operating with one foot out the door. Of the American workers surveyed, 54 percent said they'd be hunting for a new job once the economy picked up. That's significant. But the real jolt comes here: Almost *three-quarters* of eighteen- to twenty-nine-year-olds said they'd be off in search of greener pastures once the recession ended.[12] That's a heap of dissatisfaction. A terminal case of grass-is-greener syndrome? Bad choices from the outset? Growing pains?

Especially for Millennial women, the workplace often represents culture shock, sometimes of epic proportions. This is a generation of women raised with high expectations and socialized to do school well. They've been superachievers all their lives and assume they can be super-achievers at everything. We talked with feminist scholar Laura Ellingson,

PhD, a professor of communication and gender studies at Santa Clara University. She says this mentality can be appealing and terrifying at the same time. Once these superachievers get into the workplace—where they don't find the comfortable fit of college—they come up against the messy nature of the real world. And often, their paycheck comes with a job description that requires more in the way of computer skills than any knowledge of Milton or Sartre. Still, raised to believe that anything less than perfection is failure, when they confront the gulf between expectations and reality, there's that nagging feeling that "subpar" means they didn't try hard enough. Or that they chose wrong.

Which brings us to Caitlin, a twentysomething overachiever making her way in the Big Apple. She came to New York starry-eyed and idealistic, throwing herself into Teach For America. It didn't work out. She found herself in tears most nights—staying up long past midnight to prepare classes for her special-ed students—and ultimately quit. And found herself floundering. Ultimately she got a job she didn't really want at a large media corporation, and—prompted by a story in an issue of *Vogue* that she found at the gym—she began to wonder *What if?*

It was a profile of an eighty-one-year-old superstar food writer named Betty Fussell, and what she realized was that this was the same Betty she had met three years ago at a family reunion. Her grandmother's cousin. She swiped the magazine, and over Thai takeout, she decided she had to find her. And that she did—in an old Greek-Revival Presbyterian church that had been converted into apartments. "I have coffee—well, she drinks red wine—with her, and we chat for two hours about her adventures and career," she says. "The whole time I am thinking that somehow she's going to reveal the secret of life to me. I leave her apartment wanting to travel the world writing about food, of course. But between her stoop and the subway, I changed my mind about seventeen times. Maybe I could be a travel writer. Maybe I should go back to teaching, which then turns to 'nonprofits,' and then 'nonprofits abroad'—and then 'finance' as I see all the suits and ties at the happy hours I'm passing by." She gets home, exhausted, miserable, thinking about what-ifs—and finds her alumni magazine in her mailbox. "I just want to relax and think about college, where we had a core curriculum steering us, a four-year window, and immediate A's of approval. But the alumni blurbs stressed me out more—should I be networking with these people to find my dream job?

"My generation was raised to be well rounded, and involved in everything, and able to do anything," she says. "It's a lot of pressure when you suddenly think you have to make the perfect decision on a career. I moved to New York for all the opportunity, but I am realizing that with all that opportunity comes the envy and the confusion. Surrounded by all these fancy people with their killer jobs, I am constantly doubting my own start and thinking of what I should do next, or what I should have been doing last year. I have not discovered how to live in the moment and rid myself of constant indecision. I can't even decide on a Thai restaurant, of the nearly ten in a four-block radius, let alone a job. Maybe I will go back to teaching," she says with a laugh. "Turns out, Betty's fabulous writing career didn't actually begin until her fifties. Maybe we have some time."

Sure there's time. But even so, taking that baby step out into the adult world carries a world of uncertainty—even regret—for these women. It could be the lack of the comfortable boundaries they had in school—or when their parents programmed most of their waking hours. It could be the pressure to perform, and perform well: Look at me! See what I'm doing now?

Or it could be what Megan experienced as she embarked on what most of us would consider a postgrad dream gig, teaching English in

Lyon, France: the paralyzing fear of growing up, coupled with the unpredictability of living life without a script. "The thing is, I'm twenty-two, and I'm petrified of growing up," she wrote us. "This is the first autumn season in seventeen years when I have not been sitting in a classroom, studying and preparing for a life that is no longer predictable. I thought that moving to France would allow me to postpone the inevitable—adulthood—and give me something good to put on my résumé. While the latter might be true, I have found myself mercilessly thrown into the writhing realm of adulthood with little more than a worn American passport and a strong sense of survival."

THERE'S A CERTAIN discomfort, a fear of growing up—and possibly doing it wrong—that resonates especially with a generation that's been riding the treadmill since grade school, and whose decisions have been preprogrammed ever since. Which brings up an interesting paradox: We force our kids to grow up fast, at least on the outside, but then they stop.

The knock on American culture (maybe on Western culture in general) is that childhood has been compressed. Partly the media is to blame. And also consumer culture, which tricks little girls into dressing like mini-grownups before they hit double-digits. But the treadmill carries weight as well: Much of the running around from select soccer to Chinese brush-painting is geared toward the Big Kahuna—admission to a good college, which ultimately leads to, you know, *something else*. But it all starts young, like with the tween-age girl we saw in Starbucks one day. Wearing grade-school plaid and drinking a double latte, she was working with her tutor, powering through a Kaplan-style prep course for her *high school* entrance exam. (And for some reason, no one even questioned the caffeine.)

And it doesn't let up—as in the case of Anna, an accomplished college senior who reflected on the great expectations that had been riding her back for as long as she could remember. She felt that she had to do something *amazing* with her life—when all (all?) she really wanted to do was teach little kids. Is the treadmill to blame for all her angst? Could be. But then again, last we heard, Anna had flown off to Japan, where she had found a job—teaching little kids.

But here's the irony. Remember those stats from the MacArthur Foundation?

Adolescence—that period when your job in life is to define your identity, not to mention your dreams—often lasts well past the age of thirty. We could go on, but you get the drift. And we're guessing you don't need MacArthur to spell it out for you. But those numbers on delayed adulthood do bring up another interesting question: Is making commitments (marriage, parenthood, one single career) all there is to being an adult?

We think that maybe it's this: A grownup is someone who makes her own decisions, takes responsibility for where they lead her, and doesn't expect every one of those decisions to be "right."

Which brings us back to Molly, the young woman we met in the beginning of this chapter. She's landed on her feet and, at least for now, her story has a happy ending. When she was casting about, looking for a new job, she realized that deep down she'd love to be a press liaison for a politician or a nonprofit she felt passionate about. She researched political jobs and cold-called the offices of local politicians—and what she learned was that just about everyone she talked to loved what they did. "That is a feeling I have been craving: a sense of purpose," she says. "What if my job actually helped people and didn't just pay my rent?"

What she found out was that for any of those jobs, she'd need a master's, so in the fall of 2010 she started back to grad school, in a public-policy program at NYU. "Since I sent in my applications, I've just had this overwhelmingly joyous feeling, like I am making good choices for *me*, and I'm testing myself and what I feel passionate about. I regret I didn't take the time to really reflect earlier. I just spent so much time pushing away my feelings and pushing away the question—*Hey, what is it that I really want to be?*—because it was gonna be tough. Now I am feeling much more balanced, and I realize I am about to turn twenty-five, not fifty-five. I do not have to have life figured out."

THREE

THE ROAD NOT TRAVELED

Sometimes she thought, in a strange way, life was so much easier for people with no options. . . . You didn't sit around thinking, *I could have been a documentarian or a forensic psychologist or a sitcom writer.*
—Erica Kennedy, *Feminista,* 2009

THAT'S A QUOTE FROM SYDNEY, the heroine of Erica Kennedy's novel *Feminista.*[1] And it speaks to one of the more insidious side effects of a life characterized by limitless options: grass-is-greener syndrome. We've arrived at this epidemic honestly, on the shoulders of our foremothers' best intentions. With its focus on creating opportunities, feminism has brought us an expanse of open doors, but without a strategy to help us choose one. So we frequently find ourselves obsessing over what's going on behind each and every one.

Or, as Kennedy herself told us, "Too many options doesn't just apply to jobs but also to men and where we should live and what kind of life we should have. It's the predicament of abundance. As women, all these doors have been thrown open for us, but it's like, 'Oh no, which one do I choose and where the fuck is it going to lead me?!'"

Bingo.

It's like each of us is living a "Choose Your Own Adventure" story, but we're incapable of focusing on whatever adventure we've chosen. Instead—like the kid who can't resist flipping back to see how the other adventures might have panned out—we angst over the adventures we *didn't* choose, and it's an angst that's made all the more intense by having been weaned on the notion that we can have it all. And, as opposed to the women we met in the last chapter (who are in their early twenties and still pretty driven to have that high-echelon "all" they believe is their due), the women we'll meet here—who have only a few more years under their belts—are angsty over the ever-increasing realization that they probably *can't* have it all. Which is not only a bummer, but also adds a certain time-crunch to the angst.

Chloe's story cuts to the chase: "I was walking home from work, having a low self-esteem day, and I saw this sign in a storefront. It was of three smiling women, around my age, and I just thought to myself, I bet they all have kids."

Chloe doesn't even want to have children—an assertion she reiterated before admitting that, nevertheless, it didn't stop her tears. "I just feel like life is passing me by."

For the record, Chloe is amazing and enviable in her own right: She's lived and worked everywhere from New York City to Brazil, Mexico to Southern California, and she is successful, beautiful, talented, and happily married. But those things never seem to matter much when we're confronted with the green-grassed monster; when we catch a glimpse of the place where that road we opted not to travel may have led.

Julie, a reader of our blog, told us her story, too—and in its way, it's quite similar to Chloe's.

Here's some of what she wrote: "I am a thirty-year-old mother of two who has definitely suffered from the grass-is-greener syndrome. After my daughter was born, I chose to stay at home with my children while pursuing an education. I not only became extremely depressed, because I felt that I should be 'doing it all' (work, school, housewifing, and mothering), but I perceived criticism from other women for my choice. I felt like I was worthless. I did not appreciate my life and the wonderful opportunity that I had to be with my children. I was more concerned with what I thought I should be doing than with what I had chosen to do. I felt that there was something wrong with me, because I could not be the super-mom (à la Clair Huxtable) that is portrayed on television as the epitome of womanhood. When I finally decided that I needed a job, I spent the whole time I was at work wishing I was at home with my kids."

And then there's Sam, who's excelled at her job as an account manager at an advertising agency—even while she spends a fair chunk of her billable hours plotting last-minute vacays to Berlin and volunteer trips to Bangladesh and daydreaming about the road not traveled: "I majored in theatre in college, only to burn out on it and give it up after college. But now, every day, I think about that life, the performance life . . . and I wonder what I'm missing. What did I give up? Would I be happier if I had just stuck with it? Would I, could I, be more fulfilled if I were doing it right now? Oy, it drives me mad, and I keep hoping that maybe all of my going-around about it will make me so nauseated I'll actually get sick (of myself) and do something. Hasn't happened yet."

They're familiar feelings, even for those of us who outwardly do seem to have it all. And yet, for women, the whole "life is passing me by" thing is relatively new. (For men, the story's so old there's an archetype: divorce, young girlfriend, Corvette. Even, for some, a toupee. *Cringe.*) Aging, of course, is as old as time, but this particular brand of angst has less to do with aging per se than it does with the idea that, as time goes by, what once looked like a wide-open wonderland, bursting with possibility and open doors, starts looking more and more like a collage of What You're Missing Out On. That with every choice we make, we shut those other doors for good—one by painful one. It's an evil little phenomenon economists call "opportunity cost": when picking one thing means we can't have the others. And there's no model for how to deal with our feelings over what we're leaving behind Doors No. 2 through Infinity (after all, if we can do anything, the possibilities are literally infinite, right?). This bounty of opportunity is so new that we were sent off to conquer it with no tools—just an admonishment that we'd best make the most of it: *You're so lucky!*

We know we're blessed to have all these options. We get it. And so is it any wonder we want a shot at each and every one of them?

But therein lies the rub.

We want to travel but can't take time off whenever we feel like it if we're also trying to get our business off the ground—and featured on *Oprah*. We want a family, but that'd mean that packing up and moving to Cairo or New Orleans on a whim is pretty much off the table. We want to be there for our daughter's every milestone, yet we also want to model what a "successful career woman" looks like. We want torrid affairs and hot sex, but where would that leave our husbands? We want financial security and a latte on our way to the office every morning, but we sit in our ergonomically correct chairs daydreaming about trekking through Cambodia with nothing but our camera and a mosquito net. We want to be an artist but have gotten rather used to that roof over our heads. We want to be ourselves, fully and completely, but would like to fit in at cocktail parties too. (And when on earth are we going to find the time to write that novel?)

That looking-over-the-shoulder feeling is familiar to Lauren, who we first met in Chapter 1 when she told us, "I swim in a sea of confusion over my options! Being a woman who feels she is unlimited, I've spent too much time debating my opportunities instead of picking one path and sticking with it." A self-described foodie, she went on to offer the following analogy: "Have you ever felt enormous satisfaction looking at a menu with only two or three dinner options? This is good when you like the choices, but not so good if you don't. But a full menu isn't any better when you don't even know what you want (or when you want it all)."

Today, it's all on the menu, but—as it is in a favorite restaurant, so it is in life—our eyes are often bigger than our stomachs. And what might be perceived as a failure of willpower has more to do with a mantra we've been fed—a mantra that's more rose-colored than real. The positive messaging we got as kids—*You can be anything you want!*—was never coupled with the disclaimer, *But everything comes with a side of trade-offs.* That's one we have to learn for ourselves.

Here's what thirty-five-year-old Alison—a mom and former competitive horseback rider—had to say about it: "The itching that runs through my consciousness is that it is okay to think or dream or believe a girl can do anything—yet the doing and execution is what can undo her. That, coupled with a family and the people whose feelings and egos may be bruised and battered along the way. The absolute reality is that any job or hobby that evokes passion requires an equal if not greater sacrifice. The notion of 'What do you want to be when you grow up?' is not coupled with 'Okay, you can do it, but it's going to be hard.' Mom doesn't say, 'Gee little Ali, that's great! So when you fall in love and get married, make sure you can integrate all of your passions and dreams into your marriage.' That would have been the best advice anyone could have given me.

Instead, I plunged headlong into a decision before I had the courage to really declare my dreams, and the ramifications of those dreams."

We don't want to believe we'll have to give anything up—and why would we? We can have it all, damn it! Except for when we can't.

Even Erica Kennedy herself—a *New York Times* best-selling author—isn't immune. "I regret making my career into something bigger than it should have been, because I don't really get much fulfillment out of it," she said. "But I've wasted my whole life focusing on it. A lot of my friends had children when they were younger, in their twenties, and I wish I had done that."

Which brings up another aspect of the grass-is-greener game: comparing, competing, worrying about whether we're missing out or measuring up. It's a bit like when you were little, and you wanted a perm, or a belly ring, or a tattoo, and your mom said no, and you'd whine "But mo-o-oooom, everyone else is doing it!" And she'd say, "If everyone else jumped off a bridge, would you?" (And then, if you were feeling especially petulant, you might say something like, "Well yeah, because there'd be no one left to play with.")

And in a way, that feeling never really goes away. We know life isn't a race. We know we're not in competition with our friends. And yet, watching as their picks lead them to different adventures, it's all but impossible not to wonder what we're missing out on. What our lives might be like had we taken their road. And, like the kid who's convinced all her friends are all jumping off the bridge, no one wants to be left behind.

How often are the things that we choose for our lives influenced by a little unconscious—and not-so-unconscious—desire to head off being left behind? How often are the milestones (marriage, advanced degree, corner office, fat apartment in the city, fat home in the 'burbs, fat baby in the stroller) we shoot for not—if we were to really think about it—

personal goals we've set after honest, careful assessment of what we want for our lives, but just sort of assumed? *Everyone else is doing it…*

And if we do follow our friends off the bridge, how often are we left looking over our shoulders, wondering where that lonely path we *really* wanted to take might have led?

As games go, the "comparison" one is pretty much a lose–lose, serving only to compound the issue of too many choices: There's something about the way we play it that leaves us unable (or unwilling, or both) to imagine that the roads we didn't choose might well be every bit as imperfect as the ones we did. And worse, when we find ourselves lost in the Technicolor-green mirage of our neighbors' grass, we're categorically incapable of noticing that our own lawn might in fact be pretty damn green.

Which brings us to Bridget Jones. Or, more accurately, to Renée Zellweger. Early in 2010, it was reported that, though she'd like to do another *Bridget Jones* flick, the prospect of packing on those famed pounds once more had her opting out.[2] Now, much as we love the relatable, perpetually plumpish character—and even despite the reported $20 million payday—a part of us can understand Zellweger's decision to forego the gravy this go-round on the gravy train. We enjoy the occasional frosting-binge as much as anyone, but gaining twenty pounds on command doesn't exactly sound like our idea of fun—never mind the counterpoint: crash-dieting to lose it all in time for the media tour. More interesting, though, is why Zellweger allegedly said she didn't want to go yo-yo again: She believes those extra pounds had something to do with the demise of her relationship with Jack White, and she doesn't want the same thing to happen with her current (at press time, anyway) beau, Bradley Cooper. And, to quote Erica Kennedy, who dug her teeth into the tidbit on her own blog: "what the article doesn't say but I will go ahead and add—especially since she's forty now and childless."[3]

Let's leave aside the obvious rant here (or let's not: pasty rock star can't deal with his girlfriend sporting a rounder frame for a couple of months? *Boo, hiss.* There, done), because it brings up an interesting point: No matter what we have going for us (*ahem,* twenty-million-dollar payday much?), we can't help but focus on what we don't. (Remember what Kennedy said? How much would you like to bet some of those friends of hers who had kids in their twenties are regretting not chasing—and catching—the kind of career success Kennedy has had?)

What's the problem here? Are we just spoiled? Or is part of the human condition the absolute inability to focus on what's in our own backyard—blinded as we are by our imaginings of what's going down on the other side of the fence? Perhaps there's a lesson to take from Zellweger's scarypants-sporting counterpart: It's a little bit like Ms. Jones's lamenting over her "smug married friends" who, while married, were nowhere near as smugly so as Bridget imagined . . . or her inability to realize that a Colin Firth in the hand might be worth two Hugh Grants in the (proverbial) bush. But it brings us right back to an inconvenient truth of the grass-is-greener game: We seem somehow unable to imagine that the path we didn't choose might, in fact, be as rocky as the one we did.

Once upon a time, we had no choice: Our yard was our yard, so we dealt with it. Perhaps we planted some rhododendrons and called it a day. But now we're operating according to the assumption that any one of those lawns can be ours. And, as with all things undecided, despite the good intentions of empowerment and opportunity, the message *You can do anything you want!* has an evil flipside—and it's a restlessness, a dissatisfaction, a nagging preoccupation with what we're *not* doing. And we've found that one of the ways this plays out is as a raging case of commitmentphobia. To recall Chloe's words from Chapter 1: "For our generation, commitment is a kind of death."

She's right, of course. It's an ideology that's fed by the current condition—a condition characterized by abundant choices—and the message we've absorbed about that abundance. That it is a blessing. And given that, it follows that we'd feel that to commit to any one of those options is to be, at best, a fool; at worst . . . well, dead. Stagnated.

Let's take the mother of all commitments: marriage. Several recent works suggest that, for women today, the reluctance to commit has more to do with too many options—and the fear of missing out on too many of them—than cold feet.

In a piece she wrote for *Elle* magazine, forty-two-year-old Elizabeth Wurtzel, author of *Prozac Nation,* lamented the loss of her looks, her loneliness, and the years she spent fleeing commitment, sabotaging stability, believing she'd always have options (and a wrinkle-free face). In the piece, she wrote: "The idea of forever with any single person, even someone great whom I loved so much like Gregg, really did seem like what death actually is: a permanent stop. . . . Every day would be the same forever. The body, the conversation, it would never change—isn't that the rhythm of prison?"[4]

(Reader, she cheated on him.)

As journalist/blogger Hannah Seligson wrote of her book *A Little Bit Married,* "'A Little Bit Marrieds'. . . don't share the cost of anything, 'just in case.' Each thinks the other is marriage material, but how can they commit when there are untraveled continents and career paths to explore? Everything is great—but what if there is something better out there?"[5]

What if, indeed? It's a trademark conundrum of our times—with all those bright and shiny options surrounding us, only a fool would choose to shackle themselves to one option that may turn out to be less than perfect. And the easiest way to ensure we don't do this is to avoid commitment altogether, to keep the doors open, to see for ourselves whether that grass is greener. Or, at the very least—and more to the point—to reserve the right to take off at any time and see for ourselves about that grass.

In a 2009 *New York Magazine* cover story entitled "The Sex Diaries"—inspired by the magazine's ongoing online series in which New Yorkers of all walks anonymously chronicled their sexual exploits for a week—writer Wesley Yang offered an analysis to anchor the salacious tidbits, describing the assignment as a way "to develop some kind of taxonomy of contemporary sexual anxieties." He came up with a top-ten list of "things that seem to be making our playful, amorous youth crazy,"[6] and guess what? The top three had to do with choices.

Number one unsurprisingly was, "The anxiety of too much choice." And in that item's explanation, Yang spotlights the undeniable influence of something so ubiquitous, we hardly give it a second thought: the cell phone. Of it, he wrote, "One carries in one's pocket, wherever one goes, the means of doing something other than what one is doing . . . a distinct shift in the way we experience the world, introducing the nagging urge to make each thing we do the single most satisfying thing we could possibly be doing."[7]

And cell phones aren't the only e-scapegoat here. In an interview with *The Ticker*—an independent student newspaper at CUNY's Baruch College—psychology professor David Sitt takes issue with modern technology as a whole, saying, "Since technology has propelled us forward, it creates a speed where everything is immediate, and the window for gratification has narrowed."[8]

Case in point: Hannah, whom you met in Chapter 1, says, "My biggest problem is if I don't like something, I walk. Like, there is no giving it a chance. I'll give it a liiiiittle bit of a chance, but if I don't like something, I walk. There's no trying to make it work in my world; I'm like, I'm going to find something better."

In our modern, interconnected, always-on world, is all of this choice—or maybe more importantly, this illusion of limitless, constantly available choice—*the* modern person's dilemma? And does it mess with our heads in every realm? Is this why when we're working one job, we spend our time daydreaming about all the other things we could be doing? And does our überconnection to our cyberlives and techno-friends and Facebook profiles make it worse, keeping us from being fully present in our own here-and-now? From appreciating what we have—rather than jonesing for what we don't? Does the fact that we have one foot in our own life and the other in hundreds of others leave us that much more inclined to constantly worry over what we're missing? Or so overwhelmed by all the choices that we sometimes find ourselves wishing for a life with no options at all?

But back to the bedroom. (It's a fun metaphor, after all.) This issue was riffed on by *New York Times* writer David Brooks, who did a piece in response to "The Sex Diaries." In his piece, Brooks contrasts the "Happy Days era" (in which courtship, and all of social life, was governed by a very specific script) with the reality of the modern era (in which we're governed by nothing but an urgency to get a taste of everything that's out there, settling only when we've struck gold.) "Social life comes to resemble economics, with people enmeshed in blizzards of supply and demand amidst a universe of potential partners. . . . If you have several options perpetually before you, and technology makes it easier to jump from one to another, you will naturally adopt the mentality of a comparison shopper."[9]

And—as we've seen with Erica Kennedy and Julie and Alison and Chloe and Sam—the limitless choices of the modern era leave us antsy in *every* realm, not just relationships; leaves us approaching *everything* from the mentality of a comparison shopper. Listing pros and cons. Building cases for and against. Weighing our options. Hedging our bets. Refusing to commit.

PART AND PARCEL with commitmentphobia is a compulsion to "keep the doors open." Which makes sense: Despite all the drawbacks, there's a certain comfort that comes from knowing we have options. It mitigates risk. We're told, after all, that keeping all one's eggs in one basket is a bad plan. (Unless one's plan involves making a large omelet.) But, as Dan Ariely points out in *Predictably Irrational: The Hidden Forces That Shape Our Decisions,* there is a price for keeping all those "but what if" doors open—and we pay that price with the energy and commitment that those doors siphon away from the ones that are really worth keeping open.[10] To take his advice to heart would be to decide, once and for all, *This is it! Those roads not traveled? Screw 'em!*

It's a liberating idea—and a sobering one, too. Of course, what Ariely's saying makes sense. Closing a bunch of those proverbial doors— deciding, *Okay, I'm never going to sail around the world solo/become an orchestra conductor/get my PhD*—probably *would* go a long way to easing the pain of the grass-is-greener syndrome, but somehow, suggesting we just stick to the path we've chosen and forget about all the others can sound like blasphemy.

We were told we can have it all!

But most of us can't. Most of us would likely—if only after being subjected to several rounds of waterboarding or prolonged starvation or forced viewing of *Jersey Shore*—allow that, yes, having it all might, in fact, be a big ol' myth. But allowing it and living it are two very different things.

When everything is on the menu, it takes an awful lot of willpower to say, "You know, I'm not really that hungry." Even if you're really *not* that hungry. Even if, in fact, you're stuffed. But when your history involves a certain amount of deprivation, when you're told how lucky you are to be there, you approach that buffet with gusto: "I'll have some of that, and some of that. . . ."

And our feminist foremothers *were* deprived. "The problem that had no name" that Betty Friedan wrote about in *The Feminine Mystique* was characterized by housewives stuck doing the laundry and dusting the end tables and fetching their husbands' Manhattans immediately upon their return from the big, wide world while silently wondering, *Is this all there is?* (Mad *Men*? Mad Women was likely more accurate.) And feminism's second wave brought that problem out into the open and taught women to give voice to their dissatisfaction.

But don't get us wrong. Thank God for that! Thanks to the women who admitted their longing for something more and drove the changes of those years, we're free to seek out better. We no longer have to settle for unsatisfying jobs, bosses, or sex lives. And we've gotten pretty darn good at voicing our dissatisfaction—and, from there, setting our sights on greener pastures. But the lure of "better," the implicit promise of "better" . . . well, that's where it gets tricky.

Naomi Wolf suggests that the years of aspirational messaging that were the striving, climbing handmaidens of Western feminism have in fact created "a perpetual, personal restlessness. . . . Our girls and young women are unable to relax. . . . We are raising a generation of girls who are extremely hard on themselves—who set their own personal standards incredibly, even punishingly high—and who don't give themselves a chance to rest and think, 'that's enough.'"[11]

"Enough." What a concept, huh? It's simple—and yet utterly foreign. To choose (and let's face it, this *is* a choice we're talking about here) to be content, to choose not to entertain the notion that something better might be out there . . . well, it's seen as sort of sad. Unmotivated. Unenlightened. This is America! Home of the all-you-can-eat buffet, after all. And when you're told you can have it all . . . well, to settle for anything short of that is to settle. To turn in your plate before sampling the goods at every station is to miss out on your money's worth.

But maybe it's worth looking to the buffet line for a lesson. Maybe we should set the same kind of goal in life as we do in the dining hall: to cultivate the kind of awareness that allows us to pass up the mini-quiches we kind of like so we'll have room to really enjoy the crabcakes we adore; the kind of awareness that places us fully in the moment of bliss that is a mouthful of warm brie rather than the distracted, "Did I really just eat fourteen cheese puffs"–variety blackout; the kind of consciousness that allows us to recognize the point at which we're full—and to actually stop there and enjoy the fullness.

But is it realistic? Can we really find a way to be content with our choices, to blind ourselves to the other roads we've yet to travel, the other doors we've yet to open? Much like a virtuous display of willpower at a buffet, it's a noble dream. But the blessing and the curse of these modern times is this: No matter how much we might buy into the idea that closing a bunch of those doors would make our lives easier, no matter how much we might want to pretend that those other doors aren't out there, the fact remains—they're there. And as long as they're there, we're going to wonder what's going on behind each and every one of them.

FOUR

CHASING THE MIRAGE

I say, 'me,' knowing all the while it's not me.
—Samuel Beckett, *The Unnamable*, 1953

DANA IS A WRITER, ACTOR, and single mother of two college-aged daughters. She lives in Hailey, Idaho, a small town outside of Sun Valley. We're discussing with her the "iconic self"—that image we construct and aspire to, and which sometimes turns around and kicks us in the ass. She gets it.

She grew up in Connecticut, going to plays on Broadway every Saturday with her mother, which fed her dreams of being on stage. She majored in theater, minored in journalism. Moved to New York City in her twenties and found that, dreams notwithstanding, it was not a time for "quirky-looking people" to be hired. She got into production work, more writing. Then life intervened. And because it did, she understands the role of expectations; the lingering nag of what might have been.

"All of it's right," she says now. "Every bit you say. We are drawn to an ideal, and then we try to fit ourselves to the notion. My dream: to be an actress and writer. Years later, after having done both in a really small way, marriage and children came along. One reason I got divorced was that I didn't fit in with his family's ideal of what a wife should be."

The family found her refreshing—until she married into it. At which point she was expected to settle down. Become a suburban house-wife. Stop playing like one of the boys, running around with her hus-band and his three brothers. "Apparently, I was too much of a rebel, too much of a New Yorker," she says now. And so she left. Moved out west to the small town where she expected to stay about two years. Close to two decades later, she's never left. These days, she writes for a living and acts, occasionally even getting paid to do it. "Yet it nags," she says, "because that's what people do: second-guess and nag themselves over the road not taken, the poor judgment calls, the missed opportunities. The 'Who would I have been, *could* I have been, if only . . .'"

If only. As a wise woman once said, the nice thing about low ex-pectations is that you'll never be disappointed. Consider this story of a woman who grew up many years ago in a small seaboard village in Sweden, where as a young girl she was known for her beauty, and where as an adult—as the wife of a sea captain—she held a position of promi-nence. When she was in her forties, her husband died, and with it, her identity: no longer the young beauty, no longer the prominent wife. The story is a clear reminder that until fairly recent history, women derived their identity from their looks or their husband, or both.

Jump ahead a few generations, and suddenly women could be the sea captains—or whatever. And so we began to derive our identity from what we *do*. When once we were defined as someone's wife or daugh-ter, we're now defined as someone's doctor or lawyer. But slowly we are learning that that's not right either.

It's a conundrum, this search to define our authentic selves—and it's something we'll tackle in depth in our last chapter. But for now, consider: Because it's new, because we haven't quite learned how to do it, do we end up defining ourselves in terms of our fantasies, our aspirations? In the process of our quest to define ourselves, do we get seduced by the icon? We dream of who we *want* to be—the swashbuckling reporter, the fearless photog, the edgy artist, the rail-thin supermodel, the über-wealthy CEO—and make life choices that fit those expectations and the image that accompanies them.

And then, if those dreams don't pan out, or we decide to stop the chase, the iconic self becomes a nagging reminder of the road not taken. We second-guess our choices. Feel we've failed, when of course, we haven't. And back to those great expectations we're constantly shouldering: Are they one reason we are always trying to cater to the notoriously hard-to-please iconic self, who is always whispering that we don't measure up? Is our iconic self one manifestation of those high expectations? And is that why she is so notoriously hard to please?

Look no further than Facebook. Or Twitter. Writing in the *New York Times Magazine,* Peggy Orenstein confessed that, while spending some glorious time with her little girl listening to E. B. White reading *Trumpet of the Swan* one day, a nasty thought intruded: *How will I tweet this?* She admits that the tweet she decided on ("Listening to E. B. White's *Trumpet of the Swan* with Daisy. Slow and sweet.") was, as she says, "not really about my own impressions: It was about how I imagined—and wanted—others to react to them."[1]

A recent study on social networking found that sites like Facebook provide the perfect environment for managing the presentation of self—commenting and sharing obsessively, all with an eye toward self-promotion. And in most cases, the researchers found, these carefully cultivated online identities were not always in sync with real-world personalities. "Online environments enable individuals to engage in a controlled setting where an ideal identity can be conveyed," the author wrote. "[T]hey provide an ideal environment for the expression of the 'hoped-for possible self,' a subgroup of the possible self. This state emphasizes realistic socially desirable identities an individual would like to establish, given the right circumstances."[2]

Marketing folks might say we're branding ourselves in our profile pictures, our status updates, or our tweets. *We* say that maybe we're feeding the iconic self, the self-image we've constructed, which, in ways big and small, is the face of our great expectations. She's kind of a tyrant too.

Charlotta Kratz is a communication professor at Santa Clara University and a scholar who tends to see things clearly—and pithily. She makes an interesting point about the iconic self: "Anytime there is talk of images and self, I think of Narcissus," she tells us. "There is something to it, I think. Women spend a lot of time perfecting the outer image of themselves, and maybe we let that behavior guide our professional choices too. We are so used to seeing ourselves as images, and selves that are never good enough. Maybe we go about choosing careers the same way we go about choosing foundation or shoes—the image we create of ourselves is more important than our real lives. That's why choices become so scary. They will hurt not our self, but the image we have of our self."

Another professor, Kathy Long, who specializes in organizational communication, tells us that she finds a certain resonance between the concept of the iconic self and the work of sociologist Erving Goffman, who famously posited that life—or managing our identity—is an interactive performance: We act for our audience, which in turn is made up of other actors.[3]

Okay, that one gets our heads spinning. But for many of us, this self that we've cultivated is worked out in detail, with little tolerance for deviation. Swarthmore's Barry Schwartz tells us that while he hasn't specifically looked into the ways in which the iconic self can influence our choices, "it doesn't shock me if that's true," he says. "What I will say, which may be relevant to this notion, is this: Nowadays, everything counts as a marker of who you are in a way that wasn't true when there were fewer options. So just to give you one example: When all you could buy were Lee's or Levi's, then your jeans didn't tell the world anything about who you were, because there was a huge variation in people, but there were only two kinds of jeans, you know? When there are two thousand kinds of jeans, now all of a sudden you *are* what you wear. . . . What that means is that [with] every decision, the stakes have gone up. It's not just about jeans that fit; it's about jeans that convey a certain image to the world of what kind of person you are. And if you see it that way, it's not so shocking that people put so much time and effort into what seems like trivial decisions. Because they're not trivial anymore."

In fact, let's go there. Clothes are a good metaphor for what we're talking about here. They do more than keep us warm and safe from indecent-exposure citations. They are a form of self-expression, and they say something to the world about who we are. And who we want to be perceived to be. Chuck Taylors or Jimmy Choos? Superficial, yes—but your choice likely speaks to much more than your preference in footwear. And even if it means nothing to you, well, the world is waiting to foist judgment based on little more. (Think no further than Hillary and her pantsuits.) But there's more to it: Fashion is often how we express our identification with certain groups; shorthand for our iconic selves— and Shannon has a good story to illustrate just that.

She was in New York for a book reading—an anthology to which she'd contributed an essay. Off she went, sporting an Outfit-with-a-capital-O. After all, she *likes* clothes and, like many woman who work at home, jumps at any chance to discard the daily attire that most kindly can be described as scrubs. And, you know, if people were going to be looking at her, well, she wanted to look good—and be comfortable (except for maybe her baby toes).

But here's what's funny. She was staying with the intelligent and beautiful woman who had edited the anthology—who was purposefully dressed down. Why? She told Shannon she felt she had to dress that way in order to be perceived as a Serious Writer. You know, the kind who's so busy being a Serious Writer she doesn't have time for silly fashion. She said she even had a pair of fake glasses. The irony, of course, being that *she* loves clothes too. At the reading that night, Shannon couldn't help but take note of what the other contributors wore, wondering as she did what her choice of duds communicated about her: Fabulous and fashionable? Or literary lightweight?

Which makes you wonder if the iconic self sometimes serves yet another purpose: It's the armor that protects us from those we fear will judge us. Isn't it easier to slap on a costume, play the role, and see it through to the end rather than hanging our sloppy, indefinable self out there for all to see?

That's why we found Rachel Shukert's 2010 memoir—ironically titled *Everything Is Going to Be Great*—so refreshingly honest in its portrayal of the less-than-great way she led a certain very messy period of her life.[4] In an early review of the book, Jezebel writer Anna North declared that the book "does something unfortunately rare in women's writing: celebrating mistakes."[5]

Later, in the *Wall Street Journal,* Shukert proclaimed herself thrilled at Jezebel's review—but said her mom's reaction was somewhat different in that she couldn't fathom why her daughter would want to publish an account of her drunken escapades, her sexually and romantically unconventional (and frequently disastrous) shenanigans, when the women of her generation were "supposed to grow up to be physicists and judges and CEOs."[6]

But what's really interesting is her take on *Eat Pray Love,* by Elizabeth Gilbert, who she says fell into a familiar trap, compelled to present herself in such an exacting way: self-deprecating to a (well-documented) fault on the one hand, yet—according to Shukert anyway—happy to leave out the real, unflattering details about the demise of her marriage on the other. But really, who could blame her for exchanging "honesty for likability," Shukert wonders. Her book took out a long-term lease at the top of the bestseller list, and Julia Roberts plays her in a movie. Who wouldn't want her iconic self embodied by "America's sweetheart"? Not to mention sleeping with Javier Bardem. Or James Franco. So often, and especially for women, it's just easier to pick a self and stick to the script.

Which brings us back to our point. On the one hand, you have Gilbert offering up her iconic self and being rewarded for it. And we all love that, because we really don't know what to do with someone—even ourselves—who can't be compartmentalized. But we secretly love Shukert too. Simply because she allows herself to be messy, which is what earned her book its props. Not good, not bad. Both. That's pretty rare to see, because we like our women—and ourselves—to be well defined. One or The Other. It's just so much easier to pick a self and make all else fit.

That's also why we also love this comment that flew into our blog from Natalie, a woman who had achieved high levels of success in the Wall Street world of finance but who still hadn't found what some of us might define as the parameters of an iconic self: an overarching passion.

She's a new mom who lives on Central Park West, across the street from The Dakota. She expressed a sentiment so raw and honest that, well, we needed to include it:

"I feel like I have dealt with this issue my entire life, just on a slightly different level. What if you don't have a passion? It always seems to come up: What would you do if time, money, and experience didn't matter; how would you spend your time? Honestly, I have no idea. None. I probably wouldn't do much of anything. Maybe travel, but where? I am even in a pickle there: I love to visit places, but *hate* to fly. After talking with several people over the course of many years, I have found that many are in the same boat. They don't have a passion, and if they do, it certainly isn't what they are being paid for. When I did my corporate job for ten years, I did it well, but it wasn't what I lived for. I worked to live, not lived to work. My real life was always on the verge of something else. The verge of what? Who knows.

"I was talking with a friend this weekend who basically thought it was pointless to work in a job that wasn't emotionally, spiritually, and creatively fulfilling. I thought, *Good for her, but what about everyone else?* I kept thinking that this is a first-world problem and really doesn't apply to much of the world. Most people don't care if they are living their passion, or at least working toward their passion. They care if they have a roof over their head and food on the table. Even people in the United States: Many just work to provide for their families. . . . Enough with the pressure already. Maybe just getting through the day is enough. The fact that at the end of the day my family is happy and healthy is enough for me. And if I am missing finding my passion today, that is okay.

"Women have it so hard; we are expected to do it all: take care of our families and be incredibly successful in our careers. We are supposed to have it all, when in reality that is impossible. You can't have everything at the same time. Even a statement like that is pretty loaded. Since you can't have it all at once, you are still supposed to have it at some point. Why? Why do you have to do it all? Maybe if we just slowed down a bit, did one thing at a time, we could find that missing passion. And if we don't find it? Who cares, enjoy the ride anyway."

AND SO IT'S complicated, the way our expectations become enmeshed in self-definition. We might be propelled forward by the belief that we can do anything so long as we try. But if we put ourselves out there, not measuring up is a real possibility too. So then another route might be opting to travel Mr. Safe Path, lugging a sidecar of What Might Have Been. (You might call this "settling," something we get into in Chapter 6.) Fulfilling? No. But at least it keeps you safe from failure, yes? But then, there's the iconic self, wagging her manicured finger at you from the other side of the mirror: *Fail.*

And what if you're just not good enough? Sure we've been told to dream high, to never sell ourselves short. And yes, that's absolutely the right lesson. But left out of the equation is the fact that sometimes, no matter how hard you want or how hard you try, talent or resources or life itself intervenes. The iconic self might say "CEO." But what the fuck? You just tanked the GMAT. Now what?

Christine Hassler—a life coach, counselor, and speaker—calls this the "expectation hangover," a term she actually copyrighted that refers to the regret, confusion, and all-over funk you're left with when a desired result is not met. Her own story is a good example of what she's talking about, and you'll hear all about it in Chapter 7, but for now, what she tells us is this: "I think that expectations sabotage all of us. . . . Expectations mean a lot of futuristic thinking, and they create a lot of stress and anxiety, because it's sort of like a when–then [scenario]: When I get this done, then I'll be happy; when so-and-so asks me out, then I'll be happy. So it's constantly living in the future. And the other thing is, I think expectations create tunnel vision, when we are only looking at what we think should happen or what we want to happen. Often we miss out on other signs from the universe that may come in later, or other opportunities. It all creates a lot of pressure, because we're constantly operating under *shoulds*—along with these expectations from society, parents, peers, worst of all ourselves, which create a constant state of stress and anxiety."

All of which, she says, is compounded by all the options now out there and, thanks to our digital lives, by how exposed we are to so much input at all possible times. And there's something else: the fact that expectations often beget more expectations. And we've never figured out when to say "Enough."

Tricky stuff, especially because we're so new to this game. Let's listen to a woman we'll call Lori—a poet, a grantwriter for a nonprofit, and, when we first checked in, pregnant with her first child. She's got an interesting backstory: an MFA in poetry, several years of teaching English at a private boarding school that combined wilderness education with high-level academics, and then a few years as an accidental reporter for small newspapers in Colorado.

"I wonder if some of our frustration is about the fact that it's virtually impossible to excel at everything—wife, writer, teacher, runner, in my case—and so we're always worried about the area in which we're not measuring up to our own expectations," Lori says. "It seems to me that when women went back into the workforce in the '60s and '70s, many weren't trying to climb the corporate ladder. I'm generalizing here, but I know my mother always says she and her friends were pushed to be teachers, secretaries, or nurses. And I think those are the sorts of jobs where you can drop out for several years to raise kids—if you want to—without feeling like you're hurting your career.

"My friends, on the other hand, largely think of themselves as having careers with climbable ladders. I just went back to Chicago last weekend to see eight other girls I graduated from college with thirteen years ago. Every one of us has an advanced degree. We're lawyers, doctors, nonprofit leaders, PhD candidates. And I think we're a little more conflicted about leaving our careers to raise children—or even working part-time—than we would be if we were all secretaries. On the other hand, we're conflicted about having children and putting them in daycare forty hours a week."

When it comes to all this work to appease our iconic selves, we're not just talking motherhood. Lauren, the accomplished writer we first met in Chapter 1, weighed in as well. She's brilliant, she's talented, and you'll hear lots more about her later. But at one point, when she was more than likely mulling options of her own, she reflected on this whole idea of expectations and the iconic self. Here's what she told us: "I wonder if part of our problem is that we struggle to find a single self in order to satisfy a cultural need to justify our relevance, when in actuality, we are wonderful because we are each a combination of so many selves," she says. "To be one self requires a sort of museum-like static perfection that may work for Barbie, but how can it work for the rest of us? If I think I sort myself out one day, the next day something happens to challenge the new myth I created—and accepted—the day before.

"Perhaps true liberation comes from accepting that what makes us beautiful, powerful, successful, creative, or whatever it may be, comes from a combination of potent self-images working together. Are we limiting or paralyzing ourselves by struggling to become an icon for this or that? Are we treating our lives too much like advertising campaigns, wherein a product's purpose must be clearly defined (or at least extremely seductive) to be accepted and desired by the public?

"I'm not suggesting we propagate the Wonder Woman image of being many things at once, but perhaps we need to cut ourselves some slack and let the French pastry chef inside of each of us live harmoniously with the Nobel Prize–winning author we dream of becoming. Maybe if we take the pressure off ourselves to "become," we might find that we actually "are." Is a great piece of music any less so because we don't know its name or how to classify it?"

She has one last thing to add, and you get the idea that it may be a product of her own personal struggle to let go of an icon. "I wonder if our illusion of choice—if we're calling it that—comes from a bigger idea that we are burdened by our need to produce a life," she says. "Are we seeing the possibilities for production as choices, when they are in fact not within our reach, or possibly not even interesting to us in the first place? If we felt less of a burden to make something of ourselves, might we indeed then see fewer choices but have more direction and more focus?"

THERE'S ANOTHER BURDEN at play here too—something else in our backpacks that we call the tyranny of the shoulds: the definitions, thrust upon us by the mainstream, which in turn often make us feel like the outsiders and thus keep us flailing. No question, there's a certain smug comfort in taking on the role of the outsider—which may be why so many of us continue to channel our inner Molly Ringwald (the late John Hughes's "poster child and alter ego"), who, according to *New York Times* writer A. O. Scott, "represented his romantic ideal of the artist as misfit, sensitive and misunderstood, aspiring to wider acceptance but reluctant to compromise too much. . . . The paradox is that most people feel, and want to be, different. Not to smash the system or flee its clutches, but rather to find a place within it where they can be themselves."[7]

All of which brings to mind a speech at East Carolina University by feminist icon/journalist/activist/Playboy-infiltrator Gloria Steinem. In her speech, Steinem rightly connected feminism with every other social justice movement and talked about the media myth that has proclaimed time and again that the feminist movement is over. But what stood out was this: "It goes deep, and we are subject to these myths," Steinem said. "And it's part of the human condition that the general social myth is so powerful for us that we sometimes think we are the strange exception, when really, we are the majority."[8]

Which makes you think: In the same way that feeling we are somehow out of the mainstream—that we are the "strange exception"—can affect how we choose to define ourselves, it can also mess with the decisions we make . . . and often, the really important ones. The ones that take our lives in one direction or another.

Take, for example, those who just want a "paycheck job," the kind you show up for at nine, leave at five, and don't think about again until nine the next day. But we've absorbed the idea that it's not enough—that there's something wrong with us to merely want a job when we can have a Career, so we kill ourselves to meet some grand milestone we think we should want, quietly wondering all the while, *Why am I doing this, again?*

Maybe the conventional ideas about the American Dream are the ones that tug at us: steady career path, home ownership, husband, kids. Everybody else seems to want those things, right? Surely we must be insane for being more interested in adventure than security. So we opt for the safe path, while daydreams of running off to join the circus grow all the more tantalizing with each mortgage bill.

Maybe it's the notion of having it all—the Superwoman icon—that keeps us quiet. We see other women smoothly managing it all. Or so we think. So we struggle to keep our heads above water, never letting on that we're one cupcake away from going postal, never even questioning what parts of "it all" we really want, what is really worth wanting for us—because, well, let's be honest, who has the time?

Or maybe we've made our peace, but because we're burdened by the shoulds, we have to slap a socially acceptable label on our choice in order to legitimize it. Case in point: another story by Peggy Orenstein in the *New York Times Magazine,* this one on the new "femivores"—extreme homemakers raising chickens in their own backyards. These "chicks with chicks," she writes, "are stay-at-home moms, highly educated women who left the work force to care for kith and kin. I don't think that's a coincidence: The omnivore's dilemma has provided an unexpected out from the feminist predicament, a way for women to embrace homemaking without becoming Betty Draper."[9] Or without *thinking* of themselves as Betty Draper. The photo with the story shows a pretty woman, low-lights glinting in the sun, leaning up against a weathered wall covered with climbing roses. She's wrapped in a soft pashmina and cradles a chicken as if it were a puppy. Behold: the Earth Mother, circa 2010.

A few months later, the *Mail Online* did something similar in a feature on the reemergence of the highly educated housewife.[10] Kind of a retread, except for the label: "feminist housewife." According to the article, this new breed of housefrau is a young, well-educated Britster who has decided to throw career to the wayside and instead stay home and bake cakes. The article's picture shows a smiling mum in a flowered frock with a toddler in one arm and a feather duster in the other. More feminism backlash? Possibly. But maybe it's this: Women have to frame raising children or chickens as "feminist"—and of course, do it perfectly—in order to legitimize their choice and/or assuage their ambivalence over choosing it. Rather than just arguing, "This is what I'm doing, and screw you if you don't think it's okay, because, you know, what you think doesn't really matter to me."

It's hard to go there though. Because these icons, these shoulds, sometimes weigh heavily on women who really just prefer to make a life for themselves without needing it to be the grand performance Lauren was talking about. Which leads us back, in an unexpected way, to what Steinem had to say: If cultural myths are so strong, so pervasive, how much do such myths infuse our life decisions with the suffocating weight of the shoulds? How often do we steer ourselves into what we believe is the culturally approved path (what we should do, what we should want) simply—even partly—because we're assuming we're the oddball exception rather than considering that we might in fact be a part of that great, silent rule?

In which case maybe our iconic self wouldn't be such a scold. We might in fact be more willing to allow ourselves some inconsistency. Some discovery. Or the space to explore the forks in the road.

What we might figure out, if we gave ourselves that permission, is that when it comes to our dreams, our expectations, our iconic selves, we are works in progress. And that progress is often really hard.

At fifty years old, Dana has that pegged. As she's gotten older, she says, she's discovered that for her, what it's all about is giving back. "People say, 'Well, in journalism, isn't that what you already do?' And I say, 'Yeah, maybe, when I write about nonprofits. But now I want to *be* one of those people, to do good'." To that end, she's involved in local programs that promote sustainability and eating locally, and she helps produce a concert series whose proceeds go to local charities. As far as her daughters are concerned, what she wants them to internalize is that, when the day is done, what's important is to know that they've made a difference.

Lori, too, votes for this idea of iconic self as work in progress, especially when it comes to figuring out the balance between the expectations of our evolving roles and a world that hasn't quite caught up: "Maybe it's that society is telling us all that we have to be successful career women—but the world has forgotten to mention that if we want to do that, we can let go of worrying about our pound cake," she says. "Or maybe it's just that the mold of womanhood has been broken, and now it's up to all of us to make up our own versions. That's incredibly empowering—because it means we get to make things up as we go along—but also scary and hard.

"And there's not a lot of guidance, because we're one of the first generations to do this. When our mothers told us we could be whatever we wanted, they may not have had the life experience in hand to warn us that, by the way, if what we wanted was to move to Louisville, Kentucky, to take a better job, we'd better cowboy up for two weeks of intense discussions with a husband who can't see how this move will benefit him in any way. Or that if we want to pursue an advanced degree while working part-time and while raising children, we need to be prepared to have it take three times as long as it's supposed to. Or that while we could be whatever we wanted, we might someday settle for a lesser job, or finish our advanced degree at a lesser university—because those choices were better for our family.

"I think what's most empowering to me is when I see women who can joyfully acknowledge that they don't give a damn about some aspect of womanhood—motherhood, their career—that they know they're supposed to care about. That is, when my friends acknowledge that they can't be good at everything, so they're just going to let some things go. . . . Several have decided to work part-time for awhile—and are perfectly comfortable, when people expect them to still be available at four o'clock on a Saturday, emailing to say they'll handle that crisis on Tuesday, when they're back in the office, thank you very much."

Lori had her baby, by the way. A little girl. She's headed back to work—part-time.

FIVE

SYNAPSE TRAFFIC JAM

Indecision may or may not be my problem.
—Jimmy Buffett

SEE IF THIS SOUNDS FAMILIAR. One desk. To the right, a wobbly stack of books, papers, and files—some dating back, oh, to last year.

To the left, a collection of to-do lists, very little crossed off. There's a Day Planner somewhere, you can't remember where. Center stage, a computer screen with unopened emails in the triple figures. Your cell keeps pinging, and a steady stream of folks buzz down the hall or into your office itself. Kind of like a roving cocktail party, sans drinks. The lack of cocktails: not necessarily a good thing.

Meanwhile, you're low on clean clothes, your hair is stringy, you need a megatrip to the grocery store—if only you had time to make a list—and you've got some bills that are teetering on the edge of past due. They're in a stack on your desk at home and, oh yeah, so *that's* where your passport is hiding. And right now you're so overwhelmed with stuff that you can't decide what to have for lunch, much less what to tackle next. It's enough to send you running for the chocolate cake.

Oops, we're getting ahead of ourselves.

We all agree that limitless options have left us stuck in neutral, reluctant to commit, and always second-guessing ourselves when we do. But rather than beating ourselves up over it, consider this: Science offers an out—we literally can't help it. Plenty of research shows that the human brain just isn't wired to deal with an abundance of choices. This stuff, this data, this überstimulation that clutters up our workbench is a good metaphor for what's going on in the little gray cells too. And so you have to wonder: Has all this information left us not only overwhelmed, but also chronically undecided?

The science says yes. What you find, when you dive into the body of research on choice, is that when we're undecided——when we can't figure out what to do with our lives—one reason is that there's some significant shit going down in the space upstairs.

There are a number of reasons why we have trouble with multiple choices, but the first has to do with the curse of the digital age: too much information. If you input too much data, studies show, the gray cells revolt. Which may be why, as Malcolm Gladwell told us in *Blink,* "To be a successful decision maker, you have to edit."[1]

Put another way: If you can't for the life of you make up your mind—or you're constantly jonesing for that road not traveled— there's a lot of science that helps explain why the more choices that confront us, the less likely we are to make one (or to be happy with it when we do). And while many of the studies might deal with choices about jam, cake, and online boyfriends, extrapolate the findings to life choices (coupled with the newfound number of options facing today's women and the pressure that comes with the message that we're so lucky to have them), and you get a sense of why indecision and the inability to commit has become a staple of modern life.

One of the pivotal studies showing how difficult it is for an overloaded brain to function dates from the '50s. In a classic paper entitled "The Magical Number Seven, Plus or Minus Two," Harvard psychologist George Miller demonstrated that the rational brain can only hold about seven chunks of information in working memory at any given time.[2] Any more, and the conscious brain can't handle the processing and often just throws up its hands in defeat. Too much information, too much to handle.

What psychologists have figured out since, is that when the cognitive brain gets too full, decision making—if it gets done at all—gets appropriated by the emotions. Because the rational brain has, in effect, logged off, there's less rational control over gut impulses.

Enter the chocolate cake.

Some fifty years after Miller's essay, Stanford marketing professor Baba Shiv put an interesting spin on this epic battle between heart and mind. In his study, he asked students to memorize either seven digits or two, then afterward offered both groups their choice of a reward: fruit salad or gooey chocolate cake. What he found was that the seven-digit group went with their gut instincts. They overwhelmingly chose cake.[3] "We distracted the cognitive side so that people were more likely to go with emotional impulses," Shiv later told *Business 2.0 Magazine* writer Andy Raskin.[4] The two-digit folks? They made the rational decision and chose a snack that wouldn't spoil their dinner: nice and healthful fruit salad. The rational and emotional sides of the brain are often competing for attention, Shiv later explained on NPR's *Radiolab*.[5] When there's a tough choice, and the rational brain has too much to keep track of, it hollers "Uncle!" and the emotional side takes over. (Is it any wonder why on a super-stressful workday we sometimes find ourselves diving into the stale doughnuts we normally wouldn't touch?)

A number of other studies have also shown that, if nothing else, making choices wears us out. Kathleen Vohs, an associate professor of marketing at the University of Minnesota, found that when shoppers— or college students—faced too many choices, they had a tough time staying focused.[6] Even making pleasant choices (you know, like shopping for that perfect little black dress) takes its toll on your ability to concentrate later. Call it decision fatigue. But the experiments themselves are pretty shocking in the way they demonstrate just how unfocused we manage to get.

In one experiment, Vohs's crew asked random shoppers at a mall about the choices they'd made that day, and then asked them to do some simple math problems. What the researchers found was that the more decisions the shoppers had made, the worse they performed on the math test. Similarly, in experiments with college students, researchers found that too much decision making not only affected the students' performance on the math problems, but screwed with their self-control too. Students asked to make a number of choices ended up spending more time later playing video games or reading magazines than studying for a test.

It's not just the choosing that makes you tired. It's what goes into the choosing—prioritizing, weighing the options. And when the options aren't really that different? Step back (and bring on the cake). So take the act of decision making and muck it up further by making Choice A not that much different from Choice B, and you're really in a pickle. Think back to those perception tricks from psych classes where you had to decide which line was longest. The closer in length, the longer it took to make your choice. And you were usually wrong anyhow. In 2009, a group of behavioral economists studied comparative judgment in terms of benefit analysis. What they found was what you'd expect: The closer the benefits of each choice, the more time—and cognitive effort—to decide between them. They call it optimization theory.[7]

But suppose instead of two choices, you have ten. Or more. You know, as in unlimited options? Makes us crazy, right? (Need convincing? Take a field trip to the Cheesecake Factory, open the menu, and try to choose what to have for lunch. Can't do it, can you?)

Which leads us back to that iconic jam study we brought up in Chapter 1. It found that when there is too much to choose from, we're unlikely to choose at all. (Which might explain the fact that, with cable TV and a remote in your hand, you might well channel-surf two hours of junk rather than committing to a movie.) Here's how the study— one of the most-referenced on choice—went down: Sheena S. Iyengar (author of *The Art of Choosing: The Hidden Science of Choice*[8]) and Mark Lepper set up shop at Draeger's, a swanky Northern California grocery store where you find bottles of imported balsamic vinegar in a glass case under lock and key. They alternated tasting booths for high-end jam: One table held six jars, the other twenty-four. What the researchers found was that shoppers were more attracted to the table of twenty-four, but the folks who stopped at the table of six more often chose one and walked away pleased. Those faced with twenty-four were more likely to walk away empty-handed.[9]

The researchers tested their theory twice more: Students in a social psychology class were given the opportunity to write an extra-credit assignment—choosing from either six or thirty topics. Those with six topics to choose from were more likely to do the extra credit. In the third part, students were confronted with either six or thirty Godiva chocolates to sample. Those with thirty to choose from *enjoyed* the process more (hello, who wouldn't?), and yet, given their choice of a reward for participating in the study—either a box of Godivas or five bucks—they were more likely to take the money and run. Why? Choosing the best chocolate truffle from among a bunch of them not only becomes hard cognitive work, taking the fun out of eating them, but introduces the potential for regret, too: maybe you chose wrong. All of which makes taking home a box of them a lot less desirable. The question, the researchers pointed out, was why opportunity seemed to lead, well, nowhere: "Perhaps it is not that people are made unhappy by the decisions they make in the face of abundant options, but that they are instead unsure—that they are burdened by the responsibility of distinguishing good from bad decisions."[10]

All of which makes infinite sense to a relative of ours, an avowed fashionista who loves to shop. She had her "colors" done back in the '80s and found out she was made for shades of orange and green. She tells us that it changed her life, and she means that literally. "It's great," she says. "I go into a store and it immediately reduces my choices by 90 percent." (The irony? She's a judge. All she wears is black.)

Lately, online dating sites have been seeing some action too, at least in terms of showing how cognitive overload leads to lousy decisions. Two recent studies showed that when it comes to choosing a dude off the Internet, having too many choices leads to duds. One of the studies, out of Taiwan, suggested that the more potential beaus to choose from, the less likely you are to make a good choice.[11] Too many choices, the researchers concluded, make the online date-seekers distracted, and they end up spending less time on each prospect. Another study, done in 2008, also found that the more you search for Mr. Right, the less likely you are to find him.[12] According to Michael Norton—a Harvard Business School professor who coauthored the study—one issue is expectations. The online dating scene gives the illusion that there are a huge number of options for potential matches, which raises expectations too high, and which in turn results in an "often fruitless search for an ideal person who may not exist."[13]

Lori Gottlieb—author of *Marry Him,* a bestseller about settling for Mr. Good Enough—couldn't agree more. "It's not just too much information that makes online dating confusing—it's too many choices. Aren't there five new 'matches' that arrive in your email box each day? Even if none of them is remotely interesting, doesn't it still give you hope that of the next five, one might be The One?"[14]

ALL OF WHICH helps explain why we can't decide. But there's more work out there that shows why we're often unhappy when we do.

The definitive word comes from Barry Schwartz, whose book *The Paradox of Choice: Why Less Is More* suggests that an overabundance of choices leads to two negative effects. The first is paralysis: Confronted with too many choices, some people have a hard time choosing at all. The second is "opportunity cost": Choosing one option means *not* choosing others, and when those others are also attractive, you focus on what you missed and are less satisfied with what you have.[15] In an entertaining and accessible TEDTalk, he points out that this inability to choose and this tendency to continually second-guess yourself are functions of escalating expectations. As we mentioned back in Chapter 1, Schwartz, in this talk, uses the example of shopping for jeans . . . in a world where there are lots of them. Confronted with too many choices, he says, you can't help but assume that one of them must be perfect. And thus, a choice that is merely good—if you can make it at all—leads to disappointment and regret: You shoulda-coulda done better.[16]

It's actually pretty simple. In a 2004 article for *Scientific American* aptly named "The Tyranny of Choice," Schwartz wrote, "Several studies have shown that two of the factors affecting regret are how much one feels personal responsibility for the result and how easy it is to imagine a better alternative. The availability of choice obviously exacerbates both these factors. When you have no options, what can you do?"[17]

You said it, Schwartz. Remember Jane, who said she wished she was born into a culture where everything from spouse to career were chosen for her? Makes a little more sense now, doesn't it?

Regret is apparently a big factor when we're faced with a decision: We're afraid we'll choose wrong. Much of the word on this subject dates back to a 1979 paper by the late Stanford psychologist Amos Tversky and Princeton Nobelist Daniel Kahneman, who first found that the pain of loss (real or perceived) impacts us more than the pleasure of gain.[18] They called it "prospect theory." In another study that explored this idea a bit more, Tversky and Princeton psychologist Eldar Shafir asked shoppers for their reaction to a CD player sitting in a shop window, its price radically reduced. Two-thirds were ready to pull out their checkbooks. But when another CD player, also marked down, was placed by its side? No sale. With two to choose from, there was the distinct possibility that they might choose wrong.[19] Researchers out of Oxford have explained the inability to "pull the trigger" in terms of "regret theory": the fear that what you *don't* choose might be better than what you did.[20] Especially when the choices are pretty similar.

But it's not like we're operating completely on autopilot. A lot of this choice business has to do with personality too. Those who tend to geek out over such things lay it out this way. As we teased in Chapter 1, much depends on whether you're a Maximizer (someone who seeks the best and does an exhaustive search to find it) or a Satisficer (someone who stops the search at "good enough"). Interesting stuff, and it brings us back to both Schwartz and Iyengar, who coauthored a study in 2006 that may strike a chord with those of us who always think the grass is greener. Aptly titled "Doing Better But Feeling Worse," the study followed college seniors on their job hunt and found that even though Maximizers landed jobs with heftier paychecks, they ended up less satisfied than their Satisficer counterparts.[21] "Even when they get what they want," the researchers wrote, "maximizers may not want what they get."[22] Why? Regret. Even after they had scored the fat jobs, the Maximizers (they're more likely to feel dissatisfaction when they do worse, versus pleasure when they do better) couldn't help imagining the alternatives—possibly the *perfect* alternative—that they had somehow missed or even turned down. Their expectations were higher. So were the opportunity costs.

There's something else going on that can also make us rue our decisions: familiarity. According to more research on online dating (which is apparently fertile ground for studies on choice), it breeds contempt. Consider the 2007 study by Michael Norton, Jeana Frost, and Dan Ariely. (Incidentally, Ariely is the author of the best-selling *Predictably Irrational,* which talks about all the hidden tricks that manipulate our decisions. Like the fact that when restaurants put a high-priced entrée on the menu, they make more money, even though very few people order it. Why? We're likely to go for the second-most expensive.[23]). They found that the more you know, the less you like.[24] Well, then. The authors suggest that when you know very little about someone, you read whatever you want into the person. You presume similarities, which increases your attraction. But, once your information grows, dissimilarities creep in, upsetting your dreamy apple cart. Disappointed, you begin interpreting new information as further evidence of dissimilarity: no more benefit of the doubt. The upshot? "Many prospects, whether world leaders or would-be hipsters, who looked good from afar, suddenly seem less attractive once more is known," the authors write. "Ambiguity necessarily decreases over the course of acquaintance, and the positive expectations that people read into ambiguous others diminish as more and more evidence of dissimilarity is uncovered."[25]

It's not much of a leap to imagine that the same dynamics could come into play with other choices too: Your job, for example, might seem truly exciting when everything is new, but once you get set in your routine, you begin to notice your boss is a jerk, your cube gives you claustrophobia, and you were never made for spreadsheets. But second-guessing isn't the only issue. Sometimes we just, you know, goof. Behavioral economists (consider the field the love child of psychology and economics) such as Harvard's David Laibson (whom we met back in Chapter 1) have found that because we tend to discount tomorrow when we make decisions today, we often make the wrong ones. Most of Laibson's research has to do with saving for retirement. Still, you can generalize to human behavior. As he told *Harvard Magazine,* "People very robustly want instant gratification now and want to be patient in the future."[26] The point? We often choose according to the moment—especially when the emotional brain is in charge—rather than the long term.

Other studies have shown that both fear and stress can drive bad decision making. A study out of Portugal suggests that stress can switch hungry rats' brains to autopilot, leading to decisions made out of habit rather than using any kind of thought process.[27] Well, okay, we're not rats, and we don't press levers to eat. But still, you have to consider that similar wiring may be at play when we are too frazzled to think straight. We fall back on old patterns. And if they have to do with fear, we could be in for trouble.

In *Elle* magazine in 2009, writer Louise Kamps explored the ways in which fear mucks up our decision-making brain circuitry.[28] She cites some science that says that when we relax, our prefrontal cortexes tend to follow suit, leaving us better able to see the big picture. So far so good. But when faced with a big decision—when there are more factors to consider—that big picture can get blurry. It plays out like this: "Experts say people tend to make major life decisions either out of 'a crystallization of discontent,' when a situation becomes unbearable, or out of 'a crystallization of desire,' when they feel a surge of enthusiasm for a new idea."[29] She quotes psychologist Jack Bauer, whose research suggests that deciding out of desire rather than fear leads to more satisfaction. In two studies in 2005, Bauer and his colleagues found that when we make decisions based on where we want to go—rather than what we want to escape—we're happier with the outcomes.[30] Which makes you think: When wrangling with a decision, instead of angsting over the choice itself, maybe we should step back, shift our focus, and figure out what it is we really value—what it is that's calling our name.

THAT SOUND YOU hear right now? That's your head spinning, probably because of all the information you've just jammed inside it. (Magical number seven, remember? Anyone for cake?) But wait, there's more. It makes you crazy, really, when you think of all that's going on upstairs when we're trying to choose between the red one and the blue one. Back to Gladwell in *Blink*: "Truly successful decision making relies on a balance between deliberate and instinctive thinking. . . . The second lesson is that in good decision making, frugality matters."[31]

In other words, *don't* consider everything.

But, thanks in no small part to everything from the interwebs to smartphones, that brand of frugality is a thing of the past. Because outside our own heads, beyond the firing of our own private synapses, we are bombarded with ever more information and stimulation. We are always on. Wired. Addicted to short bursts of constant information. Distracted by teasers for everything from digital news alerts to invite-only shopping sites that clutter up our inboxes as well as our heads.

Really, we have work we should be doing, decisions we should be making . . . but then there's the seduction: "Buy now!" "Free shipping!" "On sale for the next five minutes only!" Whether or not you bite, the damage is done. You're sidetracked, your concentration blown.

What we might learn from noted travel writer Pico Iyer, author of *The Open Road: The Global Journey of the Fourteenth Dalai Lama*, is that what we need to do is to unplug. As he told a rapt audience at the 2010 Sun Valley Writers' Conference, the silence ushers us into something deeper.[32] Which may be why it's now become something of an indulgence to find a coffee shop—or a luxury retreat—that bills itself as wi-fi free. We've begun to appreciate the need to unplug.

While all this technocrack has made us a nation of multitaskers, research suggests that when we are doing too many things at once—when we're at the beck and call of multiple media streams—we don't do many of them well. One 2009 Stanford study found that heavy media multitasking screws up our ability to process information.[33] The researchers found that those students in the study who were regularly tuned in to too many sources of information at once (email, chat, text messages, TV, Facebook) had trouble paying attention, remembering, and switching from one task to another. What they couldn't do was filter out irrelevant information. "They're suckers for irrelevancy," said Professor Clifford Nass, one of the researchers, in an interview with *Stanford Report*'s Adam Gorlick. "Everything distracts them."[34] What the researchers found was that the chronic multitaskers couldn't help thinking about what they *weren't* doing. There's always something *else*.

Sound familiar?

Maybe it was always so. But there's no question that techno-stimulation complicates things. In fact, some researchers—such as Stanford psychiatrist Elias Aboujaoude, director of Stanford University's Impulse Control Disorders Clinic—think that habitual Internet use has become, if not an addiction per se, at least problematic for a significant number of users.[35] More interesting is this: There's also the worry that our dependence on short bursts of information might well impact our ability to think straight. "The more we become used to just soundbites and tweets," Aboujaoude told *San Francisco Chronicle* reporter Benny Evangelista, "the less patient we will be with more complex, more meaningful information. And I do think we might lose the ability to analyze things with any depth and nuance. Like any skill, if you don't use it, you lose it."[36]

Dr. John Ratey—an associate clinical professor of psychiatry at Harvard Medical School and author of *Spark: The Revolutionary New Science of Exercise and the Brain*—agrees. He uses the term "acquired attention deficit disorder" to describe the way our modern brains are rewired by our infatuation with texts, tweets, and all else technology has wrought.[37]

In fact, a University of London study commissioned by HP suggested that the average worker's IQ can drop a good ten points when he or she is "always on" (i.e., when distracted by ringing phones and incoming emails).[38] The drop in IQ isn't permanent, the research suggests, but the effect of all the distraction is reported to be greater than the impact of a sleepless night—and more than double the effect of smoking pot. What's interesting is that the study was done in 2005—long before Twitter or smartphones became our BFFs.

We'd go into this in more depth, but, you know, we're a little too distracted.

ALL OF THIS brings to mind a *New Yorker* cover, entitled "Top of the World," that reminds us how difficult it is to savor the moment, given our umbilical ties to everything tech.[39] The illustration shows two pretty people, clearly well-heeled, at the crest of what looks to be an alpine ski slope. But instead of admiring the view, reveling in their good fortune for what looks like a killer vacation, or just getting into the Zen of it all (pick one), he's taking a photo, undoubtedly to post on Facebook. She's on her cell, presumably sharing the moment, rather than living it. It would be kind of funny if it didn't give you the recognition shivers and make you wonder if this extreme connection with cyber-reality is keeping us from being fully present in our own here and now.

And when we're not fully present, how much harder is it to make a choice? You also have to wonder if the angst goes viral when we're attached to a hundred different lives at any given time. Call it "oversharing" multiplied by, well, a number that coincides with our Twitter followers and Facebook friends. (A friend once described Facebook in terms of a cocktail party: You've got this conversation going on over here, but over there are dozens, maybe hundreds, of others you can eavesdrop on as you scroll down the page. You can also flit. Pop into a conversation at will; then, when it bores you? Ta-ta.) But while all those connections might give you a good sense of the zeitgeist, it's not too much of a stretch to suspect that either you're sitting around wishing you were doing what someone else is doing (who might be wishing she was doing what you were doing and maybe even wishes she were you)—or wishing you were someone else.

If nothing else, it's one more thing that keeps us distracted and undecided. Because apparently our brains just aren't equipped to handle all this clicking and juggling and backing-and-forthing. That's what Douglas Merrill—former Google CIO and coauthor of *Getting Organized in the Google Era*—told NPR's Renée Montagne. He says the brain uses short-term memory for what it's doing now, then stores that info in long-term memory so we can find it later. The problem is in the shift, he says. "Everyone feels like they're tremendous multitaskers. It's a little bit like Lake Wobegon: Everyone thinks they're better than average, but you're not. You can't multitask. When you shift from one context to another, you're going to drop some things. And what that means is that you're less effective at the first task and at the second task that you're try-ing to do at the same time."[40]

All of which makes you long for something that will spoil your dinner.

UNDERSTANDING ALL OF this, of course, doesn't necessarily teach us how to decide—or to be pleased when we do. But it might give us the nudge we need to take Gladwell's advice from the beginning of this chapter: edit.

Consider Rob Walker's article "This Year's Model," which appeared in the *New York Times Magazine*. It presents an interesting question: When constrained by a lack of choice, are we forced to get creative? The article centers on The Uniform Project (http://theuniformproject.com), a fundraising effort created by Sheena Matheiken, who was raised in India, where uniforms were de rigueur. Matheiken vowed to wear the same dress every day for a year, with the goal of seeing just how creative she could be with accessories, despite that limitation. On her blog, she notes that despite the uniforms they all had to wear in school, she and her classmates still got imaginative . . . and stylish too. All of which inspired Walker to state this: "Rules stifle creativity and enforce conformity. Rules can do something else too: Inspire creativity that thwarts conformity."[41]

As in fashion, so in life? Chloe (she of "commitment is a kind of death") is also pretty stylish, despite (or because of?) the fact that she too grew up wearing the requisite plaid to school. She tends to agree with Matheiken and Walker. "I think limitation or less choice absolutely leads to more creativity," she says. "Which is why great art is usually made by people who come from lesser means. I, too, did time in Catholic school, and I actually had this very observation in high school. Not that I enjoyed the itchy, ill-fitting plaid skirt . . . but it was sort of a game, a challenge to find a way to allow your personality to shine through—hair color, shoe color, nail-polish color. It just goes to show that choice—or lack of—can be a blessing and a curse. I think it really comes down to an individual's ingenuity and courage to be themselves."

And, of course, to turn down the chatter. Timothy Leary (that '60s guru of LSD fame) once exhorted the youth of the day to "Turn on, tune in, drop out." Maybe it's time to flip the switch: to turn off, tune out, drop in.

SIX

SETTLING FOR THE DETOURS

I choose my choice! I choose my choice!
—Charlotte, *Sex & the City*

LAST YEAR, A POPULAR FUROR AROSE when Lori Gottlieb's book *Marry Him! The Case for Settling for Mr. Good Enough* was published, and it's not difficult to understand why. Who the hell wants to settle?

Conventional wisdom says that, now that all the doors are open, there is no reason women should settle for anything less than perfect. In any realm. We've all absorbed the message—so perfectly captured in Maureen Dowd's oft-quoted words, "The minute you settle for less than you deserve, you get even less than you settled for."[1] And it's reinforced in the supportive girlfriend–speak we feed each other. *Go for it! You're awesome! You totally deserve the best!*

In a section of Gottlieb's book entitled "How Feminism Fucked Up My Love Life," she goes so far as to say that, you know, feminism fucked up her love life. While we'd take issue with that, one point she makes really resonates.

"We grew up believing that we could 'have it all.' 'Having it all' meant that we shouldn't compromise in any area of life, including dating," she wrote. "Not compromising meant 'having high standards.' The higher our standards, the more 'empowered we were.'"[2]

(And if you don't want to blame feminism, blame your parents! That's always a convenient option. As Barry Schwartz told us, "I think, quite inadvertently, parents who only want the best for their children teach them to only want the best for themselves. . . . I've never heard a parent say, 'I only want what's good enough for my kids.'")

Empowerment, Gottlieb said, came to mean having excruciatingly—impossibly—high standards and an unshakable belief that we can, in fact, have it all. The way such an ethos plays out in the dating field, she writes, is this: "[M]any of us empowered ourselves out of a good mate."[3]

Or empowered ourselves into a ceaseless struggle to have it all. As Erica Kennedy tells us, "Women today, we're dating and dating, trying to find Mr. Perfect. Or we think we've found him, but when the reality of marriage sets in, we're thinking about all the other fish in the sea that we could have chosen. Or we hit one bump in the road and get divorced. Or we have one healthy child but then go through all kinds of fertility treatments because we won't be happy until we have *two*. I think we're socialized to believe we should want more, but it's not until we get the more do we even consider that maybe less was just fine, if not better."

This ideology of extreme empowerment informs the way many of us choose to live our lives, even if we won't quite admit it. Never mind the way holding out for "perfect" and scrambling to score the "more" generally plays out, leaving us unhappy, dissatisfied, and wasting a whole lot of time. But the truth is that the good-enough life/job/guy/ jeans often feels like anything but. To accept the good-enough option while recognizing it as such is an affront—as though we're conceding that we don't, in fact, deserve the best.

To hear Gottlieb tell it, though, what the process of writing *Marry Him* taught her was that good enough is, in fact, good enough. Maybe even better. In an interview with CNN, she said: "Is anything less than 'everything we want' going to make us less happy? The answer is no, and it probably will make you more happy."[4]

Hold the phone. Getting *less* than everything we want will make us *more* happy?

Blasphemy!

It sounds so counterintuitive. But, as we learned in the last chapter, research indicates she's onto something. In fact, Gottlieb cites Barry Schwartz all over her book and has adopted that axiom of his as a mantra: Good enough is good enough.

As Schwartz himself told us, "I think you need to learn from experience that good enough is almost always good enough. It seems like settling, as you put it. Why would anyone settle, especially these masters of the universe. . . ? And this is something that's been coming up in the last few weeks: Starting at age fifty, people get happier. And I think a significant reason why is, what you learn from experience is exactly that good enough is good enough, and once you learn that, you stop torturing yourself looking for the best, and life gets a lot simpler. And I think it's very difficult to convince a twenty-year-old that that's the way to go through life."

And it's true: Although the idea that "good enough is good enough" makes sense intellectually, while we're still establishing ourselves—testing the waters, looking to find our place in the world— there's something about it that gets our hackles up. Because what we're really talking about here is choice—and often, because we believe (because we've been told) we have so much of it, we're convinced that surely there's something out there that's perfect. And so it makes sense that so many of us struggle with the assumption that to settle for anything less than everything—anything less than perfect—is to sell ourselves short. To settle.

To paraphrase one of Barry Schwartz's conclusions from *Paradox of Choice*, as options expand, people's standards for what is acceptable rise. The more choices we have (or even the more choices we *believe* we have), the better we think we can do.[5]

Why settle then, when something better must surely be out there? To do so feels, in some ways, like a concession, surrender—giving up. But there are some problems with perfection. Namely that it doesn't exist. And therefore, we can waste a lot of time and energy looking for it. And pass up an awful lot of "good enough" in the meantime.

Let's use gift cards as an example. How many do you currently have gathering dust on a shelf, in a drawer, in your purse? We'll wait while you count.

Ready?

Before you start beating yourself up over those unclaimed iTunes downloads and Frappuccinos, consider the points made by *New York Times* writer John Tierney in an article that spelled out what we all know to be true: We humans have a tendency to procrastinate—even when it comes to matters of pleasure. And the reasons have a lot to do with perfection.

In that story, Tierney cited a couple of studies, one of which found that people who "moved to Chicago, Dallas, and London get to fewer local landmarks during the entire first year they live there than the typical tourist visits during a two-week stay." In the other study, people were given gift certificates good for movie tickets and French pastries; some expired within two to three weeks; some in six to eight. And although the people with more time to cash in were more confident that they'd redeem their gift certificates, they actually turned out to be *less likely* to use them.

What does this have to do with anything? Well, consider. "Once you start procrastinating pleasure, it can become a self-perpetuating process if you fixate on some imagined nirvana. The longer you wait to open that prize bottle of wine, the more special the occasion has to be."[6]

All of which is interesting when it comes to using those gift cards, cashing in those frequent-flier miles, opening that killer (or so you've read) bottle of syrah. But what it left us wondering was this: What might such a psychological tic mean when it comes to our lives, and our choices?

How often do we put off going after what we really want because we're waiting for the stars to align and offer up the perfect circumstances? Of course, it's just so easy to stick to the path we're already on, opting to postpone that trip (airfare might come down), that move (sure that apartment is cute, but it's so small . . . and what if I sign the lease and then the *perfect* place opens up), that baby (next year; we should be making more money), going back to school (only if I get into my no. 1 choice), starting a business (maybe it's not the right time), changing careers altogether (maybe once the economy improves), Insert Your Dream Here (insert your excuse here): All because circumstances aren't quite perfect . . . yet. But where does that get us? With a stack of dreams piled on the shelf, gathering dust and in danger of expiring, turning to vinegar?

Dr. Suzanne Shu, one of the researchers who conducted those studies Tierney cited, described what's behind this variety of commitmentphobia like this: "[People] anticipate that they'll kick themselves later if they take the second-best option and . . . the best one is still available. But they don't realize that regret can go the other way: They'll end up with something worse and regret not taking that second-best one."[7]

Which brings us back to the impetus for Gottlieb's book. She'd been there (dates with dudes she dismissed for reasons ranging from a suboptimal first name to a head of red hair), done that (single and tormented by her ticking biological clock, she hit the sperm bank and is now a single mama, lonely for company), and was ready to take a good, hard look at her standards. And once she did, what she found was a reason—and a willingness—to let go of her desperate search for perfect. Not to mention a whole new perspective on what it means to settle.

"I'm not talking about 'settling' in the sense of lowering your standards," she told us. "I'm not asking people to settle. I'm asking them to *think*. To think about what's really important and what really makes people happy in the long-term—lasting love versus the things they think are 'settling' when they're dating (he's not tall enough, he's not charming enough, we don't like the same movies/books/music, etc.). I'm asking people to have very high standards about the important things (shared values, kindness, overall chemistry) and to let go of the things that won't matter. But letting go of anything, for many women, is considered too much of a compromise, or even settling. 'Why can't I hold out for the guy who's this tall, or more creative,' they might ask, incensed that I'm asking them to consider putting less weight on that. 'Why can't I have everything I want?' What they don't realize is, even if they get 'everything they want,' they still might not have everything they need for a happy, long-term marriage."

Again, makes sense. And likely what's true for relationships will hold in other aspects of our lives as well. And for many of the women we spoke with, when it comes to settling, the more relevant question is not "Will you or won't you," but what *is* settling in the first place? Is it really settling to take a page from Gottlieb and revise (and revise, and revise again) our aspirations?

Hollee Temple, author of *Good Enough Is the New Perfect,* doesn't think so. She was the quintessential overachiever. An unrepentant per-fectionist. Took the accelerated program at Northwestern University in order to earn both her undergrad degree and a masters in journalism—in four years. She followed that up with nothing less than Duke Law School and went straight to a large international law firm in Pittsburg (her hometown), joining the litigation group. She told us, "I worked there for four years, and I would say probably about six months in I was pretty sure that this was not what I wanted to do and I was not going to be happy doing it long-term, so I tried and tried to make it work."

She changed practice groups; saw a career counselor. "I couldn't figure out why it wasn't working for me. . . . The only thing I thought was worthwhile about the job was the pay. Everything else was not working for me. I felt underutilized; I'd be locked in a room by myself for ten to twelve hours a day. They called us 'time keepers,' which made me feel like a widget-maker or something, like anybody could do it, that I was just this replaceable commodity."

She'd spent her whole life up until that point trying to get there—and discovering she hated it was a shock to the system. "It wasn't the right fit for me, but it was hard for me to get off that linear path that I had always planned, with partnership at a law firm as sort of the natural endpoint for the career that I had developed."

After having her first son, she went back to work part-time for a couple of months. Her husband got a new job an hour and a half away, so, looking to relocate, Temple landed a job in academia, at the West Virginia University College of Law, where she's been ever since. But the move did not come without its share of sacrifices, beginning with a huge, easily quantifiable one: "It involved sacrificing more than 50 per-cent of my salary. . . . But also [the new] job was a less prestigious job. I came in with the 'lecturer' title, when I was used to always shooting for the highest rung, and that rankled. It was difficult for me to accept. I did not like it; I did not have professor in my title, and it bothered me that I was viewed by some of my colleagues as 'less than'—even though my academic credentials were as good as or better than theirs—because I had taken this less prestigious job. So in my career path I basically chose to prioritize my happiness and my interest in being present for my children over the other things I could have chosen, other kinds of success—like money and prestige and the top rung of the ladder."

Ooh, yes. The money! The prestige! The symbols! They're hard things to give up, because—let's face it—as much as we likely would rather not admit it, part of that ever-elusive picture-perfect life to which we aspire is the picture itself. How it looks.

For Gottlieb and her search for Mr. Perfect, this meant height and hair and fashion requirements, résumé stipulations, questions of pedigree. And in her quest to reenvision her image of Mr. Perfect into Mr. Good Enough, such externals were the first things to go—after extensive guidance from Rachel Greenwald, author of *Find a Husband After 35: Using What I Learned at Harvard Business School*, of course. Greenwald's advice was to ditch the objective stuff and focus on the subjective. And though Gottlieb was resistant at first, she's now a proponent of such an approach—in all realms.

"It helps you really clarify what are the essential elements, whether it's a job, or a house you're going to buy, or any decision you're making. . . . Some of the more objective things are more about status—preconceived notions of what you assume lies behind those qualities," said Gottlieb during our interview. "Like, you know, really cool jobs might seem really cool, but maybe it's not really cool. Maybe the hours are terrible or the bosses are insane . . . you know, like a Hollywood job for example."

(Alex, a producer who works in Hollywood, can attest to that. "Dude," she says, "I'm doing what I wanted to do out of college, and now I'm over it. Sometimes what we originally think is glamorous turns out to be the opposite. After ten years in this industry, I'm ready for a big change. Ideally, owning my own business and not ever having to worry about a director not enjoying his sandwich.")

Gottlieb continued, "Something that looks really enticing from the outside is usually sort of culturally informed . . . very superficial." So why, we asked, do we get so hung up on them? And in a *Helloooo* kind of tone, she told us what we already knew: "The objective things are so alluring."

Like children transfixed by a shiny object, we, too, are distracted by rock-star titles, outsized paychecks, and all the associations that go with prestige positions. But sometimes, as Temple found, the subjective stuff is, you guessed it, good enough. It's a sentiment that thirty-two-year-old Michelle might agree with. For years, she gave the "writing life in the bright lights, big city of New York" a go, only to chuck it in favor of returning home to South Florida to become a teacher. "Ugh!" (Her words—or *word*.) While in New York, she interned and worked at hip-hop magazine *The Source*—and freelanced for various other publications—for years before eventually opting out of that dream. In 2006, during her second stint (this one paid) at *The Source,* the magazine existed under a cloud of rumors about imminent takeover. The end was nigh; everyone was looking for another job.

"[One day], while walking to my umpteenth interview in Manhattan—for another office-managerial interview set up through another temp agency—I stood in the middle of 42nd Street—in between 5th and 6th, I'll never forget—and decided to return back to South Florida to become a teacher," she said. She'd been living in Jersey City, in a closet of a room (literally: her room was a repurposed closet). She had no car, no savings, no prospects to speak of. After rent and transportation, she had about $50 a week leftover for extras—like food. And she was done.

While she'd never wanted to "teach other people's kids," Michelle now has a steady job with benefits and a condo, a car, savings, and her summers off. "I always wondered whether settling for my personal happiness was worth my professional happiness. I still dream of the bright lights and life in the big city," she said. "I may not be taking assignments to interview Lil Wayne nowadays; instead, I'm giving out assignments to middle-school children."

But does she feel like she's settling? Nope. "I've done it. I've had the opportunity to live in New York, ran around the city doing all those great things, so I don't feel like I'm settling. I just feel like I'm in another phase in my life. And I'm pretty content."

Ah, contentment. We've heard of that.

But how many of us are so willing to accept such a choice—one between, as Michelle put it, professional fulfillment and personal fulfillment? And what about creative fulfillment?

That's the struggle that got twenty-nine-year-old Erin talking. A Tampa native who recently moved to Atlanta, Erin has fought the pressure to settle, which, in her case, might be code for finding a way to remain true to herself. She's creative and craves meaningful, engaging work. She's consciously pushed to develop her independence—and, at times, Erin finds herself deeply at odds with the conventions of her beloved South.

Our first conversation, on a Sunday afternoon, found her on the road, driving from Atlanta (where she'd moved a little less than a year prior) to Oxford, Mississippi—the "small pond" where she went to college and graduate school and became a self-described "big fish."

Her initial decision to move to Oxford—which she did for school (and a guy) when she was eighteen—was regarded with suspicion among her large, tight-knit family. "I just wanted to get away," she said. "Florida is like its own country; lots of people never leave—and that just wasn't me. I had an opportunity to go—I was dating a guy whose company moved him there, and I happened to visit him, and I was like, 'Oh my gosh, I love it here! It's so different from anything I've ever experienced!' But everyone was like, 'Why are you moving there? Why would anyone move there?' But it's home to William Faulkner and Ole Miss and this really great literary and cultural community that Tampa just didn't have for me. And I was really craving that."

After graduation and a brief stint in London, Erin returned to Oxford. And though she and the guy fizzled, her relationship with her adopted town grew hot and heavy. She took on some nonprofit work and then started working for a cool community-oriented independent bookstore. "That bookstore just really nurtured me, [helped me figure out] what it was that I was going to set out to do—which was be independent and be my own person."

She worked her way up to marketing director and then lucked into an opportunity to produce a "Southern-Fried Prairie Home Companion"–type radio show. In the meantime, she earned a graduate degree in Southern studies—and a solid place in the community. By the time she left, she said, "I knew everyone; everyone knew me. I was very connected with a lot of the events that went on in town, and kind of went from knowing everyone and being a person that someone might call to ask a question about something going on in town, to . . ."

To what, exactly?

Well, Atlanta. And that's where the question of settling comes up.

"I realized that if I stayed in Oxford, it was going to limit me. I needed to challenge myself yet again, so that's kind of where I was. I didn't want to go to New York, because I love the South," she said, offering a qualifier before continuing, saying she's trying her darnedest not to settle—another major aspect of which is giving up a measure of that independence she's worked so hard to develop.

"What was really difficult for me was that one of the reasons I chose Atlanta was for another guy, and I didn't want to repeat—I didn't want to do it for all of those reasons again. . . . I knew I could do just as well as I did in Oxford in any other city, but I have this wonderful guy who lives in Atlanta, so in a way, I kind of had to make a sac—" she stopped there, catching herself, then continued, "—a small sacrifice. So I went to Atlanta. And let me tell you, it is no walk in the park."

She's not so wild about the city itself, and the work she's found herself doing—bid consulting for the building industry—is not what she set out to do.

"I think that for people who are kind of like me—perfectionists, or they just have higher expectations or higher standards for themselves—you're always gonna have something where you feel like you're settling. I'm going to be thirty this year, and my twin sister is married, and my sister who's one year older than me is married and has two children. For me, settling would definitely be, 'Oh [honey], hurry up and ask me to marry you so I can have accomplished something tangible that everyone can see.' For me, that would be settling. Settling would be doing what everyone is expecting me to do."

As far as the consulting work she's doing now goes, Erin says, "I am having to take some of my creative energy and focus on more traditional income-earning. I've had to basically do things that I don't really want to be doing but that make a lot more money than what I'm doing creatively. But I don't know if that's settling, because I think settling would be just doing that and abandoning this creative world that I've created. I have this friend I went to art school with—she's a pharmacist now, but she was this amazing photographer when we were young—and just a couple of years ago she said to me, 'I'm really proud of you for staying with art when you could have easily gone into another field where you'd make more money.' So I'm not going to give up this creative stuff that I do, but I just have to be a little more creative in trying to find other work that maybe alone is not very meaningful to me but it allows me to be creative."

It can be a fight, negotiating the need for creative fulfillment and the need for, well, cash—and negotiating the longing to be your own person and the love you have for someone else. But Erin seems to have come to a tenuous peace. We said goodbye just as she came to the Mississippi border—her fifth trip in as many months. She was on her way to Oxford, where she's working on a documentary and a book about the people she worked with on the radio show, and the community there. "I haven't given up on the creative side of my life, but I realized that there's no honor in not being able to pay your bills."

BUT WHAT HAPPENS when you've landed your dream job—only to find that it's not perfect either?

That's what happened to twenty-six-year-old Lisa, a Houston native and member of the only internationally touring belly-dance company in the world. She told us the following by email: "I have performed in over ten countries in the past two years. This job was my dream job and my main goal for the last seven years to achieve—which I did, despite a huge lack of confidence from my family. But since achieving my dream, I have discovered that I might not be cut out for this lifestyle. While I am incredibly happy on the road—performing in front of thousands of people—in between contracts I am stressed and depressed. This flip-flopping of emotions is too much to handle for me, so I have decided that I might be happier with a slightly more traditional lifestyle. I am going back to school to get my teaching credential and am hoping to be a math teacher, allowing me to still tour and perform in the summers. My friends and family are split on the decision. My parents are relieved; my brother (who is in the Army) is upset with me, not wanting me to give up on my dream. I spent all week this week visiting colleges and am studying for my exams. I suppose that I am settling, perhaps taking the easy road in life, but at this point I feel that life is too short to be unhappy, and hopefully my new plan will allow me to enjoy my passion without the emotional whiplash of unemployment every two months."

That's the nutshell. But further emails and conversations revealed a lot more nuance. A self-described high school tomboy ("short hair, played the drums"), Lisa says that belly dancing was the conduit that first connected her to her femininity—and allowed her to really embrace it. "Belly dance is . . . about accessing your femininity and exploring it and being beautiful, no matter how you look, and it helped a lot with my confidence as a teenager." And despite the fact that she took her first class "just for fun," she was immediately hooked. "Obsessed," in fact. "Crazy about it. . . . As soon as I started dancing, it was just like, over. I was just like, 'That's it, that's what I'm doing.' There was nothing else for me to do. . . . That was kind of when I got excited about life."

(Wow, that grass of hers is certainly looking pretty good, isn't it? That sort of epiphany is enough to have us green with envy.)

Lisa continued belly dancing throughout college, where she worked with a teacher who would become her mentor. Upon graduation, she moved to Los Angeles in order to try to get close to the woman who was the artistic director of the company Lisa had in her ultimate sights—the company she dances with now. She began dancing with the artistic director's local troupe—a dance company that performed at weddings and restaurants—and auditioning with the touring company regularly. She was invited to take part in rehearsals even though there was no spot available—but then fate shimmied in. On the very last day of rehearsals, one of the dancers threw out her back and Lisa was offered the spot. "I gave my day job zero hours notice. It was like, 'Sorry, I gotta quit, I'm going on tour!' And I was gone on my first tour."

And for a while there, Lisa was living her dream. "It really did feel like it," she said. "The first year, I went to Italy and Morocco and England and Paris and Spain and Taiwan—and it was fantastic."

But. . . A year or so later, the artistic director she'd moved to work with left the company, which was disappointing. And then the sheen started wearing off in other ways as well. "It's a Hollywood company: It's cutthroat, it's aggressive, they never pay you what you're worth. . . . People dance because it makes them feel good and they love it, and that's why I dance. I love rehearsing and performing and everything, but all of the aggression—it's like the company turned into *Showgirls*, with people trying to stab each other in the back, and I don't play that game. As soon as the director left, there was nobody in charge, and it turned into a Lord of the Flies–type situation. And I'm having a lot of trouble deciding how much more of the stress I can put up with. And other options—like having a steady life and a dog and a house—have become more attractive to me than living on the plane and traveling and being in the dance company."

Maybe that grass over there is a little greener than the grass beneath my feet. . . .

"I see my other friends I grew up with that have husbands and [are] starting families, and they have a dog and a house and everything, and

I'm like, Okay, well, that would be nice too," she says. "And I don't think I'd be happy when I'm forty if I didn't have a family, like, started."

And there's a certain amount of "the creative person's dilemma" mixed in there as well, in the form of some "time to get serious" nudging from her family. "I wouldn't have been able to get this far without [my family's] support . . . but at this point, they're like, 'Okay, it's been long enough. You've been doing this for eight years, and it's time to get some stability.' So I love my parents very much and that's why I'm listening to them and not just blowing them off."

And the fact of the matter is, most dancers have to hang up their legwarmers by the time they hit their mid-to-late twenties, anyway—as has been the case with many of Lisa's friends from the company. But still, she's torn over her next move. You can hear the tug-of-war in her words. The weighing, the pros and the cons. The attempts to talk herself into (or out of) her next move.

"Visiting schools now does make me happy. It makes me scared too though, because getting used to the lifestyle of being on the road all the time, and then coming home—that whiplash of emotions, being depressed as soon as you get home because all of your friends are gone, and you're really lonely, and you don't know how to go to the grocery store and buy groceries to feed yourself because you're not used to having to do that for yourself. And then you go on tour and you see all of these amazing places and the food's all ready and someone tells you where to be—you don't have to think about anything, you're just having fun and doing your job and performing, which is a very special thing to be able to do. And thinking about leaving: That does really make me sad and scared, but at the same point I'm so stressed out when I'm home—and trying to figure out the cycles of being gone and being home—that it's almost not even worth it."

She prefers not to call it "settling." "I'm gonna try to be thinking of it as a fork in the road, but if you'd asked ambitious Lisa from a year ago if doing this would be giving up and settling, she would have said 'absolutely'. . . so I don't want . . . I'm trying not to call it 'settling,' because [that's] giving up on your potential—'How dare you!'"

And with that little aside, she kinda hit the nail on the head.

NOW, GIVEN: THE very word "settling" carries negative connotations—far more negative than its close relative, "compromise." But when it comes to achieving our dreams—and having it all—do we interpret accepting anything less as giving up on our potential?

As for Lisa, when we spoke, she was on a road trip with an equally disillusioned colleague. They were in between performances in Phoenix and Austin, and she was testing the waters for the viability of the sort of compromise she envisions for her future: teaching during the school year, dancing during the summers. She's hopeful that sort of compromise will go well with a dog and a house.

And while many of us can hear, appreciate, and acknowledge that good enough may indeed be good enough . . . well, we just can't get past the fact that we should be striving for more. Better. The picture-perfect life we assumed—and were likely told—we'd have.

But the irony here is that not a single one of the women we've met in this chapter believes herself to be settling. We know: We flat out asked each and every one of them. But some, if not most, of the women in this chapter are doing something decidedly different than what they set out to do.

Might it be that we all settle at some point—but since "settle" is a dirty word, we don't call it that, or try not to think of it that way? And so, in the end, might it be possible that what we choose to settle for isn't as important as the fact that we've actually chosen something? And then *que sera, sera*?

SEVEN

CONVERSATIONS WITH THE ROAD WARRIORS

Don't be afraid to go out on a limb. It's where all the fruit is.
—Shirley MacLaine

DRESSING GEORGE CLOONEY couldn't keep Hannah happy at *Vogue,* but you'd think that *dating* him might be enough to dig a high-achieving Hollywood agent out of a funk, right? Yeah, not so much.

We'll get back to that, but first: Talk to the road warriors, the folks in the trenches who deal with women idling in the crossroads, overwhelmed by choices, and what you hear is a constant refrain: Failure = Good. Expectations = Scary. Regret = Soulsuck. Having It All = Bullshit.

It's a form of generational anxiety borne by overly high expectations, the always-on nature of technology, and—as women venture places their grandmothers never thought possible—a lack of role models to pave the way. There's an innate tension between pleasing the internal self (or even getting to know her) versus validation via externals: titles and paychecks and the stuff those buy. A lot of the angst has to do with the treadmill and its constant companion—fear of failure. And decisions, decisions! A lot of which seem monumental, but aren't. All of which, our experts say, makes it hard for women to make choices—and be satisfied with them—the way that doctors do: by the process of "ruling out."

The chase starts early and stays late. For starters, check this: A recent time-use study conducted by a husband-and-wife team of UC San Diego economists found that the amount of time that college-educated parents spend with their kids has risen dramatically since the mid-1990s—that dads were upping their kid-time as well, and that gendered parenting roles were starting to blur. Good news, right? Well, maybe, until you find the authors' explanation for the time shift. Look no further than the title of the study: "The Rug Rat Race."[1]

Seeking an explanation for the increase in family time—especially among highly educated parents—the authors suggest that an "increased scarcity of college slots" has prompted these parental units to compete in a "rug rat race for admission to good colleges."[2] They use the word "rivalry."[3] Hello, pressure.

If seeds are sown in early childhood, they take root during high school. In 2010, CNN reported on women who *quit their jobs* to help their kids get into college.[4] No joke. According to the story, these are highly educated professionals who take a "college-prep leave" or quit entirely to micromanage their kids through the college-application process—along with the résumé-building that accompanies it. This kind of takes "parenting as a competitive sport" to all new levels of ugly—and the ones likely to pay the price are the kids, who may never get out from under the weight of great expectations. And it's worse for girls, experts say, because they're hard-wired to please. And then, of course, comes the real world. Where there are no benchmarks of worth, such as grades or fat college-admission packets.

The irony, says Barry Schwartz, is that it's all a crapshoot, anyhow. Back in 2005, he wrote a piece for the *Chronicle of Higher Education* that condemned places like Swarthmore—his very employer—for creating the cutthroat competition.[5] "We get ten times more applicants than we can take—and they're all good," he tells us. "And so you know as a high school sophomore that you've got to be a little bit better than your best friend. That's a really terrible rat race to create, especially since the truth is that no school can really distinguish—it's basically a lottery, and all these schools pretend that it's not. If we just admitted that, we'd take a huge amount of pressure off kids in high school. You need to be good, but you don't need to be the best, because who knows who the best is?"

Monica Harris is a college counselor at an all-girls high school in an affluent area of Northern California. She sees students who've been planning on college since they were in grade school—who apply to fifteen or twenty of them, only to be devastated if their dream school says no. "They are so crushed because they have been building a résumé of activities since they could walk," she told us. "I see a lot of students who are overscheduled, stressed out beyond belief, and afraid to give up some of their activities for fear it will ruin their chances to get into college, and therefore their lives. Most of them go on to accomplish great things. But I wonder if they are taking the time to enjoy life."

Dina Collins—who has served as an administrator, counselor, teacher, and director of admissions at that same all-girls school for the past twenty-five years—suspects the answer is no. Cute, petite, and boho trendy, she leans forward across her desk for emphasis as she discusses how students have changed over the years. What's missing is a sense of playfulness, she says. They're serious. Everything is traumatic, big. She sees kids who are overprogrammed and overparented, who haven't been allowed to fail, and who are afraid to take risks. It's hardwired early, she says. There are no little events.

"What I see in these kids is the fear they're going to choose the wrong thing, and it's going to mean failure for the rest of their lives," she says. "It's so apparent when they're choosing activities. Kids used to take more risks: 'I've never danced before; the school has a dance program. Maybe I'll try that.' Now, it's more like, 'I've done *this* all my life; I have to keep doing it, because if I don't, I won't get into college. And if I don't get into this *particular* college, my life is going to be ruined.' And they truly truly believe that."

Much stems from the fact that, rather than allowing their daughters to fail when the stakes are low, parents rush to intervene. Collins says, "For the longest time, parents would call the school: 'My daughter didn't make the team, didn't make it into the play—and she's always been the best.' And we'd say, 'Well, your daughter needs to go talk to the director of the play, the coach.' And the parents were appalled. 'What do you mean? You're not going to talk to *me* about it?'" In response, the school developed a written communication protocol, telling parents that when a conflict arises, they're not to step in until their daughters have exhausted the appropriate channels.

It's all part of the escalating treadmill, Collins says. "I see the kids trying to get into high school, the *right* high school, so they can get into the right college. They're thirteen. Their brains aren't even ready for that kind of thinking. And yet they're on this trail, and they can't get off it." To a certain extent, geography plays a role. Live in an affluent area like Silicon Valley, where families are highly educated, and expectations skyrocket, she says. "The girls are thinking, 'I want to make it to this next step, then I'm going to be happy,' and then they find they're not happy because there's *another* step. What we try to tell them is there are going to be steps your entire life—but you can still be satisfied where you are right now. But nothing is ever good enough. Which gives them this sense of dissatisfaction, because when they reach the goal they've set out to reach, they're immediately setting another one."

As for the alums, she sees women taking longer to decide on a career path, changing jobs several times before landing where their passion might have led them from the start. "I think they're not ready to take the risk on something they're passionate about," Collins says. "It's like they're thinking, 'I'm going to try everything everybody else said I should do first, so I can exhaust all of those; so I will know I didn't make a mistake in choosing this.' It's like, 'I don't want to take that step first, because then my mom will be able to say I told you so if it's not right. So if I do what my mom said I should do, and what society says I should do, and none of those fit, I can say I tried it all. And no one can argue with me.'" In a way, all these detours alleviate one of the unintended consequences of unlimited options: personal responsibility for choosing the *wrong* one.

When Collins talks to students these days, a lot of the chat revolves around serious stress. They admit that a lot is self-induced, but when she asks them, "Well, do you really need to take six honors courses?" the answer will be "But I *want* to." What they really want, Collins suspects, is to please. "Studies show girls have so many more problems than boys—depression, eating disorders, migraines—because girls will stick with the craziness a lot longer than boys will. Girls are hard-wired to please, which makes the pressure even bigger. They won't give up, because to do so would be a failure. And they don't want anybody to feel they're a failure, because then they'd be letting people down."

University of Pennsylvania economist Betsey Stevenson sees it too. She's the author of a pivotal study on women's declining happiness (which you'll hear more about in Chapter 10), and she found that teenage girls aren't doing so well either. She asked teenage girls to rank the importance of a number of issues—their relationship with their parents, having a good marriage, being a community leader—and what she found was that everything was becoming so very *important.* "There's this massive intensification," Stevenson told us. "Then we turn around and ask them, 'Well, how satisfied are you?' in a number of domains, like 'How satisfied are you with how safe you are, with your friendships?' . . . and what you see is that there's one clear place they've become less satisfied, and that's with personal time. This really paints a picture of these kids in that, because there are all these things that are important, they're not taking time just to hang out—and that's what they're crowding out in order to achieve all these other things. And that may be coming at the price of happiness."

AND THEN. IT all intensifies when these girls get to college. Christine Hassler, author of *20 Something, 20 Everything* and *The Twentysomething Manifesto,* runs around the country talking to thousands of college women each year. And what she sees are women struggling to deal with a culture that constantly cries out for more. A therapist and life coach, Hassler often uses her own story to show the women that a sense of self has to come before any kind of what-should-I-do-with-my-life decisions. This is where George Clooney comes in. She dated him.

A graduate of Northwestern, she moved to Los Angeles, and in no time at all found herself the youngest agent in Hollywood, living the life, going to the Oscars, pulling $90,000 a year—and yet. Not even celebrating the millennium with Mr. Clooney was enough to quell the sense that something was not right. Though she'd always defined herself by her achievements, she was miserable. So she quit her job. Went into debt. Had problems with her family. Got sick. And got dumped by her fiancé (no, not George Clooney) six months before the wedding she had already planned. All of which precipitated a promise to herself that if she got through the crisis, she'd embark on a quest to make changes in the lives of women suffering their own quarterlife crises. The next day, she says, she had an idea for her first book.

Her message? Don't look for externals to define you—or to satisfy you either. Instead, push back the big decisions until you can look inside to figure out who you are and what you want. And failure? Embrace it.

The women in her audiences are overscheduled, overstressed, and overdoing it, she says. "They're great multitaskers, but terrible with boundaries. They put a lot on their plates. I talk a lot about being an overachiever and feeling like you have to live life on a checklist." The women relate. "I talk a lot about myths—the myth of having it all, of having your soul mate, the myth that you have to find your passion." She encourages the women to embrace mistakes and even failure—much like she did herself—as a learning experience. What really resonates is when she talks about anxiety existing only in the future.

"These women were parented during a very kid-centric time," Hassler says, "with a lot of focus on *them*. Parents really put pressure on them to be 'more' and were always talking to them about their future. I also think that most of them were never given the skills to deal with disappointment, stress, or emotions of any kind—they were always defined and encouraged by their accomplishments. So all they know how to do is focus on more accomplishments, which keeps them very much in the future.

"And then I think they are so terrified of failure. They really didn't learn how to struggle, and if they did fail, their parents rescued them, so they haven't had a lot of experience with 'If I mess up, I'll be okay.' That makes making any decision scary."

Once they've made one, however, "indecision" often morphs into "the siren call of door No. 2." Call it our more/better/different society, Hassler says. "Everything we see, there's always ways to be thinner, richer, better, smarter, faster. It's constant." The prime saboteur? Expectations, the nature of which is that they escalate. "Until we all have a sense of who we are and a good sense of satisfaction with what *is,* then we're always going to be running after the golden nugget—that constant room for improvement. There's always more we expect, and from my point of view, that's not a good form of motivation."

And yet. Graduate from a prestigious university, and there's the expectation that not only will you succeed but also that your path will be etched in stone as soon as you're legal to order a cocktail. Just ask Juliette Mullin, a graduate of the University of Pennsylvania, who as a senior wrote an op-ed for her college newspaper that lamented the fact that students tended to equate the Penn seal on their diplomas with a six-figure salary. What bothered her most, she wrote, was the fact that whenever she told someone that her postgrad plans were still up in the air, she was met with "the look of slight pity and concern that I still don't have my life completely figured out, followed by a weak, 'Sorry I asked.'"[6]

Sure, it's a question college seniors have been ever asked ("Plastics," anyone?[7]), and it's been ever loaded. But add to the expectations that ride the backs of so many women today the onus of graduating from a school like Penn, and the angst multiplies, writes our Ms. Mullin. She compared the work of trying to figure out her future to the stress of taking one more class—but more so: When expectations are impossibly high, when you-can-do-anything (and for a barrel of money) becomes the emblem of the iconic self, well, the pressure becomes intense.

It's not just an issue of privilege, however. Ramani Durvasula, PhD—a clinical psychologist, professor of psychology, and director of the psychology clinic and clinical-training program at California State University, Los Angeles—deals with a student population that is predominantly minority women, many with kids. She's advised hundreds of them on career choices, and what she tells them is that the concept of choice is one tricky, slippery slope. "The agenda is still loud and clear: 'You can have it all.' My advice to all of the students is 'No, you cannot.' So often, the discourse about choice is what you are choosing," she told us. "We leave out the rather unpalatable piece about 'What do you give up?'"

Like Hassler, she offers herself up as a case study. "I'm a single mother; I went through a divorce; I'm Indian; my family wanted nothing further to do with me—so it wasn't just divorcing my husband, but literally I lost my life." She went into debt, had to find a new home for herself and her two daughters. She's working three jobs. And what she tells the young women she counsels is to think like a man who will someday be responsible for supporting a family and paying a mortgage. "And some of these girls just stare at me wide-eyed, because they never thought about this. Some look at me and say, 'I want to be a doctor,' and I say, 'Okay, four years of college, four years of med school, four to six years of residency. . . .' Then they're like, 'When do the kids come in?' and I say, 'The kids *can* come in, but something's got to give. It may be that you make a sacrifice in the arena of marriage. It may be that you don't have the 24/7 you want with your child.'"

Her point: The idea of having it all, of unlimited options, is a fantasy, and a dangerous one at that. "What women have to do is rule things out. We need to be more tolerant of giving women a vocabulary of taking chances. I think men are much better at taking chances, and I think men have a better feel for time. Women hear the biological clock ticking a hell of a lot earlier than they need to. The painful part is, this is not easy. What I want to communicate to young women is, 'You can try many of these things, but there are going to be challenges. If you think you're going to be able to screw your husband, raise your kids, clean your house, and go to work, you're mistaken. You're going to have a messy house, an unscrewed husband, kids you're not always with, and a job you can't always do.'"

It's all about the risks, she says, the willingness to make mistakes. "I always say to my students, 'You'll get over a failure, but you will never recover from regret. That's not recoverable. Go ahead and try a job you might fail at. Go ahead and take some chances.' Because where these women often get frustrated is with the paths not taken. And what I tell them is that I want them to try a lot of things—and then report back. And that's frightening, because they still feel very programmed: They want the marriage, the house, the kids, the job—but have absolutely no sense how to get all those things at the same time. And I just don't think it's gettable in a single package. Women need to live lives where they're willing to rule things out. Like I ruled out marriage. But I had to *do* it to rule it out. What ends up happening is that if you don't have the realization, you wonder."

It all becomes more problematic with the career options women have now as compared to a generation ago, Durvasula says. "When certain paths were never even possible, it obviates people from responsibility, right? While to me that's its own form of a prison, it's also its own form of freedom if you couldn't even entertain the option. So I think that can speak to the dissatisfaction you see in young women: You now have to take responsibility. If you screw it up, it's your screw up. You can't blame somebody else."

She also sees young women with no sense of the present—who,

from a young age, have been taught to live for the future. "We have been so socialized to not stay in the moment and to become acquisitive and aspirational [instead]. That's what our entire education system is based on. People are hustling to get their children into the right preschool, kindergarten, middle school, high school, college. I mean everyone's living their life looking four years ahead."

Durvasula is currently mentoring a student at a private girls' high school in a tony area of Los Angeles, and what she sees there she finds horrifying. "These girls are in a pressure cooker. The expectations are unparalleled. You need to be an athlete, a dancer, a scholar, a scientist, and a writer. And be a poised, lovely young woman. It's not surprising that the rates of eating disorders, anxiety disorders, are quite high. And these young girls look like deer caught in the headlights all the time." The girl Durvasula has been mentoring? For the past *six years* she'd been working toward early decision at a prestigious university. She got in. And subsequently checked out. Her schoolwork, her grades? They no longer mattered. "Frankly, I don't even think she thought about what the implications were of going to this university. It was just about that early decision. Her parents would go and scream at the school when she didn't get the grades she wanted and so on. That happens every day at that school."

And failure? Not an option. Which ultimately blows. Because as women continue to chart new and unmapped territory, we need the trial and error. As Elizabeth Gilbert once wrote in an issue of *O,* we'd probably all be happier if we screwed up. Early. Often. And big. "We don't have centuries of educated, autonomous female role models to imitate here (there were no women quite like us until very recently), so nobody has given us a map," she writes. "Blow it all catastrophically, in fact, and then start over with good cheer. This is what we all must learn to do, for this is how maps get charted."[8]

The point, of course, is that the only time we can know if we're doing the right thing is after we've done it. If you chose wrong, pick yourself up, dust yourself off, and rule it out—knowing that all those missteps are indeed serving a purpose: You're helping make the map. And, as Gilbert suggests, every time you blow it, consider it a gift to your little sisters. Failure as philanthropy.

AND THEN YOU grow up. Morra Aarons-Mele talks to thousands of women online every year. She's the founder of a company called Women Online, which creates campaigns that mobilize women, companies, and nonprofits. She has an MPA from Harvard's Kennedy School, is midway through an MSW at Boston College, and is a HuffPo regular. She's got a one-year-old, is pregnant with her second, and what she sees in Gen X women like herself is a lot of fatigue. "I call it 'the caught generation,'" she told us. "We have to work; we were raised to work. We want to have a great career, but it gets mixed up in all these other issues when you have to help support a family. So we're caught between our ambition and the realization we'll have to work really hard to bring in a paycheck. And all the guilt messages we still get about being a working mom. We're caught between these ideals: Part of us wants to be the fabulous career woman, part of us wants to be the stay-at-home mom. And we don't get any clear messages from older women or younger women."

Even today, she says, we're still stuck with the mixed messages. But there's also the economy. "I never knew anything but boom times, really. Then all of a sudden, I'm thirty-three. I have kids who are going to cost a million dollars to put through college, and I have to work. Work is not a luxury for me. Statistically, it's not for any women anymore. But people still write about it. And that really pisses me off. The media still frame it as a choice. I actually feel like the media—the culture at large, the zeitgeist—presents these things as choices, and when we have struggles, we're failing as a 'personal choice' versus the reality of how things are."

Did we mention she blames the media? "Truly," she laughs, a bit ruefully. "I blame it for everything. I think we're caught between all these various ideals. And I always point to the ideal of the 'organic entrepreneur mom.' We are surrounded by images of moms. It's not the mom in the old Enjolie ad—the corporate raider who's still sexy and fries up the bacon.[9] It's not that. It's 'I've chosen my own path, I have money, I do good in the world, I have these great kids.' It's this sense of this self-actualized woman who has found her own way. And that's what we get held up against. We're supposed to work really hard, but we're also supposed to have purpose. We're supposed to be great parents, but we have to work. So what does that mean? We just can't let ourselves be. We always have to strive to be more."

She connects with thousands of women each year, women like herself, and she finds that this struggle is achingly real. "We're caught between the poles of perfection and having purpose—and I blame Oprah too." She laughs. "You have to have purpose; you have to have passion. And that's really not enough. I listen to women in their sixties now talk about how there was so much pressure for them to have it all—which meant having a husband and a family and working. And I joke that, for us, it's not only that, but recycling, being a gourmet cook, being really fit and sexy." And granite in the kitchen? She laughs. "These are nice problems to have, and I don't mean to be flip, I'm really conscious of that."

Enter expectations and the iconic self. "I think it's kind of our superego, and we've externalized it to a big extent. Living in the super-media, super-information-driven culture also accentuates that sense, because we see constant examples of who we are supposed to be. The cult of the Hollywood 'power mom.' You just can't relax and figure it out anymore." All of which, she says, is exacerbated by social media. "It's a huge echo chamber. You can't be a mom on your own journey anymore. You're a mom among millions. . . . We're losing a crucial self-sufficiency and pluckiness when we have to check in with everyone else all the time." Meanwhile, because the work and life choices are so new, those decisions weigh so much more. And because everything is instantly re-verberated in the social media, she says, the angst gets magnified.

The remedy? Plan ahead . . . but not in the way you'd expect. "A lot of ink is given to the fact that we don't teach personal finance in the school, and that's a real shame, especially for women. But no one ever sits down with you when you're in grad school and says, 'What kind of work life do you want? How ambitious are you? Do you want a husband who takes equal care of your kids? Who helps with the dishes? Do you want to be a stay-at-home mom?' You have to think about these things and plan for them. If you're twenty-eight and about to take a huge job, then sit and think, 'Do I want to have children in five years?' Then build it into your career. Don't just say, 'I'll deal with it when it happens' or 'I won't need to take time out.' Because that's how we normalize things. Women say, 'I can work hard and have kids. After all, men do it.'" She laughs. "I think that's a lie."

Funny that she would talk about someone sitting you down and asking those questions. That's exactly what Stanford economist Myra Strober does. She founded Stanford's Center for Research on Women back in 1972 and has taught a class on Family and Work since the 1970s—a class that has been a staple of Stanford's MBA program since 2000. We asked her what advice she gives the women in the MBA pro-gram who still think they can have it all, and she says, without hesita-tion: "The most important career decision you're ever going to make is who you marry. You have to have someone who is prepared to support you completely in your career, whatever it's going to be. If you want a killer career, then you better marry somebody who is prepared to support you in that. And then children? Maybe you don't have to have children. Or maybe you want to have one."

We'll hear more from Strober in Chapter 11, but her point is emphatic: You can't have it all, both kids and a killer career. Especially if your husband has a killer career too. Something, someone has to give.

Daria Todor says it's all about self-knowledge. She's an Employment Assistance Program counselor, career coach, and psychotherapist who has dealt with thousands of women in the workplace for the past twenty years. One of her clients is the Nuclear Regulatory Commission in Washington, DC. Many of the women she sees there are highly focused scientists and mathematicians, and she says that the key to getting it right all comes down to a well-defined sense of self.

A lot depends on when women make their decisions, she told us. Too soon—before this process of self-knowledge takes place, and before the brain has fully matured—and the choices are likely to be impulsive. Based on the young women she sees in the workplace and in her practice, she says the result is often dissatisfaction. "They say they made a choice that was good for them, but when you sit down and talk, they'll say things like, 'Well, I didn't really give this/that much thought.'" When pressed, many admit their choices lacked authenticity. They chose to be an engineer rather than doctor, for example, because their father thought the former was the better idea. Sure, parents have always tried to push their kids in certain directions, but now, for women, with all the newly opened doors, comes much more stress. "There's a lot of stuff going on that perhaps did not have to be dealt with by boomers and earlier women," Todor says.

Get to know yourself first, she says, by tasting and trying, and you are more likely to figure out what's right. Smorgasbord as metaphor? Yep. "We mature by taking in more information, and the more information we have that is consistent with our values—the more life experiences we have that allow us to confirm or deny that we're on the right path—then the easier it is to eventually make choices, and to be happy with them," she says.

Todor herself had wanted to be a doctor ever since she was a kid, but she finally gave up the dream when she was in her forties. "I kept going back to the idea. I really revisited it. I went to therapy, went to a career counselor, and I ultimately had to make some peace with giving that up. And I think this is what will happen with many of the Millennials. They will define themselves more by what's important to them, valuewise, and then be able to say 'Have I made an approximate-enough decision, one that's good enough, so I can say I'm comfortable where I am?' I think the source of the dissatisfaction is whether the reality is hitting the ideal. And now comes the true work of maturation, of how you navigate in a world you thought was as wide as the ocean."

Here comes the wisdom: "Every decision entails trade-off, and it entails commitment," Todor says. "And with that comes the sense of grief and loss. [When] you make a commitment to one thing, you are by definition turning your back on other options. Not knowing how to grieve a loss is really powerful. And I believe that a lot of what shows up in a therapist's office as depression may be a form of this grieving that is a natural part of growing up. And so there's an avoidance of making a decision because of the pain threshold."

It's all a part of learning to live in the moment—which might be just the right place to end this chapter. "The Buddhists say the source of all discontent and unhappiness is desire," Todor says, "desire for an outcome that we in our minds think—we *know*—is the 'right thing' for us. If we tell ourselves that we have to have it all. . . ." Her voice trails off. "I do see more women now who set definite goals for themselves. In fact, I think they're more goal-oriented in terms of things they want to achieve by a certain time. . . . 'I'm going to have a house before I'm thirty.' 'I'm going to do X, Y, Z by a certain time.'"

But even when they reach those milestones, that ever-elusive sense of satisfaction refuses to kick in. Even, apparently, if they happen to be dating George Clooney.

EIGHT

THE REARVIEW MIRROR

If you want to know the past, to know what has caused you, look at yourself in the present, for that is the past's effect. If you want to know yourself in the future, then look at yourself in the present, for that is the cause of the future.
—Majjhima Nikaya, Buddhist scripture

SO, WE'VE COVERED WHAT we're going through. But what about what the women a generation before us were going through? These are the women, after all, who forced open the doors, smashed the glass ceilings, and did the pioneering work that got us to where we are now. For the women of that generation, the struggle over choices was all about getting them.

While today, we might find ourselves struggling with how to choose between limitless options, these women remember a world where choices were limited. Where education was looked at as "something to fall back on." (God forbid you'd ever need—let alone want—to use it!) Fifty-eight-year-old Susan—now a life coach and teacher who's worked in "too many industries to list"—shared her recollection. "It was a world where my concepts of 'what I could be when I grew up' were limited to nurse (not a doctor), teacher (not a college professor), and secretary (not the president of the company). I remember my father telling me that since I was good at spelling, I would be a good secretary—maybe even an executive secretary. That would mean I might earn as much as $90 a week, and that would be 'Good money for a woman.'"

Clearly, we've yet to figure it all out. But a look at what came before can help put where we are now into perspective. And, much as we'd like to, we can't fit a complete history of the women's movement into this book, so consider this chapter a CliffsNotes of sorts—one that relies more on conversations with real women than on history books. And, as Susan's quote suggests, it's hardly the case that women have always been overwhelmed by the possible answers to the question "What are you going to do with your life?"

Today, as working women tasked with nothing less than conquering the world (while still managing to, as Ramani Durvasula might say, screw our husbands, raise our children, and keep our granite-counter-topped houses clean), we are, each of us, trailblazers. Our foremothers' struggles—to give us a world blessed with access to every conceivable road—were entirely different than those we face today. And our struggle to navigate this unmarked terrain is probably something they never predicted when they were out there burning their bras.

Oh wait. That never happened. But we'll get to that.

First let's get back to Susan: "I was a good student in high school and enrolled in college. I was not completely sure I wanted to go, but my mother insisted that I do so, with uncharacteristic firmness. So off I went . . . a rather shy, fairly compliant, good little girl, who was smacked in the face by the women's movement on my campus of Douglass College, of Rutgers University. Then the transformation began!"

And hers was one hell of a transformation. While her perception of her professional opportunities was decidedly modest, she was raised with another, very clear set of aspirations. "I learned that being sweet and polite were necessary traits for a girl, and I was aware—although I couldn't define it at the time—that my 'market value' as a potential wife was a concern for my father. He was really worried that I was going to be too tall and even asked if the doctor could do something about it! I wasn't allowed to go to ballet class like my cousins, because 'ballet dancers develop big thighs, and no man wants a woman with big thighs.'"

It bears repeating: Susan wasn't born in the 1800s. She was born in the 1950s. But it wasn't just the messaging from within her own family that was so constrictive; it was the culture too. "My perceptions of what it was to be a woman were greatly influenced by what I saw on *Donna Reed, Father Knows Best, Leave It to Beaver,* and *Ozzie and Harriet.* On the one hand, the image of the mother in the shirtwaist dress with the string of pearls and perfectly coiffed hair seemed wonderful—and yet, my own mother worked in the family business every day, so I was conflicted. I recall explaining to my little girlfriends in grade school that my mother really didn't 'work,' she was just helping my father out, and didn't take money for it. I was embarrassed that my mom didn't fit the stereotype of what other moms did, and of how the TV moms behaved.

"As you might imagine, when I caught the socially transmitted 'disease' of feminism on campus, my father was less than pleased. Worse yet, I infected my mother with it, and then my father was a very unhappy man! I became fully engaged in this social movement, and in the 1970s was the leader of a local National Organization for Women (NOW) chapter, and in the 1980s the state vice president of Housewives for the ERA. My mother accompanied me in the 1978 ERA march on Washington, as I pushed my one-year-old daughter in the stroller before us.

"While there are still issues of unequal pay and unequal access to some areas of the business world, today's young women have no idea how difficult it was to break through the glass ceiling. . . . I am concerned that not enough of our little sisters are taking this seriously. . . . I guess I sound like my grandmother saying, 'These kids today! What's wrong with them?'"

What's wrong with them, indeed.

Actually, it brings to mind a quote from Gloria Steinem. She was asked if she felt young women today are ungrateful for the gains of feminism's second wave. "I hope so," she said, and paraphrasing Susan B. Anthony, added, "Our job is not to make young women grateful, it's to make them ungrateful. Gratitude never radicalized anybody. We had to get mad on our own behalf; we didn't walk around saying, 'Thank you so much for the vote.' We got mad because we were being treated unequally, and they are too."[1]

But the fact is, many Millennial and Gen X women have been raised to believe that the women's movement is something that doesn't have much to do with them—as though the struggle for equal rights is over, and the battle was won. (In the next chapter, we'll get into whether or not that's true.) Rather than the *Dick and Jane* books of Susan's youth—with Dick running around being the firefighter or the cowboy, and Jane stuck on the sidelines in her dress and Mary Janes, saying, "Oh, look at Dick! Look at what he can do!"—these daughters were raised on books like *Free to Be You and Me* and *Girls Can Do Anything,* which sixty-seven-year-old Nancy, who still works at the business she owns, bought for her daughter—and, just recently, for her daughter's daughter.

In many ways, of course, Dick and Jane and Donna Reed and Mrs. Cleaver and all the other perfect housewives in their pearls and shirtwaist dresses have indeed gone the way of the dodo (or, you know, the Beav).

Today it's all but impossible to imagine a world in which it was accepted that a woman's place was in the home—a world, in fact, which many describe as a place that looked down on a woman who worked outside of the home. But it wasn't that long ago—and that's the world in which many of the women we spoke to grew up. No wonder they changed it.

NANCY RECALLED THAT world for us, saying, "In my teen days, I recognized that a lot of women had no ability to make a purchase or make a decision or do anything, because they were totally dependent on their husbands and their husbands' income."

That issue hit home within the context of her parents' relationship. She told a story about a time in her childhood when her mom and dad were having some marital problems—a lot of which had to do with money. "I said [to my mother], 'Well why don't you just work instead of complaining about Daddy?' And the way she looked at me, you would think I had spilled poison in her mouth."

Back in the day, the perception was that only poor or *(shhh)* divorced women worked. A working woman wasn't taken at face value—the fact that she "had" to work was generally seen as a comment on her husband's (in)ability to provide. Of course, once things began to change, and that idea began to fade, women then found themselves in a workplace in which they were treated as decidedly less equal beings.

Sixty-two-year-old Linda—a professional organizer who specializes in ADD and hoarding at a business she owns—remembers that world. It was a world in which she got laid off from her retail job once her pregnancy became obvious. "And that was acceptable! That's the part that now really gets me—I wish I had stood up for myself back then, but I mean, that's how it was."

That wasn't hundreds of years ago. That was 1972.

Barbara has a tale of her own. Around the same time, a few years out of college, she took a test for a management training program for a large corporation. She scored high and made it through the first round of interviews . . . and then ran up against a "smug middle-manager."

He asked what her husband did.

He asked whether it was likely that she'd be moving if he got a better job somewhere else. And if she wouldn't be eager to start a family once her husband's career took off. Such questions were, at the time, totally within bounds. And if you're not offended yet, just wait, there's more: "On my way out the door," recalls Barbara, "this guy said something to the effect that management training was a costly process, so surely I could understand why they would be reluctant to risk all that money on someone 'who might leave.'"

Just a couple of years later (1974 to be exact) Lesley Stahl (who is now an anchor on *60 Minutes*) was gearing up for a major first: She'd be the first woman to anchor an Election Night broadcast. As she told *New York Times* columnist Gail Collins, she was quite nervous, so her boss gave her a tour of the set as it was being built, to show her just how delightful it was going to be. All the anchors would be sitting in a circle, he said, so she needn't be nervous. "And he said, 'Walter will be sitting right there.' And in front of his place, it said 'Cronkite.' And he said, 'Roger will be there,' and it said 'Mudd.' And, 'Mike will be there.' It said 'Wallace.' And he said, 'You'll be there.' And it said 'Female.'"[2]

Token Woman or Ceiling Smasher? You make the call. Although in the end, that distinction is kind of beside the point. (Though Stahl might disagree.) What matters for the rest of us is that "Female" sat in that chair surrounded by "Cronkite," "Mudd," and "Wallace," and she held her own. And went on to make an actual name for herself.

But just because some ceilings were being shattered doesn't mean everyone suddenly started playing nice in the sandbox. In 1985, Cassidy—now a high-powered corporate attorney—was in her midthirties, several years out of law school, when, she says, "I had a federal district court judge tell me in chambers, in Richmond, Virginia—in a room where I was the only woman; there must have been twenty lawyers in the room and the judge—and he looked straight at me and said, 'Little lady, I'm sure I would like to have lunch with you, but I'll be goddamned if I knew what you were doing in my courtroom.'"

1985.

Many of these "first" ladies (not presidential wives, but the many women who went places no woman had gone before in a capacity *other* than wife) grew up watching their mothers living lives that were often characterized by what Betty Friedan, in her seminal 1963 work *The Feminine Mystique*, famously diagnosed as "the problem that has no name." That book, widely credited with igniting the contemporary women's movement, put words to what so many women were feeling. And living. Friedan called out the powerful systems keeping women in the home, the problems in defining themselves solely in relation to their husbands and children, deriving their worth in mind-numbing housework, feeling trapped. And when the rumblings of the second wave grew louder, the daughters of these women were called to action. Not least because they'd watched their mothers suffer from that unnamed affliction (stuck in the home doing brainless work, unengaged in the world around them, bored to tears), and didn't want the same for themselves.

As Salon's Joan Walsh put it, "Along with a haunting depiction of desperately unhappy housewives, I saw something else in Friedan's work: That feminism had been founded by the petrified daughters of frustrated women, who ran screaming out of their unhappy homes determined never to be trapped behind a vacuum cleaner."[3]

Nancy saw that misery in her own mom's life: "My mother had headaches and stomachaches and was in and out of hospitals. . . . She was always ill. When I look back on it, I think, 'Well gee, this is called being bored to death, this is called being angry.'"

Despite their mothers' circumstances, for many women in this era, college wasn't even on the radar as a means to a life larger—and more satisfying—than the house(work). Linda says, "The only female I knew who had ever gone to college was a cousin of mine who had somewhat of a disability, so it was presumed that she *had* to go to college, because she was going to have to support herself; she was going to be an old maid. And the only other people that even talked about college were people who wanted to be teachers. Teaching was like the only acceptable career choice for a woman. . . . As a child in that era, we challenged nothing. So the option of college was just never there. And I didn't question or challenge it. I had been brought up to go to secretarial school, get a commercial diploma, learn how to type, be a secretary until I got married, and then that was it!"

Earning a commercial diploma meant that, rather than a "college preparatory" curriculum involving things like math and English literature and history, Linda learned shorthand and typing. After earning that degree, she discovered a school that offered a one-year course in retail merchandising. She jumped on it—and then worked as an assistant buyer at Abraham & Straus, a department store. Until she got married. And it wasn't until many years later, after "quite a few years" of fighting with her husband, that Linda finally went to college.

Of course, for some women of that era, college was a given. Only, as Susan said, talk of college was generally couched in a caveat, qualified with the refrain "so you'll have something to fall back on."

Cassidy and her two sisters were raised by a highly educated mother and thrice-married father, who "was adamant—even though he was from the old school—that we would never have to depend on a guy for a roof over our heads. Even though he assumed that we would all get married, and that's exactly what would happen. . . . We were raised to go [to college]; there was never a question that all three of us were going to college. But there was the parallel assumption that we would get married, and that we probably wouldn't work after we got married." (Her mother, who spoke four languages and had her master's, taught high school . . . until she got married. "But," says Cassidy, "while she was married—and even after the kids were grown and gone—nope, she did not work.")

Incidentally, Cassidy has a serious brain on her. She went to Stanford and started out, in 1965, as an engineering major. Then she discovered the Grateful Dead and opted to work a little . . . less hard. She switched to architecture late in the game, but upon realizing she wouldn't be able to graduate on time, switched again, to art studio. Which was convenient: Sculpting and painting proved a nice comedown after late nights at the Fillmore Auditorium. And while she says she never noticed that she and other women were treated differently from the way their male counterparts were until years later, she has more than a couple "Oh-no-he-di-int!" stories to tell. Many of which went down at her summer job as a secretary at an architecture firm in Manhattan and are like something straight out of *Mad Men*. (Nutshell: "I got hit on left and right.") But even at Stanford University, men weren't above putting women in their place. During her time as an architecture major, she says, "I did a drawing for a project, and I got a C. And a year later—same class, same teacher—a friend of mine, a guy, needed the same project and hadn't done it. So he used mine, and we changed it just a tiny bit, moved a couple of trees around, and he got an A-. . . . I think it was a subtle way for the teacher to say, 'Lady, you don't belong.'"

While it was assumed Cassidy would go to college (even while it was assumed she'd get married and never put her education to use), such an enlightened scenario is a far cry from what Susan went through: The women in her family always had to fight for their education. "My mother was the eldest daughter in her family, and her father didn't see any reason for a girl to go to high school," says Susan. "On the first day of high school, her two other brothers were getting up and out of the house, and she started to follow, and her father said, 'Where do you think you're going?' And my itsy-bitsy spitfire British grandmother stood down [her] rather hostile husband and said, 'You're going!' And she grabbed my mother, spun her around, threw her out the door, and slammed the door behind her."

Susan's mom got her high school diploma and dreamed of being a nurse, saving her pennies for nursing school. And then, in the face of a family crisis, she handed over that money—and with it, her dream. Years later, a rough patch in the family business she ran with Susan's father coincided with Susan's high school graduation. So Susan offered to forego college and instead stay home and help out with the family business. But her mom was the one who put her foot down—perhaps channeling her own spitfire mother who'd insisted that *she* go to high school. Of her mom, Susan said, "She was a very quiet, meek, and mild type, so I was stunned. She just—*'You're going to college!'*—she just said that, and I was like, 'Whoa, where'd that come from?' I didn't really understand at the time. But she had given away her dreams for other people's sake and didn't want me to do that."

Can you imagine? If you answered no, well, consider that evidence of how far we've come. But the fact remains that we've still quite a ways to go.

FIRST WAVES FIRST: In 1919, suffragettes, as they were called, earned our right to vote with the passage of the Nineteenth Amendment. But did you know that prior to Betty Friedan (and the "second wave" that her 1963 book *The Feminine Mystique* sparked), there was another crop of women demanding the sorts of things we still don't have today? The sorts of things that would allow women to more comfortably combine career, home, and family?

True story. In between the suffragettes and the second-wavers was another sorority, the feminists of the 1930s. Dorothy Sue Cobble—a Rutgers labor studies professor and author of *The Other Women's Movement* and *The Sex of Class*—dubbed these women the "New Deal feminists." In 1945, those women introduced the first equal-pay bill into Congress. And they reintroduced it again and again for the next eighteen years until the Equal Pay Act finally passed in 1963.[4]

And those visionaries had other changes in mind too: more-flexible policies so employees could take time off for education or to care for family members. Cobble writes, "Beginning in 1943 . . . they lobbied for 'full Social Security,' including paid maternity leave and investment in child care and early education . . . tax exemptions and tax credits for dependents and the recognition of women's unpaid caregiving as part of the calculation of Social Security benefits."[5]

Ahead of their time? Well, maybe so, maybe not—but it goes without saying that those New Deal feminists might be more than a little dismayed at the current state of affairs. It's just this sort of work that many believe to be the next step for feminism—and we'll go deeper into this in the next chapter.

A generation later, the second wave was building. First came books like *The Feminine Mystique,* which awakened desperate housewives to their common discontent. Then their daughters, forced to confront a limited vision of their future, woke up. As Linda says, "I had a sister-in-law who . . . got into the feminist movement ahead of me . . . and started challenging me, like, 'Okay, so you have these babies, and then what? What are you going to do in five years?' Because it's true, the way I was raised, I was gonna be a secretary, I was gonna get married and have kids—and you never looked beyond that. So my sister-in-law kept challenging me, and that's when I finally decided, 'Okay, I want to get back to school.'" Others, like Susan, began to put the pieces together in their college dorms, where late-night conversations—and ditched bras: the horror!—led to anger, then action.

For Susan, the talk that at first "made no sense" to her began to click around her sophomore year of college—and that click was followed by a thunderclap of anger. "I became rebellious and hostile to a lot of the things that I saw in my home, thinking back, or realizing [what] I had been brought up to think and believe about myself and about girls and women, and the blinders I had been brought up with as far as what my possibilities would be. For career or life."

Older women talked and fostered a sisterhood in consciousness-raising groups. In a 2010 story in *The Observer,* writers Susie Orbach and Shahesta Shaitly described what those gatherings were all about: "[Women would] talk about their personal decisions, their sex lives, their love lives, their ambitions, their work, their children, and their men, and discovered that the individual idioms of their lives which felt so personal and particular were, in profound and often startling ways, similarly structured and imagined."[6] They reconsidered their unhappy marriages—and ditched them. They reconsidered their uncomfortable girdles—and ditched them too. They took to the streets with their younger sisters, and the rallying cry was "Change!" The personal was political, and the timing was perfect: The status quo was being challenged in all sorts of realms, and for one sweet, hot minute, feminism was worth fighting for.

And then, well, it wasn't. Backlash hit, feminism became an F-bomb, and somewhere along the way, much of the focus got lost. No one wanted to be branded with the scarlet F lest they be concomitantly branded an ugly shoe–wearing, razor-shunning man-hater. Some believe that those associations were emphasized by a culture hostile to the cause: Make feminism unappealing; kiss it goodbye. As Gail Collins told Joan Walsh in an interview posted on Salon, "Women who fought for women's rights in the '60s and '70s did not get hosed down, or attacked by snarling dogs, or thrown in jail; they got laughed at. And humiliation and embarrassment was the great huge club that people used to keep women in line."[7]

And there were other issues that contributed to the movement's loss of mainstream steam—among them, criticisms that feminism was concerned primarily with middle- to upperclass, educated white women, and a perception that feminism privileged career over motherhood, rather than working to help women reconcile the two. Some women felt that the right *not* to have children was indeed addressed. But the common woes of working mothers—and matters of policy that might make things easier for them—seemed to take a lower priority. It was a divisive spin—even though, in truth, feminists have a long history of fighting for policies significant for mothers as well as for working mothers. In addition to coining the slogan "Every mother is a working mother," NOW's 1967 Women's Bill of Rights "called for maternity leave and daycare centers along with legislation against discrimination. In 1970–71, it campaigned for the Comprehensive Child Care Act, helping lobby it through both houses of Congress only to have it vetoed by President Nixon."[8] And NOW has continued to work for policy changes that would benefit mothers and families. But the perception remained.

Ironically, even Betty Friedan—so known for calling women out into the world, away from lives circumscribed by the chores inherent to running a household and a family—had an eye to the future . . . or to the past vision of those New Deal feminists. She "envisioned a world, and a feminist movement, that allowed women to *combine* career, home, and family."[9] (Emphasis ours.)

And yet. One result was the opening salvos of the Mommy Wars; motherhood itself became a minefield.

Susan, who for the first several years out of college and as a married woman was the sole breadwinner—supporting her husband while he finished school—remembered her ten-year high school reunion. "Here I was, the president of the NOW chapter in my area and having conversations during the cocktail hour, and everyone's going around asking, 'What are you doing, who do you work for?' And I said, 'I just had our second child,' and, literally, 'Oh!' And they turned on their heels and walked away. Whoa! That was a real cold-water-in-the-face realization that . . . what you're doing at home raising your children is not valued by other women. Holy crap!"

Some diehard feminists who also happened to have kids felt they'd somehow been abandoned. Joan Walsh wrote of her own experience in her early thirties, when her marriage was flailing—which she attributes to her inability to manage the two main loves in her life: a baby and a career in journalism, the latter of which had been reduced to the kinds of stories she could tackle from her basement office, leaving her jealous of colleagues who were trotting the globe on assignment. "I was also angry at feminism, quite honestly, feeling it had left me alone to manage these dilemmas, that it was far more interested in defending my right not to have children than in building a world that would let me have them without giving up my ambition or my sanity."[10]

Dissension. Disillusionment. Not to mention the mockery—that club to which Gail Collins referred—and lingering stereotypes of feminists as obnoxious, bra-burning man-haters. Is it any surprise that the F-word became so divisive? As the *New Yorker*'s Ariel Levy wrote of Leslie Sanchez's book *You've Come a Long Way, Maybe,* "If what you mainly know about modern feminism is that its proponents immolated their underwear, you might well arrive at the conclusion that feminists are 'obnoxious,' as Leslie Sanchez does . . . [writing] 'To me, the word feminist epitomizes the zealots of an earlier and more disruptive time.'"[11]

CALL US CRAZY, but it seems that the time Sanchez dubs "disruptive" was the time when some serious shit got done. (Oh, the bras: At the 1968 Miss America pageant, a small group of women protested by pitching girdles, makeup, high-heels, and bras into a "freedom trash can."[12] They were never burned. But it does make a good story. As Hunter S. Thompson might have said, we remember it, whether it happened or not.)

And for younger women, or even their mothers, who have always had a life blessed by the choices our older sisters fought for, feminism felt irrelevant. But what could be more relevant? The choices that paralyze us now were earned—not so long ago—by women who were dismayed (and often infuriated) by how few choices they and their sisters had. And a certain measure of our difficulty in navigating these choices has to do with the fact that they're just so new. Just as the women of those consciousness-raising groups found that their personal, particular struggles were in fact common, we're finding that ours are too. This is a problem that has no name.

Many of the women we've met in this chapter agree that we still have a ways to go. And while they're proud of the work they did to bring us to where we are today, they feel pretty strongly that young women might want to consider those who went before them. Linda says, "I still think every woman should be required, like, the first year of college, or even in high school, to read *[The Feminine Mystique]*. Because I think far too many of the young women today just think, you know, 'Okay, women have their rights, this issue is dead.' This issue is still alive. And I think young women don't appreciate what the generation or two before them went through."

SUPRISINGLY, A LOT of the women you've met in this chapter say that, despite everything you've read here—despite enduring a terribly sexist upbringing, like Susan did; despite being thought strange for having desires beyond motherhood, like Nancy was by her own spouse: "My children's father really was a little embarrassed that I wanted to work full time. He thought that was pretty odd." (Note: they've since divorced.); despite the outright harassment Cassidy endured in judge's chambers and elsewhere—despite it all, these women didn't perceive their capabilities to be limited. "It never occurred to me that I couldn't do anything that I wanted to. Never occurred to me. I didn't have that problem," says Cassidy.

And they gave us a world that reflects those beliefs about themselves. Ourselves.

So what do they make of today's women, who are moaning and groaning about all the options available to them? You might be surprised. "Well, it was something we faced too," said Nancy, who now owns her own business, with a logo that proudly boasts, A WOMAN-OWNED PUBLIC RELATIONS FIRM. "I did want to do everything. . . . I would like to see women be more comfortable in their choices. . . . I think there will always be fights for women's equality of one sort or another, and we're going to have to keep up the fight . . . we cannot forget what it took to get here."

Nor can we forget that we're in uncharted territory, struggling with a whole new set of issues. After all, these women? They're not old. And their stories are not unusual, nor are they irrelevant.

We as women—independent, educated, working women solely responsible for what we do with our lives—don't have centuries of role models to look to for guidance. We're all fumbling along, making up the rules, operating without instructions, charting the map.

We're trailblazers. Like Susan, Cassidy, Linda, and Nancy. They cleared some of the brush, but their work has led us to a wide expanse of unmarked terrain—and it's up to us to take it from here and hack our way through.

NINE

YOU'VE COME A LONG WAY, BABY . . . MAYBE

The truth will set you free. But first it will piss you off.
—Gloria Steinem

HOLD THE APPLAUSE, LADIES. We're not there yet.

We've been told the battle of the sexes is over. That we've waged the war and we have won. Feminism? Done and done.

But: When, fifty years after the passage of the Equal Pay Act, a woman still makes seventy-seven cents to every buck a man brings home; when women make up half the workforce but have yet to make more than a token appearance in the boardrooms; when women still face gender-based discrimination; when women are expected to come home from work, then work at home because workplace and social structures have not evolved—well, it appears that women's work is never done.

It's one more reason we're all living in the land of the undecided.

Don't get us wrong, we've come a long way, as the last chapter detailed. But we've still got work in terms of the persistence of the pay gap, the subtle forms of sexism that pervade the workplace and the household, and the lack of structural changes that would allow working women the same choices as their husbands when it comes to raising a family. It's not that the feminist movement is over, nor has it failed.

Check the perspective from second-waver Germaine Greer, author of *The Female Eunuch*. Writing in the *Times Online* in 2010, she issued a call to arms: "The media tend to think that the fantasies they peddle are realer than real. But in the real world, women have changed; bit by bit, they are growing stronger and braver, ready to begin the actual feminist revolution. The feminist revolution hasn't failed, you see. It has only just begun."[1]

Former *Boston Globe* columnist Ellen Goodman, who tracked women's issues for forty years, wrote that if she were to grade the movement, she'd give it an "incomplete." "A woman is now Speaker of the House, but there are only seventy-three women in that House and seventeen in the Senate," she wrote in one of her last columns. "At sixty, Meryl Streep is playing a romantic lead, yet girdles have been resurrected as 'body shapers' and girls are forced into ever-more narrow standards of beauty. Young women grow up believing they can be anything they want, just don't call them by the F-word: feminist."[2]

California First Lady Maria Shriver, too, writing in *Time* magazine, cites the "unfinished business" of the women's movement, enumerating a laundry list of inequities: "Women still don't make as much as men do for the same jobs. The U.S. still is the only industrialized nation without a childcare policy. Women are still being punished by a tax code designed when men were the sole breadwinners and women the sole caregivers."[3]

Morra Aarons-Mele (we met her in Chapter 7) thinks that the next frontier for the women's movement is work. "That's what we're going to coalesce around," she told us. "Because women are now 50 percent of the workforce, we bring home 44 percent of aggregate income in this country, and it sucks for us. I mean, it's that simple. The same way that it sucked not to have birth control, the same way that it sucked not to have the vote, I feel that strongly about work right now."

Look no further than a multiyear study by UCLA researchers who tracked the home life of thirty-two different dual-career families. They found chaos, stress, and blurry boundaries. Work–life balance? More like work–work balance, especially for mom. So-called leisure time, tracked as fragmented breathers, accounted for only 11 percent of women's waking hours at home.[4] Kathleen Christensen is with the Alfred P. Sloan Foundation, which financed the project. She told *New York Times* reporter Benedict Carey, "I call it the new math. Two people. Three full-time jobs."[5]

Carey's story also covered the impact of the study on the field workers who were ever-present in these families' lives, via camcorder: "'The very purest form of birth control ever devised. Ever,' said [one of the researchers] Anthony P. Graesch, a postdoctoral fellow, about the experience. (Dr. Graesch and his wife have just had their second child.)"[6]

Which is interesting. Even a researcher with a camera trained on the good, the bad, and the ugly of frantic families chose to reproduce. Even given what we know, many of us still choose to raise families. But it's a pipedream to expect that women are going to make like June Cleaver and stay home with the kids, especially in this economy. As the study shows, there's something broken in the way it all comes down.

On the one hand, there's the message: "Hey girls, you can do anything!" But then there's the reality: "You're going to run into challenges and compromises, and how are you going to get those bills paid, and oops, we forgot to mention that."

Ramani Durvasula thinks we *should* mention that. She calls feminism a moving, evolving target and says that we need to change the conversation. After a strong start as a social movement, feminism got ambushed in the 1980s, she told us. "The media and the government did a fabulous job of branding family as something so wonderful. What I thought was beautiful and manipulative about the whole thing was, women who were trying to work and have kids were saying, 'This kinda sucks. This is really hard.' So the media was giving these women an out, right?"

At that point, she said, the paradigm changed. The dialogue about choices continued, but the advocacy got lost. Flash-forward a few decades, and women raised to define feminism in terms of their choices are now confronted with reality, Durvasula says, which leaves them confused—and dissatisfied. The real message, she says, should be this: "We actually don't have the choices we think we have. Feminism is about compromise. And yeah, 'compromise' is an ugly word. But if we were honest about what that compromise might be, it might be a meaningful discussion, because to say that it's about choice is lying to them."

The joke is that the numbers—and the anecdotes from way back when—lead us to believe this abundance of choices, this promise of possibility, is more reality than illusion. Check the cocktail-party trivia: As of October 2009, women made up 50 percent of the American workforce.[7] Two-thirds of American families rely on mom to make ends meet.[8] We women also have serious spending power—some $5 trillion within the next few years, according to a survey conducted by The Boston Consulting Group.[9] Plus, 70 percent of families with kids have a working mom; 60 percent of college grads are women; 50 percent of those with new PhDs or professional degrees are women; and women make 80 percent of household buying decisions.[10] All of which might lead us to believe we've got the muscle—and the financial leverage—to make the structural changes we need, to call our own shots. But the reality is, stats aside, we're still playing catch-up. All of which screws with our choices, or at least our satisfaction with them. We're led to believe that the perfect option is out there, just waiting to be tapped. And when it doesn't pan out, when we go face-to-face with the challenges of daily life, we're disappointed. Dissatisfied. Jonesing for that next fix of greener grass.

IT'S A DOUBLE-EDGED sword. Because we *have* come a long way in just a few generations, it really is tempting to believe we can have it all. As Nancy Gibbs wrote in a *Time* magazine report on the status of women in 2009, "If you were a woman reading this magazine 40 years ago, the odds were good that your husband provided the money to buy it. That you voted the same way he did. . . . That your son was heading to college but not your daughter."[11] Sounds crazy, right? She also writes that, even if you had a job, your paycheck was not only considerably lighter than your male counterpart's—but that it was okay because, after all, you were probably only working for "pocket money."

Gibbs offers up some other doozies: 42 percent of high school athletes are girls, up from 7 percent in 1972; women make up 50 percent of Ivy League presidents; three of the last four U.S. Secretaries of State have been women; five women won Nobel Prizes in the same year; and, she writes, "we just came through an election year in which Hillary Clinton, Sarah Palin, Tina Fey, and Katie Couric were lead players, not the supporting cast. And the President of the United States was raised by a single mother and married a lawyer who outranked and outearned him."[12]

There's more from *New York Times* columnist Gail Collins, whose book *When Everything Changed* tracks fifty years of women's progress. The book is inspiring and optimistic, and one reminder that how far we've come has to do with pants.[13] In that same interview with Lesley Stahl we mentioned in Chapter 8, Collins recounts an anecdote about a Manhattan secretary named Lois Rabinowitz who had the audacity to show up in court to pay a parking ticket wearing, *gasp,* trousers—for which she was excoriated by the judge and subsequently thrown out. This was 1960.[14] True story. Then there was the "men only" express flight from New York to Chicago. "Nothing was illegal back then," Collins told Stahl. "It was perfectly legal to say, 'Well, we don't hire women for those jobs,' or as *Newsweek* used to say, 'Women don't write. They only research.'"[15]

At the top of the interview, Collins told Stahl that, as far as the women's movement is concerned, and despite all that's left to do, we've won. "Women being born today are going to have all kinds of problems, many of them having to do with trying to balance family and career, I will tell you, but that kind of sense of limitations that existed throughout civilization and society just is not there for them."[16]

Well then. Makes you want to slap yourself on the back and smoke a skinny cigarette.[17] Until, that is, you check the numbers on the flip side: Ellen Goodman (mentioned in the beginning of the chapter) reminds us that there are only fifteen women CEOs in the Fortune 500 and that the Equal Rights Amendment—defeated in part because people feared it would send women to war—has still not passed, even though almost a quarter-million women have served in the Middle East.[18]

From the Center for American Progress, we learn that more than half of mothers bring home at least a quarter of the family income, and that over a third of mothers in working families in all but two states are the family's primary breadwinner. In other words, some 12 million families rely on mom's income. And yet, without exception, these women earn less than their male counterparts.[19] We'll get into this pay gap in depth later on, but for right now, there's more to make you seethe.

A study from the *Academy of Management Journal* suggests that bosses assume women have more family–work conflict than their male colleagues (even though this isn't the case), which negatively impacts their chances for promotion.[20] The study's author—University of Illinois management professor Jenny Hoobler—says what's interesting is this: When she presents her research to women, even in her MBA classes, they say they're not surprised this happens, but they also don't think it will affect *them*. "Especially the undergrads. They think that discrimination is something that happened in the generation ahead of them. They sort of think that everything will work itself out by the time they're actually coming up against these things." (To paraphrase the late Hunter S. Thompson: Should we tell them now, or should we let the poor girls find out for themselves?)

And what about the fact that not every woman wants children? They at least should be safe from such bias. Er, right? 'Fraid not. Call it the nonmaternal wall: Lancaster University professor Dr. Caroline Gatrell told the *Daily Mail* about her findings, which suggest some employers see their female employees who don't want children as lacking in some "essential humanity," and view them as "cold, odd, and somehow emotionally deficient in an almost dangerous way that leads to them being excluded from promotions that would place them in charge of others."[21] Swell.

From that *Time* magazine report, we learn that 98 percent of kindergarten teachers and dental assistants are women, but only 10 percent of civil engineers, and a third of physicians and surgeons, are women.[22] There's more from *The Nation* columnist Katha Pollitt, who noted that men are not only paid more, but also promoted more, and once a woman becomes a mother, she is less likely to be hired than a woman without kids. If she takes time off to stay home with them? *Ka-ching.* For every two years that a woman jumps out of the workforce, she gets docked some 10 percent of her income—for life. And though women make up half the workforce, they're still clustered in the lower-paying ranks: secretary, nurse, elementary and middle school teacher, cashier, retail salesperson, health aide, waitress, bookkeeper, and receptionist. "There'd be more to cheer about if [women] also earned an equal share of the pay," she wrote. "It may be easier to find a job as a home health aide than a welder, but male jobs tend to pay a lot more than female ones (and, one might add, do not involve a lot of deferential smiling)."[23]

"Deferential smiling." Doesn't that just say it all? Are we supposed to smile all the way to the bank (where, by the way, the tellers are most likely to be women) with our seventy-seven cents on the dollar?

THERE'S A LITTLE-KNOWN "holiday" in April called "Equal Pay Day." While the name implies equality, the meaning is actually its opposite. Equal Pay Day marks the day *your* salary catches up to your male counterpart's . . . from last year. On average, a man makes in eight months what a woman makes in twelve.[24] That's right: Compared to the dude in the next cube, from January 1 to somewhere around April 20 each and every year, you, sister, are working for free.

Despite the fact we're well into the twenty-first century—despite the fact that the first bill President Obama signed into law was the Lilly Ledbetter Fair Pay Act, which extends the time employees have to file discrimination suits; despite trend stories on breadwinning "alpha wives"[25]; despite the fact that the Equal Pay Act was enacted, oh, some forty-seven years ago—the fact remains: On average, women earn seventy-seven cents to a man's dollar. Even less for women of color: African-American women earn 61 cents and Latinas earn 52 cents for every dollar a white, non-Hispanic male brings home.[26] In a piece on NPR, reporter Jennifer Ludden cites the conventional wisdom that accounts for the pay gap: occupational segregation, "career time-outs" to care for kids. But, she reports, when economists controlled for those and other variables, they *still* found "an unexplained gender gap of anywhere from a nickel to a dime or more on the dollar."[27]

Motherhood, lower-paying careers—they're convenient excuses, and they're handily debunked by Ilene Lang, who's with the women's research group Catalyst. "From their very first job after getting their MBA degree, women made less money than men," Lang told NPR. "On average, $4,600 less."[28]

Very first job? MBA? Well, that settles the time-off-for-kids/lesser-paid-career-track thing. And Catalyst's findings held even for women without children. For Lang, this says old stereotypes persist. "There are assumptions that women don't care about money, which is crazy!" Lang says. "There are assumptions that women will always have men who will take care of them, that women will get married, have children, and drop out of the labor force. All those assumptions are just not true."[29]

You mean we work for more than pocket money? Fancy that. But the numbers are worse than we think, according to the Center for American Progress: Working women in the United States lose, on average, $431,000 over a forty-year career. Women with a high school degree lose $300,000 on average, and women with a bachelor's or graduate degree lose $723,000 on average. In fact, the analysis shows that the more educated and professional a woman may be, the more she loses over a lifetime of work, simply because of her gender.[30]

In case you're not pissed off yet, the National Organization for Women culled the following stats from sources that track pay equity: The pay gap was fifty-nine cents in 1963, when the Equal Pay Act was passed, meaning it's taken us forty-seven years to close the gap by eighteen cents. Men working in traditionally female jobs still earn more. One year out of college, women earn eighty cents on their male counterpart's dollar, but within the next ten years, that drops to sixty-nine cents.[31]

The nonprofit WAGE Project posts even more dismal estimates: A high school grad loses $700,000; a college grad loses $1.2 million; and a doctor, lawyer, or MBA will make $2 million less over the course of her lifetime.[32]

And while there's no doubt that a pay gap exists apart from a "time-out," there's also no doubt that said time-out kicks us in the pocketbook. (According to a report by the Institute for Women's Policy Research, women are more likely to earn less—and work less—once they have kids. But for men, the reverse is true.[33] Ain't that interesting?) When caring for kids or aging parents (which is usually "women's work") gets factored into the equation, this whole pay-gap thing gets worse. Labor economists Claudia Goldin and Lawrence Katz did a gender-disparity study of University of Chicago MBAs, and they controlled for everything from business-school courses to job experience to hours. They found that for new MBAs, there was just a modest wage gap (favoring men, of course) out of the blocks. But ten to fifteen years later, the gap was a stunning 40 percent.[34] In a virtual Q & A session on the *New York Times* online, Goldin and Katz explained it in terms of "the greater number of career interruptions and lower weekly hours experienced by the women (mind you, they still work a large number of hours)."[35]

Um, 40 percent? You can guess what "career interruptions" means: everything from maternity leave to working reduced hours (read: some variation of the eight- to ten-hour day) so that you can be there for soccer games or doctor's appointments. You might think it looks like women are penalized for being female. You might be right.

How best to address the issue? Well, asking for more money is a start. A big one—and one in which many agree women might need a lesson. We don't want to be rude, pushy, or assertive, but we don't want to be broke or underpaid either. But as with a lot of things, focusing on the individual leaves a little too much unaddressed. The Paycheck Fairness Act, currently pending in the Senate, would make it easier to prove gender bias and nix the wall of silence that exists around salaries in an organization. That's a start.

And while pay inequity is something women face right out of the gate—and that is self-perpetuating, in terms of developing a salary history—there's more to it. Attitudes and biases play a not-incidental role. Consider these tidbits from a 2010 *Newsweek* story written by three young female staffers: A Girl Scouts study revealed that young women avoid leadership roles for fear they'll be labeled "bossy"; another survey found they are four times less likely than men to negotiate a first salary. As it turns out, that's for good reason: a Harvard study found that women who demand higher starting salaries are perceived as "less nice," and thus are less likely to be hired.[36] Bossy? Less nice? Ugh. Call it the curse of "working while female."

A COLD, HARSH reality that those who'd rather make the issue personal are quick to gloss over has to do with how far women *haven't* come in terms of equal representation. Those *Newsweek* writers we mentioned above boldly went there though: "Are We There Yet?" asks the headline. And the story's slug line was the kind that leaves you with a distinct sense of dread: "In 1976, 46 women filed a landmark gender-discrimination case. Their employer was *Newsweek*. Forty years later, their contemporary counterparts question how much has actually changed."[37]

How much *has* changed? If *Newsweek* is any indication, not a whole hell of a lot: In 1970, 25 percent of *Newsweek*'s editorial masthead was female; today it's 39 percent. Last year, men wrote all but six of *Newsweek*'s forty-nine cover stories. And that's apparently par for the course: Taking major magazines as a whole, there's one female byline for every seven male ones. There were countless frustrations, the women wrote, "But as products of a system in which we learned that the fight for equality had been won, we didn't identify those feelings as gender-related. It seemed like a cop-out, a weakness, to suggest that the problem was anybody's fault but our own."[38]

Maddening, that perception. What's also maddening is that the "progressive" world of Hollywood is one of the worst when it comes to equal representation—which is especially noteworthy when you consider its role in creating the cultural standards by which we often measure ourselves. In 2009, the Hollywood Writers Report found that women and minorities had not made any significant hiring gains since 2005, with women writers making up roughly one-quarter of the field. "Women, who account for slightly more than 50 percent of the U.S. population, remain underrepresented in television employment by 2 to 1 and in film employment by nearly 3 to 1."[39] Their salaries also show a discrepancy—white men $98,875, versus women $57,151—for a whopping wage gap of $41,724.[40] Is it any wonder that the fat old guy in the movies often gets the pretty young girl?

Frankly, it would seem that gender equity would be good business, but getting those numbers closer to 50–50 is easier said than done. It turns out, underrepresentation might also be self-perpetuating. One study found that women may avoid situations when they feel outnumbered. When female math, science, and engineering grads simply watched a video pitching a conference where men outnumbered women, the women showed the physical signs of threat—faster heart rates and sweating—and reported a lower sense of belonging, less desire to participate in the conference at all, and were more vigilant of their surroundings overall.[41] Which suggests one reason why women may avoid fields like math and engineering: It's not "innate differences," as erstwhile Harvard President Lawrence Summers famously suggested back in 2005.[42] It may be that we just don't feel welcome. Which maybe makes sense when we're talking technology: *The New York Times* reported in 2010 that women account for just 6 percent of CEOs of top tech companies, and 22 percent of software engineers.[43]

But what about the workplace in general? Could these "social identity threats" be one reason we are often unsure of ourselves? Why we agonize over career decisions? Why we often stick with safe, women-friendly careers (which, incidentally, fall lower on the pay scale)? Sometimes it's the threat, not the reality, that does us in.

Think about it while you consider this, also from the *Newsweek* women: "The four most common female professions today are: secretary, registered nurse, teacher, and cashier—low-paying, 'pink collar' jobs that employ 43 percent of all women. Swap 'domestic help' for nurse, and you'd be looking at the top female jobs from 1960, back when want ads were segregated by gender."[44] For the record, Susan from Chapter 8 told us that her first job (the one she had while she supported herself and her husband while he finished school) was one she found in the "women's want ads."

But there's also this, says Harvard Business School professor Rosabeth Moss Kanter: People trust the judgment of those who resemble themselves. "In top positions, men are going to prefer men who think like them," she told an interviewer in a *Harvard Business Review* IdeaCast. The good news is that people also prefer those who got their MBAs at the same schools. So, with women making inroads in prestigious business schools, they may also begin to make inroads in the boardrooms. (FYI: According to Kanter, when she was appointed to her position at the Harvard Business School, the headline in the school newspaper read, "Tenured Female Faculty Doubles.") On the other hand, Kanter said, "There's the lingering feeling that women are torn because of their families."[45]

And sometimes, even when women do cross the barrier, there's a tinge of Groucho Marx, who famously quipped he would never join a club that would have him as a member. In a couple of instances of women infiltrating the highest echelons, the spin has had less to do with how great it is that they are finally getting their due—and how society as a whole might benefit—and more to do with how little those ranks mean anyway. When Diane Sawyer took over Charlie Gibson's gig as anchor of *World News Tonight,* Karen Heller of *The Philadelphia Inquirer* wrote that what a woman in such a position really means is that no one cares about television news anymore.[46] Congratulations on your lengthy career and hard work; you've made it to the top of your game. But you know, it's really just a booby prize.

Likewise when *The Washington Post* ran a story about "The Hillary Effect" (that is, the increasing number of women diplomats): "More than half of new recruits for the U.S. Foreign Service and 30 percent of the chiefs of mission are now women . . . a seismic shift from the days, as late as the 1970s, when women in the Foreign Service had to quit when they married, a rule that did not apply to men."[47] Good news, right? It should be. As the article suggests, diversity at the top has been cited for more open-minded decision-making processes and, in some cases, a stronger focus on poverty, healthcare, and the marginalization of girls in many nations. On the other hand, what's good for the world may not be so easy for the women who are changing it.

Mary Jordan, the reporter on the story, cited ambassadors as saying that being a woman in a traditionally male field does indeed give them a special status: curiosity. Singapore's ambassador recalled showing up at a Washington restaurant and asking for her table, booked under "Ambassador Chan." She was told, "He's not here yet." Many of the women diplomats said they're presumed to be the ambassador's wife in receiving lines, and that what they miss is the "spousal support" that makes their male counterparts' jobs a little easier. But the kicker is this: Susan Johnson, the president of the American Foreign Service Association, noted that the increase in women diplomats seems to coincide with a general political shift from diplomacy to defense, and she wonders, "Is the relative feminization of diplomacy indicative of its decline as a center of power and influence?"[48]

Cue Groucho.

AS INFURIATING AS all of this may be, even more infuriating is the fact that no one seems pissed off. And, we'd venture to say, there are even some among us who read the stats and the surveys and, like Jenny Hoobler's students, don't quite believe it has anything to do with our lives.

Susan Douglas would diagnose that as a classic case of "Enlightened Sexism," and her 2010 book makes a compelling case that, because of all the advances we've made—and because of a lopsided accentuating of the positives—the stereotypes, inequities, and biases that would have once been called "sexist" go unnoticed. She suggests that all we have to do is turn on the tube, where women doctors, women lawyers, women detectives and Hillary and Oprah all conspire to convince us: *See? We have come a long way, baby!*[49]

All of which leads to a sense of complacency—especially among younger women—that keeps us from addressing the real work that needs to be done. To find out why so many refuse to identify as feminists, Barbara once interviewed a houseful of bright, kick-ass college seniors, ready to take on the world. One of them cited the fact that she'd grown up with every opportunity and had never experienced anything she'd identify as gender-related discrimination—so for her, feminism was not an issue. "It's hard to get passionate about a cause when you haven't faced the consequences of what you're fighting for," she said, then added later, "You have to be oppressed to have a movement. And we're slowly working forward."[50]

Really? See above. Maybe what it takes is a reminder. That's what we've found in a number of comments on our blog, where we once posed the question, "Are you a feminist?" One comment was especially telling: Jill, a thirtysomething attorney, explained that she had never considered herself a feminist. "I always thought that feminism involves more than just fighting the little daily fights that are personal to me (i.e., knowing I am entitled to equal pay and equal opportunities, and demanding those things for myself). Because I am not involved in feminist causes and do nothing to champion the rights of other women, I never thought the feminist label applied to me," she wrote, then added, "Maybe I am one of 'them' after all."

Well, of course she is. As is Lynn, a recent college grad, who wrote, "It's great that feminism has come far enough that [young women] don't have to deal with many of the egregious injustices that women in the past had to deal with (and probably an indicator of class and race). On the other hand, it's really the cleverest and most sinister way to stop feminism before it even begins: Just convince young women that there is no sexism and that their lives are perfect. You can go on paying them less, underrepresenting them in government, and treating them like sex objects, and they'll see it as equality."

But even if we're oblivious to the inequities at home, it's hard to deny the oppression that women face worldwide. In a *Los Angeles Times* interview, Somali refugee Ayaan Hirsi Ali—the controversial author of *Infidel: My Life*—reminds us that women in radical Islamic cultures are still subjected to honor killings and genital mutilation. In many of those countries, women cannot go outside without a male escort.[51] Laura Ling and Euna Lee—the two American journalists who were imprisoned in North Korea in 2009—were covering a story of human trafficking, in which North Korean women fled to China to escape repression, only to find themselves entrapped and exploited as online sex workers undressing for clients via streaming video.[52]

And in August 2009, the *New York Times* devoted its Sunday magazine to the plight of women across the globe. The cover read, "In many parts of the world, women are routinely beaten, raped, or sold into prostitution. They are denied access to medical care, education, and economic and political power. Changing that could change everything."[53] Among the injustices (which really is too-mild a term): persistent patriarchal values in China and India that result in discrimination (read: killings and neglect) against daughters, along with increased abortion of female fetuses; teenage prostitution in African truck stops; and young Afghan girls who risk everything to go to school. The magazine also noted studies that suggest that when women gain incomes, family money is more likely to be spent on nutrition, medicine, and housing, and consequently, children are healthier.

What does this have to do with we who are deeply privileged by comparison? Well, one way to look at it is this: Though we're not close to the finish line, we are leading the way for some of our sisters around the world. In one of the articles, Secretary of State Hillary Clinton addressed the interconnectedness of it all. Asked by reporter Mark Landler if there was a lesson that women everywhere could learn from her presidential run, Madame Secretary answered that her campaign gave heart to a lot of young women: "It is still the most common comment that people make to me: 'your campaign gave me courage' or 'your campaign made a difference in my daughter's life' or 'I went back to school because of your campaign.' So, it is unfinished business, and young women know it is unfinished business."[54]

But while we should use our good mojo to effect change world-wide, America has fallen down on the job. The World Economic Forum's Global Gender Gap Report for 2009 took its annual country-by-country measure of global progress in the lives of women and girls and found the United States was not only riding the middle of the pack, but had actually fallen three slots to No. 31. What kicked our ass, and the United Kingdom's as well, was the fact that we lack progress at the top of the food chain. "What is lagging is women's presence at the highest levels of power," wrote Laura Liswood, cofounder of the Council of Women World Leaders. "Countries that adopt quotas for business or politics often see an immediate jump in their standing once these mechanisms kick in."[55]

Quotas? Ooh, scary! And yet, as Latoya Peterson pointed out on Jezebel.com, look to our friends to the far, far north: Norway requires public institutions to promote and document gender equity. Iceland passed similar legislation back in 2000. Finland has an "Ombudsman for Equality, the Gender Equality Unit, and the Council for Equality." And Sweden employs both an Ombudsman on Discrimination plus laws in schools and workplaces to prevent gender bias.[56]

Why should we care what goes on in Iceland, Finland, Norway, and Sweden? Maybe because they hold the top four spots in that report. As Liswood suggested, while the numbers themselves can't prompt change, they should serve as a firm nudge: "And looking at a gender gap that has been indexed should give leaders pause if they are not fully utilizing 50 percent of their talent."[57]

All of which reinforces our point: It's not personal, as the young women from *Newsweek* initially feared. It's political. As Charlotta Kratz points out, you find a number of gender-equalizing structures in Sweden, where she's from: affordable child care, paid parental leave, and five to seven weeks of paid vacation per year—all of which makes it easier for the overwhelming majority of families where both spouses have careers.[58]

Representative Lois Capps (D-Santa Barbara) agrees, telling us that while it's great to be raised to believe you can do whatever you want, "the truth is that there are a lot of barriers. Gender equity. There isn't that in the workplace. There are so many glass ceilings still that young women will see if they look far enough. What they need to recognize is that it will take a lot of strength to get where they want to be and want to go."

And a lot of policy too. During the 2009 debate on healthcare reform, Capps says she made it a point to talk to different groups about the impact of the legislation—and was stunned when a group of upper-management people all zeroed in on one issue that had nothing to do with healthcare: child care. "It's such a huge barrier," she continues. "And we have not dealt with that adequately in this country. It's always been considered this soft, women's issue. Well, it's not. It isn't men, it isn't women, it's about the next generation and how we get them started. . . . There are enormous barriers there today. Huge ones."

Or, as former *Boston Globe* columnist Ellen Goodman pointed out in her farewell column: "It was easier to fit into traditional male life patterns than to change those patterns. We've had more luck winning the equal right to 70-hour weeks than we've had selling the equal value of caregiving. We have yet to solve the problem raised at the outset: Who will take care of the family?"[59]

This never-ending tension between work and family? We'll get deep into that in Chapter 11, but right here we wonder: Have we not addressed it politically because it's been labeled a "woman's issue"? And has the fallout from this lack of structural support been the foundation for women's growing sense of dislocation? We tend to think so.

Clearly, women are feeling the pinch. According to Christine Hassler (who you met in Chapter 7), they're feeling it even before their clocks start ticking, because they interpret the idea of "having it all" as "having to *do* it all." Which morphs into constant stress, often burnout and, you guessed it, indecision. "I think college women, women in their twenties, make a lot of choices based on assumptions," she told us. "They have no idea what being a wife and a mother and a career woman really entails, and yet they're planning to do it all." And they think they can.

Until they realize they can't.

Which leads us back to where we started: To be sure, there are strides here and there that signal some promise that the personal might again become political. San Francisco, for example, has instituted a Department on the Status of Women, which has written up a set of gender-equity principles, backed by a set of metrics that companies can use to gauge their progress.[60]

Londa Schiebinger—a Stanford history of science professor and the former director of the Michelle R. Clayman Institute for Gender Research—suggested that the best way to keep more women in the labs is to get them out of the kitchen. Her study of dual-career academic couples found that women scientists still did the bulk of the housework. Her remedy? Benefits packages (tailored to fit individual needs) that include housework.[61] Talk about a dream. It's a policy that could, and should, be applied to all professions, not just science, Schiebinger told *Stanford Report* writer Adam Gorlick, though she saw a special relevance in the sciences: "'It doesn't seem like a good use of resources to be training people in science and then having them do laundry,' Schiebinger said in reference to Carol Greider of Johns Hopkins University, who was doing laundry when she got the call in October that she won the Nobel Prize in medicine."[62]

Whether progressive ideas from the San Francisco Bay Area will eventually seep into the water table and head east, who knows? But it's a start as we dive back in to women's unfinished work. And where is that work headed? Let's let Gloria Steinem take that one. At a 2009 panel discussion on gender issues at Yale, a graduating senior asked whether women should feel obligated to continue in the workforce.

To which our favorite feminist icon replied: "Dispense with the word 'should.' Don't think about making women fit the world—think about making the world fit women."[63]

Done.

TEN

WHAT A LONG, STRANGE TRIP IT IS

I was too afraid to speak in public until after thirty and finally decided to speak because of the women's movement, and I still was terrified, but I realized if women can't do anything fucking right anyway, might as well do what you please.
—Gloria Steinem

WE'RE ALL LIVING IN AN ERA of option overload, so why are we so convinced that women are experiencing the psychological effects more acutely?

A good place to start is with a piece of research that inspired a blogosphere brouhaha. In May 2009, Betsey Stevenson and Justin Wolfers published a study called "The Paradox of Declining Female Happiness." The title kinda says it all, but the gist is this: While thirty-five years ago, women reported being happier than men, today's women—whether or not they have kids, and regardless of marital status, employment status, income, geographic location, and ethnic background—report being *un*happier than men.[1]

At first blush, it's surprising, as the past thirty-five years have seen so many advances for women (remember Chapter 8)? Even Betsey Stevenson was taken aback. "Absolutely, I was surprised!" she told us. "It's certainly not what I'd expected to find."

As one might imagine, dozens of articles came out in the study's wake, riffing on the whys. The *Sunday London Times* got to the crux of the issue, as we see it. The article quoted Helen Parker, a twenty-seven-year-old executive, as saying this: "There's plenty more opportunities for women than there used to be—but then again, that means you are always questioning whether the moves you have made are correct, or whether you should have done something else."[2]

Well, yeah, we'd tend to agree, as you might have gathered. But of the myriad interpretations, some stood out—and got our hackles raised. A few months after the study was released, a Huffington Post piece—trumpeted as the beginning of a series—benefited from some pimping, courtesy of an email from none less than Arianna herself. In a message entitled "The Sad, Shocking Truth about How Women Are Feeling," Ms. Huffington summed it up: "Women around the world are in a funk."[3] . . . And then turned it over to management thinker and author Marcus Buckingham, who'd offered this tidy cause-and-effect interpretation of the study during an interview for *BusinessWeek*: "Better education and job opportunities and freedoms have decreased life happiness for women."[4]

In other words, feminism = bad.

The more cynical of us might wonder why Huffington appointed a man to take it on. The poor, confused, unhappily liberated women need a man to lead us out of the woods? The bigger hackle-raiser, though, was this particular man's recommendation: "To focus on moments rather than goals, plans, or dreams."[5] *Don't worry about your goals or dreams, little lady, smell the roses instead!* Talk about a paradox.

We're all for smelling the roses, but we think there's more to it. Like living—and working—in a world where the structures have not caught up with the idealized messaging, with socialization that doesn't translate to the workplace. Like subtle—and overt—sexism. Like trying to capture the impossible "All" we were promised. Only to realize, as Germaine Greer put it, "When we talk about women having it all, what they really have 'all' of is the work."[6]

In fact, Betsey Stevenson thinks that our newfound aspiration to have—and do—it all may indeed be driving the phenomenon. "It may actually be that there's an accounting difference . . . that women are less happy because they're aggregating their happiness over more domains." And, as we saw in Chapter 7, when Stevenson described the "massive intensification" they found when slicing the data to look specifically at teenage girls, "everything is just becoming more and more important." The pressure we put on ourselves starts early and stays late.

How does it play out once we've outgrown our curfews? As Maureen Dowd wrote, "When women stepped into male-dominated realms, they put more demands—and stress—on themselves. If they once judged themselves on looks, kids, hubbies, gardens, and dinner parties, now they judge themselves on looks, kids, hubbies, gardens, dinner parties—and grad school, work, office deadlines, and meshing a two-career marriage."[7]

When you look at it that way, what Stevenson and Wolfers dubbed a "paradox," we might be more inclined to call a "well, duh."

Another interesting point came from a guest post on our blog, in which Charlotta Kratz—who's Swedish born—observed that America's conflicting values system might play a role. According to a World Values survey, the United States scored among the highest on two sets of values: "self-expression values" and "traditional values."[8] That's a pretty intense conflict from which American women are operating, no? While both women and men learn that self-expression is important, women may lack support in fulfilling their wants and needs if they go against traditional family values, says Kratz. "American women are caught in a crossfire between change and tradition."[9]

Dowd went further, adding that women are more hormonally complicated and biologically vulnerable than men, that they are harder on themselves, and that "America is more youth and looks obsessed than ever, with an array of expensive cosmetic procedures that allow women to be their own Frankenstein Barbies."[10]

We are overwhelmed by choices, judgment, and expectations— and the pressure to appear happy, young, and gravity-resistant while we deal with it. It's new territory, with no mapped-out trails to follow. As Marcus Buckingham himself said: "Choice is inherently stressful, and women are being driven to distraction."[11]

Dowd ended with a silver-lining take on that idea: "Stevenson looks on the bright side of the dark trend, suggesting that happiness is beside the point. We're happy to have our newfound abundance of choices, she said, even if those choices end up making us unhappier."[12]

Interesting. And, in fact, we'll get into that when we talk about happiness in Chapter 13. But we think there are some other, subtler factors at work in this paradox too, factors that make navigating our newfound "freedom to decide for ourselves" particularly treacherous.

Not the least of which is the fact that we were never taught to be the navigator.

We've found that a measure of the second-guessing, the sense of overwhelm, that paralyzes women in their twenties and thirties (which includes most of the women we've profiled in this book) stems from an uncertainty as to how to find their way in the unfamiliar turf of the postschool world. Sure, women do the role of student well. But the workplace? Different kind of rules.

Kratz contends that higher learning, at least in the humanities and social science, is collaborative (that is, female) in attitude. Which is great . . . while we're in school. But once we're outside that environment, once we're faced with a workplace that's set up totally differently—it's a little jarring. There's an unfamiliarity that exacerbates the uncertainty we already feel over the choices we face, and whether we've made the right ones.

"Maybe this learning environment has made the young women who graduate today unprepared for what faces them outside of the university: same old world, where women can be professionals, but only if they check their female-ness at the door," Kratz wrote. "I think young women walk out into the world expecting to be heard, and I think they feel disconnected and depressed when they are not. . . . The skills they've developed don't work."[13]

But there's more to it. From ancient times, men have been raised knowing their job is to slay the dragons, and that they will be alone in doing it. For generations, men's roles have been predetermined and unquestioned: go, seek, conquer. Provide. And workplace—and social—structures have evolved to support this model. For women, though, relatively new to this world of work, roles are in flux. (And the structures are an additional step—or ten—further behind.) We never learned to slay the dragon—we were the pretty princesses waiting in the castle—and often, we're a little bewildered by the nature of this man-constructed world as opposed to the comfortable fit of school. It throws us off our game. How do we fit in? Should we fit in? Do we even *want* to fit in?

Additionally, there's a certain deep-seated need for approval, something women are trained to seek from the time we're little girls. From hugs from Mommy and Daddy, to stickers from our first-grade teachers, to acceptance from our adolescent peers, every step of the way, we've been raised to worship at the altar of "What will people think?"

Take Jane's story. When we met her in Chapter 1, she was so overwhelmed by her options that swapping them for a life in a country where everything from spouse to career was chosen for her was sounding like a good deal. She wrote us some months later with an update—and a plea for help. The problem? Jane found a job that she loves. In an email, she wrote, "I wake up every morning excited to go to work!" (Actually, she wrote, "EXCITED." Really.) This, of course, is not the problem. The problem is that, after several interviews she went on—motivated primarily by a little healthy "what the hell"—a friend who doubles as the president of a wildly successful start-up offered Jane a job.

Jane consulted with everyone—her current boss (who said she was planning on retiring in five years . . . and turning the company over to Jane), her parents, her aunt, her boyfriend, her ex-coworker, and all of her friends. She wrote, "I've been 100 percent in and 100 percent out about six times each way. I have a 3-page pro/con list. Literally. . . . And now I'm here. With probably the most difficult 'Who are you?' decision I'll face for a while (ever?). And you know how I feel? Like I'd rather take a swan dive off the Space Needle than make this decision. What if I'm wrong? What if I hurt someone? In the middle of a recession, I have two amazing opportunities, and instead of seeing that, high-fiving myself, and getting to the decision, I want to cry. Or throw up. And I want to take back ever going to that first interview."

What should Jane do? We had no idea, though we picked up on something in her email: "What if I hurt someone?" To wit: "It's so odd how emotional and relationship-driven this is for me, in addition to the fear of making the actual decision. A huge factor on my list involves hurting people. Instead of being proud, I feel like a selfish, sneaky, ungrateful turncoat."

Who couldn't relate to that? Girls are raised to be sensitive to others' feelings, to be empathetic, to be sweet. And it's not just the sugar-and-spice nurture that's to blame here; nature has us hard-wired for it too. After all, back in the loincloth days, we had to keep the babies—the very tribe—safe and sound, anticipating and taking care of everyone's needs, while the menfolk were off bringing home the buffalo.

The trouble is, some of us become so good at empathizing—such experts at feeling others' feelings—we have no idea how to parse them from our own. "*I* don't care; what do *you* want to do?" becomes a refrain. And when we're deciding where to go for dinner, hey, we're the perfect, easygoing companions. We even convince ourselves that we really *don't* care—never mind that we've had Indian twice this week already. (After all, who doesn't love a good curry?) But it can become a habit. And then what happens when we face a choice like Jane's, where we're the only one who can make the decision—and the only one who's going to have to live with the consequences?

As Jane put it: "If I could really figure out the answer to everyone's question 'What do *you* want?'—I'd do that! But how do I know what I want?"

Good question.

And in a way, it's compounded by this modern world. You know, the one that's populated with the six-degrees-of-separation Facebook faux-*migos* who check our status updates, look at our vacation pictures, spy on us from the pages of our cyber-yearbooks.

How much are our choices influenced by attempts to impress the tribe of "friends" we've amassed with a few clicks of the mouse? Do all those eyes somehow urge us to stick with what's socially correct on the one hand? Or prevent us from exploring options they might find prosaic—or somehow impolitic—on the other? Could all those eyes be one reason we are so eager to please? Why decisions come so hard? Why we judge ourselves by the judgments cast by others?

And have you noticed how the nuances of friendship (real friendship, not friends of the "How do I know you again?" Facebook variety) play a role in our choices—and how our choices play a role in our friendships? Conflicts, particularly between women, have a lot to do with choices. Defending what we've chosen for our lives—and what we've chosen to leave behind. Judging our friends' choices. Interpreting the fact that our friend has chosen something different as her judgment (and rejection) of what we've chosen for ourselves. The distance that grows when we feel like (because we've chosen differently or believe we would choose differently were we in her shoes) we can no longer relate to the women to whom we're closest.

When we're deep in the throes of a "Which way should I go," part of the angst is often the knowledge that no matter which way we go, we will be judged. In all sorts of ways. In ways that men aren't, and in ways that are often contradictory. And the damnedest truth of all: We often do it to each other.

The inconvenient truth here is that we care what other people think—whether we're talking about our boss; the mean girls from seventh grade who we've refriended, and are hoping to impress with the way we've chosen to live our current lives; or our real friends who've made different choices than we have—and who might or might not be dropping some snark about our own choices when our backs are turned. When it comes to our choices, the "what will they think" factor is more powerful than we'd care to admit.

BECAUSE THIS SECTION will piss you off, let's begin with a cartoon a friend described to us. Imagine if you will, one frame in which a pretty woman looks into the mirror in horror: Her mirror image is heavier, uglier, and facial-hairier than her real self. The next frame shows a balding, beer-bellied man smiling happily as he gazes upon his reflection, which features a chiseled physique and a full head of hair.

Funny . . . or is the joke on us?

Depending on where you look, there's plenty of evidence to indicate that, indeed, the joke may be on us.

Exhibit A: Aaron Traister's Salon story entitled "And May Your First Child Be a Feminine Child." Here's the slug line: "People did victory laps when my wife gave birth to a boy. Why was the reaction to our next baby, a girl, so cold?"[14]

Ugh, right?

"A kind of pitying, you-lose sentiment was common among dads without daughters. . . . As for women, well, they never went that far, but even their enthusiasm seemed dialed down." He continued, saying the one thing everyone agreed upon was this: "Boys are easier than girls, and girls are difficult and demanding, and then they turn into teenage girls and then they're at their worst."[15]

But one guy's experience is hardly representative of the world at large, right?

Maybe.

In "Did You Mean That, Google?" *Salon Broadsheet*'s Mary Elizabeth Williams was in for a shock when she searched the term "bad fathering." Google's response? "Did you mean: bad mothering?"[16]

Seriously.

"The very first thing at the top of the page when you search for 'poor fathering' is 'Mommie Dearest (poor mothering ability).' The first two true results for 'bad fathering,' meanwhile, are for a band called Bad Fathers and 'First time father deserves a bash.'"[17]

Who knew Google was a sexist pig? Although frankly, the fact that it is but a soulless algorithm makes those results even more disturbing. While we'd venture to say there likely exist as many examples of poor fathering as of poor mothering, they're clearly not written about (or read about or searched for) as often. Like the cartoon couple at the beginning of this section, some of us are inclined to seek out our flaws, while some of us are . . . not.

As one might imagine, Traister's piece ignited more than a little online unrest. One response, from *Double X*'s Amanda Marcotte, offered a common take (if a touch victimizing for our taste). She attributed the cause of our inclination to work harder for less money as "partially sexism, and partially women's lack of entitlement due to lower self-esteem. We put our noses to the grindstone, never . . . draw attention to ourselves by asking for more, and suffer from imposter syndrome . . . when you're told that you're less valuable than boys from the day you're born, you . . . believe it."[18]

Ugh again.

But taken together, the thing we wonder about is a chicken-and-egg kind of conundrum. What comes first, the inferiority complex, or the assumption that we should have an inferiority complex? And can the latter be every bit as damaging?

On the Offensive Sexism scale, Traister and Google score relatively low. We could write an addendum to this book equal to the length of this book filled with worse. We bring them up not to cry foul, but because they get at an interesting question: How does all of the above—which is so decidedly at odds with the "You can be anything you want!" mantra we've been chanting since preschool—play into how we make our decisions?

How many of us put on a brave face while silently picking ourselves apart in front of the proverbial mirror? A picking apart that's made worse because we know we should be thinking, *I can do anything I want!*

That silent self-doubt can leave us on shaky ground.

Uncertain.

And how this uncertainty plays out is interesting too. We're sure you've heard this one before: Women are less assertive than men, as evidenced by the way we soften strong statements with hedges ("sort of," "maybe"), disclaimers ("I don't know," "that's just my opinion"), and tag questions ("Don't you think?" "Isn't that right?"). It's a favorite topic of women's mags and students of communication, and it's often taken as a given, but recent research suggests there's more to it. UC Davis communication professor Nicholas Palomares conducted a study showing that "Women hedge, issue disclaimers, and ask questions when they communicate, language features that can suggest uncertainty, lack of confidence and low status. But men do the same."[19]

Hold the phone. Men do the same?

Yep. Palomares found that—in written (email) communication, anyway—men were tentative when discussing stereotypically feminine things ("One man, believing he was corresponding with a woman, wrote: 'maybe girls prefer the quality of products at Sephora over other major department stores? I don't know.'"). Women were tentative when discussing stereotypically masculine things (insert requisite how-to-change-a-tire anecdote here). Palomares found "no difference in tentativeness" when he asked his subjects to write emails on topics that were gender neutral— such as a recommendation for a good restaurant.[20]

But what of all those studies showing that women are less likely to ask for raises and promotions? More on that in a second. First, this study's tidy wrap-up:

"Some topics cause men and women to think and communicate in terms of their gender, which leads to tentativeness when the topic is inconsistent with their gender."[21]

Inconsistent with their gender. Hmmm. Stay with us. Could it be that, because for so long women have had such low status at work, that the very environment can feel foreign—maybe even masculine? Coupled with a touch of the inferiority complex (or the assumption that we should have an inferiority complex), so graciously illustrated by Traister, Google, and Marcotte—might that be why we don't demand the raises or promotions we deserve? And could it be, because for so long women had so few choices about what to do with our lives, could it be that one reason we hem and we haw—that we analyze to the point of paralysis, that we second-guess ourselves at every turn—is because making confident life choices based on what we really want seems a little . . . bold, assertive . . . *ahem,* manly?

I mean, I don't know. That's just our opinion.

Just imagine how much spare brainpower we'd have if we could let it all go, if our belonging, our acceptance, our equality was a given, and if our internal critic turned into the kind of ally that would make looking in the mirror an empowering experience. Maybe there's a lesson to take from the guys here: Maybe the next time we say to ourselves, "I'm not good enough," we should say instead, "Wow! Who knew I was so fabulous?"

IT'S A MENTAL switch worth flipping as early as possible: Two of the key findings in "The Paradox of Declining Female Happiness" are that women grow less happy as they age, and that, by the time they reach age forty-seven, they are overall less happy with their lives than men are with theirs.[22]

Hmmm, wonder why.

For all his postulating, Marcus Buckingham didn't give the issue any more than the most cursory of acknowledgments: "A youth-obsessed culture that is harder on women than men?"[23]

Uh, ya think?

Yet with that, he dropped the subject like a hot potato. Hardly unexpected. After all, the only thing less appealing than an unhappy forty-seven-year-old woman is talking about why that forty-seven-year-old woman is so darn unhappy.

Moving on: the requisite media scapegoating. The year 2009 saw the premiere of a television series featuring a single, fortysomething woman as its protagonist. The show was charmingly dubbed *Cougar Town*. In it, our heroine comes in the form of an amazingly well preserved, extremely beautiful Courtney Cox, on the prowl for a taste of much-younger man candy. Not that there's anything wrong with seeking out some hot sex with a (very) able-bodied partner. But somehow, the message is off. For what we're given is a fortysomething woman— beautiful, successful, self-sufficient; with a healthy son, career, friends— and yet, here she is, measuring her worth in terms of sex appeal. Approval from the boys. Post–forty!

While we've got the media on the stand, there's something else to consider too, something far subtler. As journalists, we're trained to be conscious of the damage done by unwitting stereotypes, which often comes in the form of a reporter's shorthand. One of the most insidious tactics that affects marginalized groups is overcompensation: "gee whiz" features on seventy-five-year-old marathoners, for example, or inspirational stories on the academic success of so-called "model minorities". . . or the way Meryl Streep's over-fifty sexual being in *It's Complicated* was framed: as a novelty, the exception who proves the rule.

Of course, it's not just the characters she plays—the fact Streep continues to get leading roles at all is considered a "gee whiz." She reports, "There was a big fight over how I was too old to play [the female lead in *The Bridges of Madison County*], even though Clint Eastwood was nearly twenty years older than me. The part was for a forty-five-year-old woman, and Clint said, 'This is a forty-five-year-old woman.'"[24]

The leading man needs only a recognizable name. His female costar, on the other hand, needs not only a name—but must also be young and beautiful too. Men in their fifties and sixties not only get to be leading men who still get the girl, but in the real world, they also get to run companies and countries. They've got status that is earned by (wait for it . . .) *age*. Their female counterparts, on the other hand, generally are considered redundant at best, silly at worst. Or the gee-whiz exception to the rule.

So back to the study. When you live in a society that doesn't value older, naturally aged women—to the point that the popular culture refuses to even show you what one looks like—it's entirely possible that you're not going to be so happy about becoming one. You might, in fact, be a little bit pissed off. (Again, why is the decline in women's happiness called a "paradox"?)

Then again, a lot of women claim to really come into their own with age. (And in fact, as we'll see in Chapter 13, other studies show that just as everything else starts getting its sag on, our happiness begins to climb.) To be much happier, much less concerned with what others think. *The New York Times's* Judith Warner wrote, "Most women in their forties, however conflicted, however sometimes confused, aren't actually spiraling into self-doubting despair, but are actually working their way toward some greater degree of self-acceptance. . . . Many come into their own, creatively, professionally. And in motherhood, in friendships, in romantic relationships."[25]

(Gee whiz!)

But getting there is scary, probably (and maybe counterintuitively) scarier the *younger* we are. When you've absorbed the message that your value does nothing but go down as your age creeps up, every decision becomes that much more loaded, that much more stressful, when played against the backdrop of a ticking clock. We think it's a huge part of why women's decisions are so tough. We've gotten the message: "Time is short. Choose wisely. And fast! You're only going to be relevant for so long."

Biology plays a not-incidental role as well, of course. This story from Kris lays it out pretty succinctly. "My husband and I were talking about a man who had a super career, made lots of money, and retired at age fifty. He married a woman twenty years his junior. Now he's seventy and is having health problems. But he still has his wealth, children—and a younger wife to care for him. A woman couldn't have that life plan—we have to build our careers, find a partner, have [and] care for our children, and make our fortunes all at the same time. Men can move through life's milestones sequentially. Because of biology, and more so, societal norms, women can't. Because that's not the norm, we all worry about leaving the workforce, getting older, being passed over and left behind."

She makes some real points that serve to illuminate why women's choices are so much more loaded. The bottom line being: Thanks to cultural messaging and biology itself, women are extra conscious of the clock. It's an underlying worry that seeps into everything, intensifying the pressure every time we find ourselves at a crossroads. On the one hand, we're told we can have it all. On the other, we're told that idea is a fantasy predicated on bullshit. But if we really can't have it all, we know we better pick wisely. And in a hurry. The clock's a-tickin'.

AS WE'VE MENTIONED, we women are rather hard on ourselves. In our attempts to have it all, often what happens is we wind up trying desperately to *do* it all. And because it is impossible to do everything, we feel we should be able to do those things we choose to do really, really well. And if we're not doing those things really, really well and they're sapping some of our time and energy that could be spent on something else, we feel guilty. Double the failure, double the fun!

In "Work–Life Balance? The Mantra That Balances What Matters," Fawn Germer illustrates this particular source of angst to a cringeworthy T. She writes about one night, years prior, when some friends came to her and her then-husband's home before heading out to dinner. She was in the midst of a monstrous investigative project ("the most challenging and important work I'd ever done"), and, bogged down in the thick of it, she'd taken to stashing mail and other sundry junk in the guest room. And this night before dinner, her husband opened the door to show everyone the mess. "In the midst of some of my greatest accomplishments as a journalist, I was exposed for the one failing that trumped everything. I'd failed in my traditional role as wife."[26]

Germer's story hits pretty close to home. Successfully juggling all the roles we take on is difficult—when it's not flat-out impossible—and the judgment we heap on ourselves when we fail to measure up in any one arena is harsh. There's the being judged, the need for approval, and then there's the guilt.

When in our valiant attempts to do it all, we fall short, we beat ourselves up and feel guilty. Guilty because we can't do it all, yes, but also guilty over our choices: When we choose to focus on something in one moment, we feel guilty about all the things we're neglecting. Former U.S. Secretary of State Madeleine Albright (who was a journalist, researcher, full-time single mom to three daughters, and professor, all before ever stepping foot into the White House), when asked about work–life balance, said, "There are no easy choices. Every woman's middle name is guilt."[27]

There's no doubt that guilt weighs heavily on our choices. It complicates things, loading each choice down with some additional—and not necessarily relevant—worry. In the same way that factoring others' feelings and our fear of being judged out of our decisions requires conscious work, so does eliminating the guilt factor. How often do we do things we don't want to do, out of guilt? Say yes when we don't mean it? And women, with our oversized to-do lists and our underdeveloped sense of balance—well, it's probably not too wild a stretch to suggest the two are related.

But back to Germer's guest room of shame: What strikes us most about her story is that failure on one scale can trump all our other successes. It's a familiar feeling and makes us think: Is it a uniquely woman thing? How many men do you know who consider their successes at work irrelevant, or even slightly diminished, because they don't vacuum enough?

IT'S EASY TO rant about, but how do we get over it? An easy answer might be to consciously choose what's most important to us and forget what's not. But for women, often it's just not that simple. Opting to drop the balls that don't matter as much to us as the others? That's contrary to the messaging we've heard for years: Have it all, do it all. Be all things to all people: friend, employee, wife, mother, daughter, domestic goddess, sexual superhero, and a triathlete who can speak intelligently on any number of subjects and tackle the Sunday crossword in pen. On some level, we want to. We feel like we should be able to be superwoman, even while we call out that unholy icon as bullshit.

So we keep those balls in the air. And we watch our sisters, with their balls in the air, and think, *If she can do it, I should be able to do it too. What's the matter with me?* Rather than *I bet she's as overwhelmed as I am. Why are we doing this to ourselves again?* But if we could throw caution to the wind and let a few of those balls drop, would we perhaps find ourselves a little happier, our sisters a little less stressed by the juggling act they're trying to pull off, our lives perhaps a little less balanced—but tilted more in our favor?

IN THE FACE of all this, what's an appropriate rallying cry for the overworked, underbalanced, overjudged, undersupported women of today?

Get more sleep.

So proclaimed Arianna Huffington and *Glamour* magazine editor-in-chief Cindi Leive, anyway, in their "Sleep Challenge 2010" call to arms.[28]

Don't get us wrong. We're sure that when they implored women to start "sleeping our way to the top" their intentions were good. But, as Feministing's Jessica Valenti put it, "What Huffington and Leive are really talking about is sexism, not sleep."[29]

Let's back up, shall we? The Huffington Post piece quotes Michael Breus, PhD—author of *Beauty Sleep: Look Younger, Lose Weight, and Feel Great Through Better Sleep*—as saying, "Women are significantly more sleep-deprived than men. . . . They have so many commitments, and sleep starts to get low on the totem pole. They may know that sleep should be a priority, but then, you know, they've just got to get that last thing done."[30]

Tell us something we don't know, Breus.

He goes on, "Women often feel that they still don't 'belong' in the boys-club atmosphere that still dominates many workplaces. So they often attempt to compensate by working harder and longer . . . fueled by the mistaken idea that getting enough sleep means you must be lazy or less than passionate about your work and your life."[31]

Maybe. Or maybe it's more to do with the fact that many of us are so overloaded with tasks and to-dos, first shifts and second shifts, attempting to succeed in the "boys-club atmosphere that still dominates many workplaces," there simply isn't enough time left for sleep.

Sleep deprivation, of course, comes with all sorts of nasty side effects, as the HuffPo piece points out. Illness, stress, traffic accidents, weight gain (let no fat card go unplayed!). We know how it feels to slog through a busy day in a fog of exhaustion. We know we should get more sleep.

But the fact is, the modern workplace—of which women are now the majority—is still set up as though the workers who fill it were Don Draper clones, men with a full-time Betty at home, able to take care of all the stuff that keeps a life running smoothly. But the ladies (and gentlemen) of today don't have a Betty. She took off to Vegas, baby. So we do our best Don—and then we do Betty's job too. We work our full day—and then we fold the clothes. Do the grocery shopping. Arrange the playdates. Pick up the dry cleaning. Attempt to cook healthy meals (or contend with the parking lot at our favorite takeout joint). Exercise, socialize, and—if there's time—sleep.

As Lisa Belkin put it on *New York Times*'s Motherlode: "The reason women don't sleep as well as men is . . . because the world, as it is constructed, gives women more to do . . . the social expectation is that [housework] is still a mother's job, and shaking it requires more than a simple declaration that we will get more sleep."[32]

It's enough to make us cry out for our blankies! So what are we to do—and, more importantly, why are we even bringing this up?

We think the sleep challenge offers a good opportunity—one that doesn't involve shut-eye, but rather its opposite: to start recognizing the deeper truths in "personal challenges" like this for the eye-openers that they are.

It's much like what went on with certain interpretations of "The Paradox of Declining Female Happiness" study, where, by focusing on self-reported, empirical measurements of happiness, it became all too convenient to miss the harder point—making what is, at its core, a societal issue personal instead.

And the sleep issue is another instance in which something societal and systemic is trivialized by framing it as personal. Don't get us wrong: It's important to smell the roses and bank some shut-eye. But such platitudes can serve as a smokescreen, keeping the discussion light and distracting us from the harder questions, the more elusive answers. Sleep, happiness—they're easy to individualize, but it's what's behind them that needs a harsh light cast upon it. And this way of framing such issues—for which solutions are so desperately needed—is precisely why there aren't any solutions. Working women are operating against a bevy of structural obstacles, and when we make the struggles personal, we lighten the load, trivialize the deeper issues, take the burdens off the institutions and put them squarely onto our own backs.

So, get more sleep—and while you're at it, dream of a society that's awake to the reality of women's lives . . . and willing to do something about it.

WHILE MUCH OF what we've gotten into here might have you feeling a little gloomy, convinced we're all doomed to an existence of nonparadoxical unhappiness, we don't see it that way. On the contrary, in fact, we contend that women, as a whole, are in a place characterized by growing pains.

The *Washington Examiner*'s Marta Mossburg had this to say about "The Paradox of Declining Female Happiness" study, and we tend to agree: "Too many choices . . . can paralyze. . . . Men are used to this. For women, opportunity is still a relatively new phenomenon. . . . Women's declining happiness in the face of greatly expanded freedoms should come as no surprise. But neither should a reversal of the trend once they . . . get used to it."[33]

Our experience—defined, as it is, by choices—is a generationally new one, made all the more difficult by the structures, socialization, sexism, ageism, and guilt that get in the way. There's a lot we're fighting against, making the landscape of limitless choices that much more difficult to traverse. But we've battled bigger boogeymen before. And, much like flipping on the light was all you needed to make the monsters under your childhood bed disappear, a good dose of daylight can illuminate those things that silently hold us back. And make them a whole lot less spooky.

ELEVEN

LIFE IN THE CARPOOL LANE

Most of us have trouble juggling. The woman who says she doesn't is someone whom I admire but have never met.
—Barbara Walters

HERE'S WHERE IT ALL GETS COMPLICATED—trying to carve out a life for yourself, despite the fact that you're stuck in a workplace designed for someone with a wife at home to take care of business.

It's another reminder that when Mom told us we could have it all, she might have fudged the details. Certainly she never told us about the new workplace math in the Age of Overwork: that the forty-hour week now equals fifty-two. Or that the technology that was supposed to make life easier means we never get away from work.

Let's face it. The workplace is still structured like a set for *Mad Men,* when you're expected to make work your life, and leave it to Betty to handle everything else. But whose life looks like that, regardless of gender? Men and women are single longer; they likely have hefty commutes; and most married folks have a spouse who works full-time too.

Getting a hit of free time, exploring a passion outside of work? Balance? Not until structures—and traditional gender roles—change.

One more reason we're so undecided?

Admit it. We've got one hell of a disconnect, which likely accounts for the glazed eyes you see in women rushing past at Starbucks or Safeway. It also partially accounts for the results of a 2009 survey that found only 37 percent of the generation that grew up with *The Brady Bunch* said they planned to stay in their current jobs after the recession ended.[1] Lack of career mobility, reason No. 1. But right up there? Better work–life balance. Likewise, a 2009 Catalyst study of that same age group found that over two-thirds of women surveyed "cited a commitment to personal and family responsibilities as a barrier to women's advancement." Only 38 percent of men felt the same.[2]

In other words, if you decide to have kids, it all gets excruciatingly more complex. Because it's likely that the daily juggle is all going to fall on you, sister. Take a high-powered attorney we'll call Joan. It's summer—easily the worst time of year to be a working mother—and she tells us she's ready to throw it all in. Stay home. And do what? Who cares.

It's not the law that's the problem. She likes what she does. She's good at it too. In a public-sector job, she supervises a bunch of lawyers who in turn oversee a bunch of other lawyers. She's got a teenaged daughter who goes to a pricey high school where she's involved in sports, music, and a competitive slate of college-prep courses. Joan travels some, and though her husband has slightly more flexibility when it comes to carpool duty, she's fried. Bring up the term "work–life balance," and what she says, without hesitation, is this: "It's all a crock of shit."

A big lie. It's where the promise that we can have it all becomes definitively exposed as illusion. Where indecision meets dissatisfaction.

Beyond the fact that no one ever told us that trying to combine work with life is not only hard, but—if you want to do well at both—darn near impossible.

"Can you have it all? You can't," Stanford's Myra Strober tells us emphatically. "The notion of opportunity cost is taught within the first hundred pages of any economics textbook. If you're doing A, you can't be doing B. By and large, if you're playing basketball, you can't be reading Jane Austen. Now, can you have both work and family? The answer is yes." But. Where it becomes problematic is for highly educated women with demanding jobs—jobs with a lot of travel and even more responsibility, she says, "particularly jobs that were traditionally men's jobs, and where accommodations for parenthood have not been made."

Clearly, it's a question of privilege (we should be so lucky, right?). But as options increase, more of us grapple with the have-it-all fantasy. Joan's a case in point. The idea of work–life balance, she says, may be great in theory, but in practice? Hardly. It's a concept just beyond our grasp, this idea of being able to manage both work and a life—whether or not we have kids. Which leaves so many of us in one hell of a pickle.

And speaking of that, why is it always pegged a woman's issue, Joan wonders? Or framed as a matter of personal choice?

Or, for that matter, defined in terms of daycare? Take the case of Ashley, who was part of a focus group for a committee investigating strategies for improving work–life balance at her university. After a lengthy session with the powers that be, she got the picture: Proposed work–life policies translated to onsite daycare, which ultimately caused her to explode, "I'm not straight, I don't have kids, I don't plan to have kids. What's in this for me?"

In fact, most of the debate around work–life issues (as evidenced by the statistics, the research, and most of the policy discussions) centers around families, as if caring for small children were the only consideration. What about longer vacations? Shorter work hours? (According to Thomas Geoghegan, a labor lawyer in Chicago and author of *Were You Born on the Wrong Continent? How the European Model Can Help You Get a Life,* Americans work the equivalent of nine extra forty-hour weeks a year in comparison to their German counterparts. "We don't have any material value of leisure time, which is extremely valuable to people," he told *Salon* writer Alex Jung.[3])

Apart from this lack of downtime, however, once you do add kids to the mix, the conflict grows ever more intense. Indeed, says Barry Schwartz. He told us, "It's worse in many ways for women than it is for men because of the great lie of the feminist revolution, which is not simply that women can do anything, but that women can do *everything*. There's a sense that men can think that too, but society hasn't changed enough for men to have the same kind of investment in their nurturing role as parents that women do. To have a high-powered career as a woman, every day is torture."

Schwartz says that back when he and his wife were raising their kids, he took pains to tell his students that his family life was an anomaly: "I said, 'Listen, I have a job two blocks from my house, and I only have to be in the office six hours a week—the rest of the week, no matter how hard I work, I get to choose where and I get to choose when. You can't do this if one of you is a lawyer, the other is a doctor. So don't kid yourself. We got lucky. The world is not set up for this. You will discover it.'"

Discover it we do, and with that discovery comes layers of ambivalence. The first is with the term itself. "I thoroughly detest the term 'work–life balance,'" says Ellen Galinsky, president and cofounder of the Families and Work Institute, a leading think tank on the changing workforce. It's a Friday afternoon, and she's working at home, jamming on a deadline. "I use 'work–life fit,'" she says. "Because 'balance' doesn't fit the research. Research shows there's no such thing as 50–50: You're kind of prioritizing this, that, and the other, all the time. There's a shifting dynamic. And 'balance' is a word that makes people feel terrible."

Morra Aarons-Mele agrees. "I think we're still struggling with the fact that, for women, work is part of our lives, always," she told us. "I actually don't believe women are expected to have careers the same way men are. I think there's a lot of ambivalence in our society around that, once you enter the childbearing years. The ambivalence is in the women, it's in the men, it's in the older generation, it's in the powers that be, it's in the media."

That ambivalence grows from a whisper to a roar once we slam up against either the prospect or the reality of trying to combine work with family life. Suddenly, career choice becomes a matter of careful calculation. Women raised to be masters of the universe are pulled in opposite directions: Meaningful career? Meaningful family life? Maybe we've come up expecting to achieve the male model of success; now we realize it's an impossibility. Or we're agonized because, with all this grand opportunity, we find we don't want that kind of success anymore. As the "declining happiness" study suggests, grasping increased options has been harder on women: Career choices have evolved, but responsibilities at home have stayed the same. Whether or not we can "have it all," we're still expected to *do* it all. And the social structures and policies that might allow women to have the same work–life fit that men take for granted? Not there yet.

Barbara Hewett, PhD, is the senior assistant director of the Career Center at the University of Pennsylvania, where she works with undergrad business students from the prestigious Wharton School. They are highly motivated students with sky-high expectations—which, she says, are pretty realistic. Most have stellar job offers by Christmas break, and most are pretty pleased with their career paths. Until—for the women—the issue of work–life fit comes in. What she hears from some of them five to ten years later—when they've had a kid or are thinking of it—is that they might want to move closer to family, or that they might even want to drop out of their career for a while.

Myra Strober sees an added wrinkle for women in high-level careers. They often marry men with equally demanding jobs, and if he makes the fat paycheck, she might well leave the workforce because of the logistics of daily life, she tells us. "Those men often have what I call 'killer jobs.' So they are not able to share parenting. So the woman faces the following choices: Am I going to be a stay-at-home mom and also manage the household, since my husband is traveling constantly? Or am I going to have some kind of job that is less than a 'killer job'? So now these women face the issue: They can't really *have* the exciting jobs they were trained for. They have to make a compromise, and sometimes they say they would prefer not to work at all, and do volunteer work, rather than take a lower-level job."

But for most of us, opting out is not an option, and in fact, one of the most annoying aspects of this work–life debate is the way it is often framed: personal rather than political. Sociologist Paula England studied several decades' worth of workplace numbers to find out whether women with college educations were "choosing" to stay in the workforce. (They were.) Referring to the "cultural ambivalence" that surrounds the issues of women and work, she told *New York Times* blogger Judith Warner: "On the one hand, people believe women should have equal opportunities, but on the other hand, we don't envision men taking on more child care and housework, and unlike Europe, we don't seem to be able to envision family-friendly work policies."[4]

BACK IN 2009—just about the time women became the workplace majority—Ellen Goodman offered an update on the recession's creepy underbelly. Those paying the biggest price (underpaid, overworked, and often powerless to complain) were women, especially those with kids.[5] Blame the so-called maternal wall: discrimination, pure and simple—especially during tough times. Goodman cited both the rising number of pregnancy-discrimination complaints, as well as calls to the Center for WorkLife Law at the University of California Hastings College of the Law.

About the same time, polls by the Sloan Work and Family Research Network at Boston College found that 70 percent of those surveyed thought their employers were less supportive of flexible work arrangements. And the majority of respondents said they'd never used the Family Medical Leave Act. Most telling was this comment: "I used the FMLA after the birth of my first child. I had income from short-term disability insurance, and it worked well. But for my second child, I wasn't eligible, because I hadn't met the hours threshold, and for my third child, I wasn't eligible, because my employer had too few employees to be covered. Like a lot of women, I took these ineligible jobs because they offered flexibility. So I've come to think of the FMLA as the Firstborn and Medical Leave Act—because you're most likely to be covered at the point where you've been the ideal full-time worker before you've started your family."[6]

Okay, we're riled up by the fact that maternity leave gets linked with disability insurance. But the main point: Have we ever heard of "business daddies" dealing with discrimination when their wives are pregnant? Or worrying about how they will take time off to care for kids? Or, for that matter, having to take a lower-paying job just because they needed flex-time? Nope, thought not.

The reality, Ramani Durvasula told us, is that children are the death knell for women who aspire to career success. Ouch. "In the absence of tremendous financial resources, the hard labor of raising kids—and maintaining a home and family—often obliterate any chance of pursuing a meaningful career, and self-care typically flies out the window." The antidote? Stop selling women and girls a bill of goods, and switch out the "happily ever after" fantasy for "breadwinner," she says. "Imagine if young women thought that in order to be valuable spouses, they would have to do the earning. Perhaps this would translate into *truly* family-friendly policies and a stop to the castigation of women who choose to pursue paid work."

Numbers back her up. According to a 2009 Pew Center report on working mothers, a solid three-quarters of the American public believe that husband and wife should both contribute to the family income. But still, women are conflicted. Kim Parker of the Pew Center writes, "Working mothers in particular are ambivalent about whether full-time work is the best thing for them or their children; they feel the tug of family much more acutely than do working fathers. As a result, most working mothers find themselves in a situation they say is less than ideal."[7] Other interesting stats from the report: 40 percent of the working moms said they *always* feel rushed; 27 percent of the women without jobs say family responsibilities keep them out of the job market; and a whopping 62 percent say they'd rather work part-time.[8]

It's not just the question of who should raise the kids, but the fact that even when pop steps up, women still own the second shift. The 2008 American Time Use Study surveyed married parents with full-time jobs from 2003 to 2006. (Those were the latest stats available when we went to print.) The researchers found that mom was more likely than dad to do both housework and childcare: 71 percent of moms versus 54 percent of dads spent time caring for their kids (1.2 hours for mom; 49 minutes for dad), and 40 percent of moms versus 23 percent of dads spent time on carpool duty. And housework? Women again won the sweepstakes: 89 percent of moms versus 64 percent of dads spent time on household chores: (2 hours a day for mom and slightly over 1 for pop). As for leisure? Approximately 2.9 hours for mom versus 3.7 for dad.[9]

THE WHOLE DEBATE took on the appearance of a street fight in the summer of 2009, when Jack Welch—former CEO of General Electric— famously pronounced that women who want to climb the corporate ladder have to choose between taking time off to raise their kids and making it to the corner office. "There's no such thing as work–life balance," Mr. Welch told the Society for Human Resource Management's annual conference in New Orleans on June 28. "There are work–life choices, and you make them, and they have consequences."[10] His blunt talk ignited a firestorm—not because he implied that women can't have it all, but because he defined the choices in midcentury terms: Family or career, girls. Not both. Nowhere did he suggest workplace policies to make it less than a zero-sum proposition. Nor did he address the fact that neither he nor his male contemporaries ever had to make such a choice.

All of which echoes that study by Jenny Hoobler that showed that women were perceived as having greater family–work conflict than their male counterparts. They were thus seen as less promotion-worthy and less dedicated to their jobs, and were often denied the most challenging assignments. It's all part of that maternal wall. But here's what's crazy: The study found that these attitudes were prevalent among both male and female supervisors. And it didn't matter whether the women employees had kids or not.[11]

Hoobler told us that it showed "this lingering stereotype that women aren't as dedicated to their careers because they are or *will* at some point take the primary responsibility for caregiving in the family."

It's a double hit. Not only do women have to do more of the work, but they're also penalized for it. "People think this is something that has gone away," Hoobler says. "While men are doing a lot more than their fathers did, in dual-career families, women are still bearing the lion's share. But what our study showed was that even when women *did not* have those responsibilities, their bosses felt they still did."

Hoobler also suggested that anything that called attention to caregiving—using onsite daycare, for example—reinforced the bias. Even, say, snapshots on the bulletin board. "Pick up any businesswoman's guide to career, they'll tell you stories about that," Hoobler said. "If a man has a picture of a child in the office, it makes them look like they're stable—like a good, solid, trustworthy employee—but if a woman has pictures in the office, it looks like, 'Uh-oh . . . will she leave early to pick up her kids? Will she take an extended maternity leave? Will she even come back after the birth of her next child?' It's ridiculous that in 2010 these stereotypes still exist, but they're still out there."

(Contrast: A study on fathers out of the Boston College Center for Work and Family found that the dads confirmed that having a baby enhanced their image at work in terms of reputation, credibility, and even career options.[12])

The bottom line is this, says Hoobler. "People who want to do a good job in their career and want to be a great parent? They only have so many hours in the day. And we have this structure of work where the hours we work are still based on the model of 'the breadwinner, and someone to stay home and take care of the kids.' So if you're both breadwinners, it's almost structurally impossible to do an excellent job of childrearing at the same time."

Our point exactly.

All of which echoes what Joan Williams dubbed "the myth of the ideal worker." She wrote about this myth in her book *Unbending Gender: Why Family and Work Conflict and What to Do About It.* According to Williams—who's a professor at the University of California Hastings College of the Law—the workplace is designed for an employee who can work forty years straight, without taking time off for childbirth or carpools; for someone who won't balk at overtime and who has someone else at home to take care of business. That means men. "Women may choose not to perform as ideal workers," Williams wrote, "but they do not choose the marginalization that currently accompanies that decision."[13]

Williams—who directs the Hastings Center for WorkLife Law—recently authored a report with the Center for American Progress that suggests things have not much changed since 2000, when she wrote the book. Women in high-level jobs are often pushed out when their jobs demand 24/7 availability and when "full-time" means fifty hours a week or more. "As a result, professional women who need hours more like a traditional full-time job of forty hours a week often find themselves 'doing scut work at slave wages,' as one professional woman put it."[14]

And don't forget the "mommy track"—a term coined by the *New York Times* and based on an idea that Catalyst founder Felice Schwartz proposed in a *Harvard Business Review* article back in 1989. That article suggested that businesses could accommodate the growing number of working mothers by offering them alternative career paths.[15] Good perhaps in theory, but in practice, what it meant was that women who bought into such arrangements were stereotyped as less serious about their careers. The upshot? Rather than corporate America changing structures to accommodate those who wanted/needed a life outside of work (um, *all* of us?), many women had the choice made for them and found themselves sidelined.

NO WONDER MANY women carve their own alternatives—though they almost always involve career sacrifice. Take Casey. She's a bright thirtysomething mom with a master's degree from a top-ranked journalism school. Ever since she was a kid, she's said that if, for some reason, she couldn't be president of the United States, well, she wanted to be the press secretary. Today—four days from the birth of her second child, and one week after quitting her job as media liaison for a public agency—she is talking about her decision to stay home and do freelance consulting.

She lives in a pricey coastal town, and her decision would not be possible if her husband were not making serious money. Still, hers is a familiar story: She landed a job as a reporter at a daily right out of grad school, then moved to the opposite coast when her husband started a prestigious MBA program. After he graduated, they moved back, and Casey found that her paper—and all the others within commute distance—had hiring freezes, which ultimately led her to the job she just left. She liked the work and learned a lot. Then came child No. 1. Her mother helped with childcare, and the agency let her negotiate a part-time position: two days in the office, a half-day at home. Her husband traveled a lot, so flexibility was key.

"I initially thought I had hit the jackpot, but I've realized that [the part-time position] came with its own set of hazards," she says now. "My own expectations were too high. News seemed to hit on days I wasn't in the office. I had only co-ownership over my position and therefore less power. And I seemed to disappoint my boss regularly, just by virtue of the schedule. It's a tough adjustment to go from being a valuable team player to a part-timer who has to be out the door at five and won't be in tomorrow. Also, there was no hope for advancement, and it seemed ridiculous to go hunting for another job with more responsibility while only being willing to work part-time." She felt trapped.

A recent report from the U.S. Joint Economic Committee showed that in 2009, some 17 million American women worked part-time— approximately one-fourth of all working women. And while part-time arrangements can be a good compromise, the bad news is that they not only present their own glass ceilings, but they pay less too. The report found that part-timers (nearly two-thirds of them are women) make less per hour than full-timers—even for the same work. In sales, part-timers receive 58 cents on the dollar. For those in techno jobs, part-timers receive 63 cents. The report also found that many part-timers "do not receive the same health benefits, paid time-off for vacation or sick leave, or pension benefits that full-time workers receive."[16] So sure, a part-time slot is an option, but for how many women?

A growing number of working moms—dubbed, somewhat dismissively, "mompreneurs"—have decided that if the rules don't accommodate them, well, they'll make their own. (One is the quintessential Gen-Xer, Soleil Moon Frye—a.k.a. Punky Brewster—who cofounded an ecofriendly baby-products business called The Little Seed.) According to a 2010 report by the National Women's Business Center, in 2008 there were 7.2 million businesses in which women were majority owners, generating $1.1 trillion in sales. The study also found that over one-third of all self-employed people were women.[17]

Morra Aarons-Mele says the rise of women entrepreneurs represents a flat-out rejection of the mommy track, which she writes is "shorthand for (primarily) women with children who don't want to work extreme hours."[18] She also finds that, in a world where there's still ambivalence about working mothers, it's deemed okay for women to start mom- and kid-related businesses (read: nonthreatening), and they often do it from home. But whether the business involves kids or computers, the trade-off is not always what it's cracked up to be. Those home-working moms often find they're always "on"—working longer, harder, and faster, and often juggling several things at once.

Finally, there are those few women who opt out entirely—a non-trend that caused its own media firestorm. It's been a controversy ever since 2003, when Lisa Belkin wrote a piece for the *New York Times Magazine* entitled "The Opt-Out Revolution." In the article, she reported on a group of fast-track women who'd "opted out" of their high-flying careers once they had kids.[19] Ever since, a debate has raged as to whether the story reflected an actual trend—backed up by numbers—or if it was based on anecdotal information from a select group of women. Census stats that came out in 2009 suggested the latter was the case.[20]

"The *New York Times* has been breaking that story regularly since about 1986," says Hoobler. "Because it's really sexy. Sensational. To me, it's backlash against women's progress. It's like, 'See, women didn't really want to play with the big boys anyway.' Also, it gets companies off the hook: 'Oh, I guess we don't have to do anything for them, because apparently, it's their choice.' And I do think a lot of it is structural. Especially women who have a high need for achievement, [they] feel like, 'Oh my god, I can't be excellent at both things, I'm going to have to choose something.' But I don't think it's that women don't desire the same things that men do in their career. We want advancement. We want the big bucks. We want the challenging assignments."

But absent structural and societal changes, the conflict between work and family often involves retooling the dream. In 2010, *Harvard Magazine* ran a feature on a study showing that women who'd gotten their MBAs from Harvard were far less likely to both have kids and a full-time job at the time of their fifteenth reunion than were MDs. And in both cases, working mothers chose less-demanding areas: The story pointed out that women make up 41 percent of new doctors nationwide, but only 30 percent of ER doctors or general surgeons.[21]

The story was somewhat unremarkable (sorry, Harvard), except for the dialog it provoked. One comment from a twenty-nine-year old med student named Erin was right on point. About to choose her specialty, she confessed that she thinks she was made to be a surgeon but knows that she'll never go into that field. She writes that she can't figure out how to be a good mother someday and factor in the hours—and the lack of flexibility—required to be a good surgeon. "I hate that this conflict exists," Erin writes. "I hate that I keep running into a roadblock. And I also hate that my male counterparts don't have this same internal dialogue."[22]

Which brings us back to Casey. She realizes she's lucky to even have the option to stay home with her kids when they're young. And she knows she'll pick up her career later. But still. "I've thought so much about this issue over the years—dating back to when I was in college and weighing law school versus [journalism] school," she says. "I am trying to embrace this next stage. . . . I reassure myself that I can reenter the arena when I want to. And who knows if I even will. But at the same time, I find myself jealous of my husband heading to the office in the morning because he has such an important responsibility in supporting our family. I just love the action and the challenge of working, especially in a newsroom. A small part of me would like my back against the wall and the pressure on. . . . Unfortunately, being a woman, your career is not as linear as men's. And so, I end up wondering, if I did have a linear career, how high I could have gone. And I'll never know."

SO LET'S TALK policy. In 1971, both houses of Congress passed the Comprehensive Child Development Act, which would have provided for a national daycare system. President Nixon vetoed it. Since then, the closest we've come to any federal family policies is the Family Medical Leave Act, passed in 1993, which provides for twelve weeks of unpaid leave for maternity, adoption, or family illness in companies with over fifty employees. That's it. Which, as of 2010, makes the United States the only industrialized country without any form of paid parental leave. The last holdout was Australia, which in June 2010, established a taxpayer-funded eighteen-week parental-leave program, where the parent on leave—either mom or pop—will receive the equivalent of minimum wage for eighteen weeks.[23] The other countries with no paid leave? Three: Papua New Guinea, Swaziland, and Lesotho.[24]

And, as a joint report from the Center for American Progress and the Center for WorkLife Law points out, we're also missing federally mandated "paid sick days, limits on mandatory overtime, the right to request work-time flexibility without retaliation, and proportional wages for part-time work." The report also notes that "90 percent of American mothers and 95 percent of American fathers report work–family conflict."[25]

Approaching a good work–life fit takes more than policy, and Ellen Galinsky is the first to tell you that work has to "work" for both employer and employee. But national policy can prompt priorities that trickle down. Let's look at Sweden, which subsidizes preschool and elder care—and provides thirteen months of paid parental leave that can be taken in any increments until the child turns eight—reserving at least two months of that leave for fathers. As a result, 85 percent of fathers take parental leave. And those who don't, suggests *New York Times* reporter Katrin Bennhold, might face the stink-eye from family, friends, and coworkers. It's part of a decades-long initiative to ensure gender equality—and it works. Because companies expect both genders to take parental leave, no one gets penalized. According to Bennhold, mothers' earnings increase by 7 percent for every month dad takes off—rather than perpetuating the gender pay gap when mothers were the only ones to take a time out. And 41 percent of companies made "a formal decision" to encourage fathers to take leave. A system of workplace flexibility has evolved—either parent can leave at 4:30 P.M. to collect children, no questions asked, so long as they log in at night—and family-friendly policies have become a recruiting tool.[26]

There's no question the initiatives were controversial at first, and state money provided an incentive. What's more, in a country like the United States, which prides itself on individualism, mandated policies might never take shape. But as Kratz (she's from Sweden, remember?) points out, these family-friendly policies came about because of this: What Americans consider private choices, Scandinavians consider public policies. She writes, "These programs have been put in place after public discussions. That means that unlike in the United States, childcare, just to take one example, is an issue that gets public attention. . . . It doesn't mean Swedish families have it all figured out, or that the tension between career and family doesn't exist. It does. Swedish women are tired and frustrated too. But they talk about it. Society talks about it. Politicians consider it. In 2009, in Sweden, the experience of being a woman is of public interest."[27]

By contrast, in spring of 2010, Congress failed to pass the Work–Life Balance Award Act (HR 4855), a benign bill that would have established an award for businesses that develop and implement work–life balance policies. It failed, 249–163.[28]

Weird, when you consider public attitudes. According to a 2009 report issued by the Families and Work Institute, young women want jobs with more responsibility every bit as much as men do—and moth- erhood does not change those ambitions. But the study also found that men spend more time with their kids than their fathers did, and that— as gender roles have begun to shift—men's stress over work-and-family conflict has increased.[29] Ellen Galinsky, an author of the report, tells us that this suggests that the idea of work–life fit might move out of the pink ghetto and start being framed as change that benefits all of us.

Some might snipe that it's time already that men feel the conflict too. But Galinsky believes that, as the generation of men who are (or who expect to be) more involved at home climb the ranks, they're likely to be more amenable to family-friendly policies. She said their studies find that when supervisors—regardless of age or gender—have respon- sibilities for kids or elders, they are seen as more supportive of work– life policies, because, says Galinsky, "when you go through it yourself, typically you feel different about it."

What's more, she says, when men as well as women leave work to pick up kids—or if dad does the drop-off at the onsite daycare center— the stigma, and that maternal wall, starts to go away. "In an ideal world," Galinsky says, "work would work for you and your employer, and there are some policies that would help you do that, but where the rubber hits the road is how your supervisor and coworkers treat you. You can work at a company that has fantastic policies, or live in a country that has fantastic policies, and you can still have a horrible situation. There has to be a culture where people value personal and family time."

The appetite for change is there. Polls conducted in 2009 by the Center for American Progress and California First Lady Maria Shriver found that "overwhelming majorities of both men and women—includ- ing both conservatives and moderates—said that government and busi- nesses need to provide flexible work schedules, better childcare, and paid family and medical leave." A full 85 percent of those surveyed agreed that businesses would risk losing good workers if they failed to adapt to families' needs, and 75 percent agreed that employers should be required to provide more flexibility.[30]

One sign of life was a White House forum on flexibility in March of 2010. First Lady Michelle Obama immediately earned cred with working mothers in her opening remarks by recalling a job interview when she was still on maternity leave with Sasha. She couldn't find a babysitter and ended up taking the baby with her. Sasha slept through the entire interview, and Michelle got the job. The point? "I know that I was lucky, number one. I was interviewing with the president, [who] had just had a child himself and was very understanding and open-minded."[31] Later, the President closed out the forum by saying that the "disconnect between the needs of our families and the demands of our workplace also reflects a broader problem: That today, we as a society still see workplace-flexibility policies as a special perk for women rather than a critical part of a workplace that can help all of us." He also cited a White House report that found that companies with flexible workplaces had lower absenteeism and turnover, and higher productivity.[32]

HARD TO TELL whether presidential advocacy will translate to action, but demographics might be on our side. The Pew Center reports that Millennials—who make up roughly a third of the workforce—overwhelmingly rank being a good parent (52 percent) over earning a fat paycheck (15 percent), even though only about a third of them have kids.[33] Add to that a 2010 Accenture survey that found that Millennial women believe they can have both a rewarding career and a fulfilling personal life.[34]

Let's not forget the money, either. Women make up half the workforce, and in 22 percent of marriages, they bring home the fattest paycheck.[35] As our numbers rise, and with it our economic clout, we girls may finally be in a better position to push for the kinds of changes that work for us. "Once a woman starts bringing home equal or more money," Morra Aarons-Mele told us, "things change. There's been a rallying cry for thirty or forty years, but we haven't had the critical mass in terms of percentage of the workforce or the money we control. That's new."

Optimism or naivete? There's a caveat, and for that, we turn to Barry Schwartz, who said to us: "What I worry about is that there's a kind of tournament, and the Millennials who win the tournament are going to be the ones most inclined to play by the older generation's rules by the time they get there. In a position to make the rules themselves, they will have forgotten they had a notion about how they should live their lives." Pause. "But maybe not," he says. "There's no reason not to be a little optimistic."

Stay tuned.

TWELVE

TRAVELING THE REVOLUTIONARY ROAD

You'll never be a man. Be a woman;
it's a powerful business when done correctly.
—Joan, *Mad Men*

ANYONE OLD ENOUGH TO HAVE BEEN a working girl in the '80s—or to have seen the movie *Working Girl*—might have some idea what we refer to when we describe The Shoulderpad Effect, in which, through fashion, a not-so-subtle belief became manifest: To play with the boys, one must pretend she is one of the boys. Lest tragic workwear of yesteryear seem too passé a reference, call it, if you like, The Sarah Silverman Effect.

Actually, comedy writing is a fascinating lens through which to take a look at the play-like-you're-one-of-the-boys phenomenon.

As we mentioned, Hollywood is one of the worst offenders when it comes to gender equality—especially in the writing room. And the oft-outnumbered women comedy writers—who, quite literally, deal in the crude, the offensive, the politically incorrect—are forced to walk a tenuous line: To shut up and nut up, or to stand up when something crosses the line and risk being written off as a wimp, a wuss, a . . . woman.

They are an extreme case, to be sure; but even still, lines get crossed. Take this example, from a 2010 *Salon* piece by Lynn Harris, in which an experienced female writer let fly some good "asshole ex-boyfriend" anecdotes as potential script fodder, prompting "another writer to start ranting—angrily, not riffing—about how women 'always date jerks.' Another narrowed his eyes at her. 'A guy acting like an asshole? That's what makes you spread your legs?'"[1]

The perfect illustration of one of the key buzzkills of the blend-in style of work: an unwillingness to say "uncle." "'It's hard to speak up and say, 'I'm offended as a lady,' because the whole point is you're trying not to be different.'"[2]

It's reminiscent of a tidbit from the intro to Gloria Steinem's *Outrageous Acts and Everyday Rebellions,* in which she lamented all sorts of subtle instances of discrimination she'd endured, culminating with, "a lifetime of journalists' jokes about frigid wives, dumb blonds, and farmers' daughters that I had smiled at in order to be 'one of the boys.'"[3] Here's the super disturbing part: She wrote that in 1983.

And yet. Even today, writers from the Harris piece say, "There is pressure to prove that you're impossible to offend . . . which causes some to 'overcompensate by being incredibly dirty.'"[4]

No matter how well they can stand the heat—how much they might, in fact, thrive on the heat—these women are outnumbered and, by virtue of that token status, feel forced to endure sexist missives, to out–gross-out the guys, to keep their mouths shut for fear of being called out as "that girl"—even when they hate themselves for doing it. With all that to contend with, it's a miracle these women are funny at all.

Imagine how funny they'd be if they could just be themselves.

It's an extreme version of what so many of us face every day, when trying not to be "different" leaves us in a no-man's-land, stuck between trying to blend in (to get a shot at beating them at their own game) and standing out and striving to change the rules altogether—but risking our acceptance. And it makes you wonder: How much does our own performance, our contribution, suffer when we're expending so much energy managing our image? How much better could we be, at *whatever* we're doing?

But "be like a man" continues to be the party line. For example, consider one particularly annoying instance of a man taking it upon himself to tell women as a whole, "You know what your problem is?" New York University professor Clay Shirky's blog post "A Rant About Women" decreed that our problem is this: "Not enough women have what it takes to behave like arrogant, self-aggrandizing jerks . . . self-promoting narcissists, antisocial obsessives, or pompous blowhards, even a little bit, even temporarily, even when it would be in their best interests."[5]

In other words, not only should we behave like men, we should behave like the very worst of them.

We'll concede he might have a point. We're underpaid and underrepresented—and perhaps our reluctance to demand that pay and representation is partly to blame. But it's awfully convenient not to mention how women are not socialized to behave like, well, douchebags. Or how, when we *do* summon our inner "pompous blowhard," not only are we not rewarded for it, we are in fact judged, smacked down, written off as "hormonal"—even when our male counterparts engaged in the same sort of douchebaggery might be, as Shirky himself suggests, rewarded for their efforts.

But worse is the message that we should look inward rather than outward, that we should change ourselves rather than the world. As Jezebel's Anna North points out, the trouble with such a strategy is that sometimes it works. Change to fit in, gain acceptance—only to find that you "still have to work within the existing power structure. . . . Those who are marginalized by a system are often those best able to see its flaws, and teaching those people to just work around their marginalization is a great way to keep them quiet, and to keep anything from ever changing."[6]

Don't get us wrong. If you—at your deepest you—are a pompous blowhard, then you go! You blow hard and long, sister. If, in your heart of hearts, nothing makes you happier than a gross-out competition, you be grosser than gross. But why is it that the same standards we apply all over the rest of our lives don't apply here? Which is to say, when was the last time you advised someone that their surest route to success was to try to appear to be something they are not?

AS WE SEE it—and as scientists prove it, and as feelers sense it—we women are different. Not different bad or different good, just different. ("Whether that's nurture or nature—I don't really care anymore," Elizabeth Lesser told us. She's an author and cofounder of the Omega Institute for Holistic Studies and the Women and Power Conference. She's also one of the aforementioned "feelers," and we'll hear much more from her later.) And we think a certain level of our frustration is a result of the fact that we've been so loathe to own it, that we instead absorb the ubiquitous message "To be successful, act like a man." When you're told that to be yourself is to risk being accepted, to risk being taken less seriously, decisions are made all the more confounding. Not least because every time we act in ways that are out of alignment with who we are, we become a little bit more of a stranger, even to ourselves.

Not only that, but more often than not, playing by these established rules—fitting ourselves into the prescribed roles; following certain, defined paths that lead to certain, defined symbols of success—leaves us feeling somewhat hollow. As Naomi Wolf wrote in a 2010 *More* magazine piece, "After forty years of women trying to fit into a postindustrial Western 'male' model for work, we've seen that women can achieve it just fine, and often they even outperform men—but that doesn't mean it is the right model for most women's deepest satisfaction."[7]

We've proven we can play their game. But despite the fact that playing it has left us pretty dissatisfied, we continue to play it. We're after a truer fit—yet we're reluctant to say so. We dance around the idea, then pull back, perhaps fearful that to claim a difference is necessarily to claim a weakness. Or to somehow forfeit our feminist card. It's as though we're willing to walk right up to that line, but we're afraid of what will happen if we step into the abyss beyond it. (All of which made the research and reporting for this chapter more than a tad frustrating.)

This dissatisfaction and discomfort are bad enough, but we wonder if playing by these rules for so long has left us blinded to what may be our biggest strength of all: The fact that we are different. And that by virtue of that difference, we have something valuable and, you know, *different* to offer—something that all too often gets squelched by The Shoulderpad Effect.

But it still remains controversial, taboo, to suggest women and men are different. When we spoke with Elizabeth Lesser, she too acknowledged this, saying that although she does "intuit that the way a woman's brain and values and heart function [is] different from men," this conversation is a "very, very interesting, complicated, dangerous [one]."

Let's have it anyway.

IN 1990, DR. Judy Rosener published a paper in the *Harvard Business Review* that ignited a firestorm. Why? Well, in the paper, called "Ways Women Lead," she suggested that women and men are different.[8]

The horror!

The controversy is understandable, then and now. And frustrating. In fact, Dr. Rosener—now eighty and working on a book called *Organizational Intercourse,* about how organizations can benefit from utilizing these differences—still seems mildly exasperated by it. She told us, "I never said women are better. I said they were different and they led differently . . . it was very controversial, again, because if you say men and women are different, immediately people say, 'Are they better or worse?' My crusade has been they're not better or worse; they're different. And difference does not mean deficiency. Difference means added value, and I kept trying to say this. Look, because they're different, that means you get two different ways of doing things, without one being better than the other. But I want to tell you, that is a very difficult message!"

Why, though? After all, it's indisputable that men and women are physically different. But historically, the resistance—especially from women—to such a message makes a certain amount of sense. Plotted against the timeline of the modern workplace, we're still relatively new to the game. It was logical that, upon our initial entrée, our strategy was to blend in, to play like the boys, even to look like them (one word: shoulderpads). Like the comedy writers, we downplayed our differences, concerned that, if men smelled fear, insecurity, or Chanel No. 5, we'd be at an immediate disadvantage. Or kicked out of the club for good. To focus on our differences would have been a risk. It could mean conceding a point or two to those who'd happily use it against us: "See, you don't want to be in the boardroom, sweetheart. Wouldn't you rather be home, making that nice tuna noodle casserole you do so well?"

And that may do a little to explain why, when Dr. Rosener's paper was written up in the *New York Times* Business section, she said it was "particularly women who said, 'We're not different,' because again, they said, 'If you're different, you're deficient.'"

Part of this bias surely has its roots in early—and lingering— medical and psychological theory, where the bulk of the research and observation was based on men, and then applied to women. But as recent research on physiology, disease, drugs, exercise, and neurobiology (which we'll get into in this chapter) has begun to show, women are not just small men.

Nor is a woman "a man in a skirt," as Susan Bulkeley Butler put it. The author of books including *Become the CEO of You, Inc.* and *Women Count,* Butler was one of five women in the first undergraduate class at Purdue's business school to include women. She was also the first female hired by Arthur Anderson—one of the "Big Five" accounting firms—in 1965. Even then, she refused to be anyone but herself, and she managed to work her way up the ranks, focusing on making "things happen for myself"—although she does say she remembers eating a lot of lunches alone. She made partner in 1979, went on to become managing partner, and since retiring in 2002, has mentored women "so they could see I'm not a man in a skirt"—and helped them to realize they don't have to be one either.

So if a working woman isn't just a man in a skirt, what is she, exactly?

Sucking on a chocolate, Dr. Rosener rattles off a laundry list of the differences between men and women: "Men are linear thinkers; women are holistic thinkers. Men communicate on one level at a time; women communicate on more than one level at a time. Women view power as a means to an end to do something; men view power as an end in itself. Women negotiate in a win–win manner; men negotiate in a win–lose manner. Women are interactive leaders; men are commanding leaders.

Women are concerned about process as well as outcomes; men are concerned primarily about outcomes. Women see relationships as an end unto themselves; men see them as a means to an end. Women are sensitive to subliminal cues; men pay little attention. Women are multithinkers and multitaskers and are comfortable with ambiguity."

They sound like age-old stereotypes—ho-hum, unenlightened clichés—and yet, you know what they say about clichés: They get to be clichés because somewhere, there's a grain of truth. And more and more research is demonstrating that, in this instance, that grain of truth may be biological in basis. Yes, rather than whether we played with trucks or dolls or some nice gender-neutral Play-Doh as little kids, it's looking increasingly like hormones are in the driver's seat. And they've commandeered the navigation system too, plotting out the pathways our reality-processing neurons will frequent even before we've gulped down our first breath.

Dr. Louann Brizendine—a Yale-educated, Harvard Medical School faculty member and director of the Women's Mood and Hormone Clinic at UCSF—is somewhat of a pioneer in this area. And her 2006 book *The Female Brain* is a bible of the biology behind our behavior. (You may know her from one oft-repeated finding: On average, women use two to three times as many words per day as men. Extrapolate from that what you will.)[9] Of course, upon its publication, even she was put on the defensive. In a *Newsweek* piece ahead of the book's release, she was quoted as saying, "It's not politically correct to say this. . . . I've been torn for years between my politics and what science is telling us. But I believe that women actually perceive the world differently than men. If women attend to those differences, they can make better decisions about how to manage their lives."[10]

But as Dr. Rosener said, the idea that women and men can be

different without one or the other being deficient is an incredibly difficult message. And, as one might expect, Brizendine's tome was met with some fierce resistance. That *Newsweek* piece cited Dr. Nancy C. Andreasen—a psychiatrist and neuroimaging expert at the University of Iowa's medical school—as saying, "Whatever measurable differences exist in the brain . . . are used to oppress and suppress women."[11]

Granted, that was 2006. But the sentiment is not as out-of-date as one might expect. It remains controversial to go there. Even Jenny Hoobler—author of the "maternal wall" study we talked about in Chapter 11—believes it is still taboo to suggest that there's some essential difference between men and women. She told us, "I think it feeds into the stereotypes of women as nurturing and caregiving and communal, which all the research shows is the direct opposite of what people think of as a prototypical excellent leader of a company. You need to be hard-driving, you need to be individualistic, you need to take risks—so that 'think leader, think male' is really bolstered when you talk about the differences between males and females. I think that's destructive, actually, to women's progress." Hoobler says she believes that such perceptions are starting to change, but we're not there yet, and identifying those qualities in ourselves—nurturing, caregiving, community-driven—is to risk fanning the flames of perceived inferiority.

But when you look at Dr. Brizendine's research—which happens to jibe pretty closely with that laundry list of Dr. Rosener's—it becomes harder to dismiss the power of nature when it comes to the differences in the ways men and women operate. And that our differences actually mean we excel in a lot of areas—areas that are pretty key, in business and in life.

Brizendine's book describes the development process our brains go through in utero, beginning with the fact that all human brains start out female. Then, around the eighth week, a male fetus's brain is saturated in testosterone, which shrinks its emotional center (insert "insensitive man" joke here) while increasing the areas responsible for sex and aggression. In the non-testosterone-soaked female brain, however, "The fetal girl's brain cells sprout more connections in the communication centers and areas that process emotion."[12]

"There is no unisex brain," Brizendine wrote. "[Girls' and boys'] brains are different by the time they're born, and their brains are what drive their impulses, values, and their very reality."[13]

A person whose brain has bigger communication and emotional centers, she says, is a person for whom communication and emotional sensitivity are "the primary values . . . a person who [would] prize these qualities above all others."[14]

Because our brains were never hit with that shot of testosterone—which stunts the brain's centers for communication, observation, and emotion-processing—our potential to develop such skills is simply better. And these innate tendencies only intensify once we're out in the world. "Girls' well-developed brain circuits for gathering meaning from faces and tone of voice also push them to comprehend the social approval of others very early."[15] So maybe it's not neuroses that have us so concerned about what other people think, it's just that our brains are wired to be more attuned to such indicators—imagine that!

She even likens our heightened ability to listen ("girls can hear a broader range of sound frequency and tones in the human voice than can boys"[16]) to that of bats. So perhaps it's not that we're *too* sensitive, it's that we're *more* sensitive—sensitive enough to pick up on subtle cues that really are there, but which men are simply unable to discern.

According to her research, hormones (and their potent effect on our brains) also underlie women's tendency to be more stressed by emotional conflict than men—and our superior ability to observe emotions in others. We can tell from looking at someone if we're being listened to or not, and, she's said more than once, the combination of increased capacity in areas of emotion and memory explains why women remember fights that men insist never happened.

Ahem. On that note, we'll rest her case.

REGARDLESS OF THE SCIENCE, the fact that we are fundamentally different from our male counterparts is something we all know, deep in our DNA (if you'll excuse the expression). And yet, hearing that "Yes, you are woman! You are different!" can come as a revelation.

Judy Pearson, a leadership coach and author, told us, "The women in my workshops come up to me and say, 'That's nothing I didn't know, but I never thought of it that way before, and I have a whole new appreciation for who I am and what I am.'" When we spoke with her, she was deep in the throes of writing her forthcoming book *A Different Kind of Courage,* which focuses on much of the current brain and hormone gender research. Of our differences, Pearson had this to say: "No more than I could will myself to be a redhead or an Asian woman or five inches taller—we can't will ourselves to those things—why would we think we could will ourselves to behave differently, as men?"

Why indeed. (And we can both attest that willing oneself taller, sadly, is an exercise in futility.)

And yet. Corporations still drop serious coin on sending women to workshops designed to do just that. In fact, it's a major beef of Dr. Rosener's. "We spend millions of dollars on workshops trying to get women to act more like men—[to] be more decisive, all this kind of thing . . . making women fit into a male model. . . . But based on what we now know about brains and hormones, these differences have to be acknowledged."

Not least because those hard-to-measure things at which we naturally excel are proving beneficial to the bottom line.

For example, did you know that, according to Catalyst, companies with significant numbers of women in management have a much higher return on investment?[17] Or that when work teams are equally split between men and women, they are more productive?[18] And then there's this: According to a study from the Center for Women's Business Research, women-owned businesses generate about $3 trillion in revenue and employ 16 percent of the workforce—nearly double the number of the fifty biggest companies in the country combined.[19]

And, you know, we're not above pointing out the fact that the most male-dominated industries haven't exactly done that well by the world. Take, for example, finance. Or oil. Ugh. 'Nuff said? In fact, in the wake of the 2010 BP oil disaster, *Ms. Magazine* published a blog post titled, "Women Clean Up After BP's 'Man-Made' Oil Spill."[20] The article pointed out the work that women-led groups including Coastal Women for Change and Code Pink: Women for Peace were doing, early on, to address the crisis. Additionally, the piece suggested that if more women had been in leadership positions at BP, it's possible the disaster never would have happened. The author pointed to research showing that women are more concerned about the environment, that they engage in more environmentally conscious behavior, and that they are more interested in a company's environmental practices. This is the sensibility we bring to the management table.[21]

And time and again, women have demonstrated that it's us—and not the men—who are brave enough to act as the conscience of our organizations.

In a July 2009 story on *Double X* entitled "Why Corporate Women Are More Likely to Blow the Whistle," Maureen Tkacik introduced us to "a veritable Davos of Bitches Who Told You So," including Enron whistleblower Sherron Watkins; Brooksley Born, former chairman of the Commodity Futures Trading Commission, who spent three years pushing for derivative regulation, only to be shushed by Alan Greenspan and Larry Summers; Sheila Bair, the only government regulator who can credibly claim to have seen the crisis coming; and Genevievette Walker-Lightfoot, an SEC attorney who smelled a rat in Bernie Madoff–land way back in 2004.[22]

Such examples are all the more amazing when you consider not just *who* and *what* these women were speaking out against, but also how few women there *are* in the positions to speak out on such issues in the first place. And that, outnumbered as they may have been, they did it anyway.

But back to Sherron Watkins, who after Enrongate was named one of *Time* magazine's 2002 "People of the Year."[23] At that time, when asked whether she thought women were somehow more ethical than men, Watkins said no. But it seems that with the passage of seven years, came a change of heart. And a willingness to claim *la différence*.

Of this, Tkacik wrote, "[Watkins] thinks women are more likely to blow the whistle than men, for reasons that have as much to do with nature as with nurture. . . . Watkins became convinced whistle-blowing was one of the few types of 'risk' that come more naturally to women after meeting Judy Rosener."[24] Yes, that Dr. Rosener.

Now, it's long been believed that, in the battle of the sexes, men are the natural-born risk takers. But according to Rosener, it depends what kind of risk we're talking about. The kind of risk that one takes with the encouragement of an audience (think *Deal or No Deal* or shortsighted shareholders) is the kind at which men tend to excel. The other, which Rosener calls "moral risk," is the kind that one takes *in spite of* the audience's disapproval. And that is the kind where women excel.

All of which is not to say that men suck. Judy Pearson—the leadership coach and author we mentioned earlier in the chapter—thinks we'd do well to consider that, when women and men work together, the result is often greater than the sum of our respective parts. As it is in the bedroom, so it could be in the boardroom. "By nature we are collaborative, nurturing, and inclusive. Men are by nature aggressive and competitive . . . but just as our physical differences we find attractive, it works for making babies," she tells us; if we are able to appreciate our other differences, we might find that they work well together. "Where men are aggressive, that is offset by our nurturing. And men are competitive but that's offset by our collaboration. Men want to win at all costs and then stomp on the loser, but we're inclusive, so if you lose, we're going to love you anyway. . . . Corporations are now realizing that when they have women on their boards or in the C-suite, their profitability goes up immeasurably, because women bring those additional aspects to the table."

BUT ABOUT THAT table: Do we really want to be there?

Interestingly—though perhaps not surprisingly—despite the fact that women are officially half the workforce, we are more than twice as likely as men to be thinking about calling it quits. In a 2009 *Harvard Business* blog post entitled "Are Your Best Female Employees a Flight Risk?" by Sylvia Ann Hewlett, the founding president of the Center for Work–Life Policy—Hewlett wrote that "in the wake of last year's financial crash, high-powered women were more than twice as likely as men—84 percent compared with 40 percent—to be seriously thinking [about] jumping ship. And when the head and the heart are out the door, the rest of the body is sure to follow."[25]

That's a pretty staggering stat—and as you might imagine, much riffing ensued.

In "Why Are Women So Unhappy at Work?" a follow-up post on the same blog, Sean Silverthorne wrote, "Certainly there are career opportunity questions. If women believe they don't have as good a chance as their male colleagues of advancing, of course they should be considering options. But a 2X factor suggests something more deep seeded [*sic*]. Something about the nature of work in the modern company."[26]

His post earned a slew of responses, citing reasons for our "wandering eye" ranging from discrimination from the good old boys' clubbers, to a need for more corporate support for work–life balance, to female "dogs in power that insist on running the place like a sorority."[27] No woman really wants to take part in the proverbial workplace pissing contests (and even if she did, she's not properly equipped).

All legit.

And yet, we find ourselves again convinced that there's something deeper to explain why women are so unhappy at work. This comment on the post gets at it: "There's a fundamentally different paradigm that can exist in female-oriented workplaces, and it takes us away from the whole aggressive money- and progress-oriented approach to work—it is [a] collaborative, nurturing, fun approach . . . it's like a circle, not a hierarchy."[28]

Naomi Wolf addressed the square peg/round hole issue in that *More* piece we mentioned earlier in the chapter. "Women evolved to survey the environment, gather, produce goods and food, and raise small children in an entrepreneurial, flexible context in which every element is part of the greater whole," she wrote. So we're dissatisfied, unhappy, and out of our element when we're "compartmentalized in a bleak manmade workspace, isolated from family and social life and alienated from [our] larger context."[29]

And in an October 2009 *New York Times* op-ed, Joanne Lipman made another, related point: "Women define success differently. . . . They also define themselves differently. I'm in the unfortunate position of witnessing many friends and colleagues [get] laid off. . . . But the women are less apt to fall apart . . . even for the primary breadwinners—because they are less likely to define themselves by their job in the first place."[30]

We think they're all onto something. We define success differently, differently than men do, and differently from the way it was defined in the early corporate structures (and in the structure of our very society)—structures which were built pretty much exclusively by men. So is it any wonder that we find the whole game more than a little unsatisfying?

The fact that the typical workplace, as it is currently configured, isn't set up to recognize (or, for that matter, to utilize) women's strengths certainly doesn't help either. Dr. Rosener put it this way: "It isn't the women that are the problem; it's the policies and practices that all value male attributes. There's just no doubt in my mind. Because male attributes can be quantified. How many clients did you see? How much money did you make? How many widgets did you make? The women's attributes are not quantifiable. Picking up subtle cues, developing relationships, working in teams, creating a sense of unity—how do you put a number on that? So if you can't measure it, you usually don't think about it. So when women get looked at for promotions, they are not looked at in terms of what their qualities are; they're looked at in terms of male qualities."

Given that, is it any wonder a monstrous 84 percent of us are considering jumping ship?

But if we want the structures to change, we have to stick around. As Susan Bulkeley Butler told us, "The organization can't change by itself. The culture of the organization is based on the people [who] are at the top—and we all know who's at the top at the majority of the organizations. And they are who they are, the organization is what it is, and it's just not going to change overnight. . . . Women say to me, 'Well, I don't want to be like them,' and I say, 'I wasn't like them.' But we can't make change happen unless we're there. . . . I'm tired of waiting on them to make change happen. So it's up to us. And we've got to realize that it's up to us."

SO, WHAT IF we were to embrace our truest selves—and somehow refashion the workplace and modern society to reflect it? What might that look like?

It's a huge idea, and requires thinking way outside the box. And, just to start out big, consider the words of Liberia's president, Ellen Johnson Sirleaf (the only female head of state in Africa), in a 2009 interview with the *New York Times Magazine*. When she was asked whether wars would still exist if women ran the world, she replied, "No. It would be a better, safer, and more productive world. A woman would bring an extra dimension to that task—and that's a sensitivity to humankind. It comes from being a mother."[31]

Not all of us are mothers, of course. But what she's alluding to is that essential female *thing*. That *je ne sais quoi* that science-minded types like Brizendine use the lab to define, whereas women like Elizabeth Lesser take a different tack. We've covered the science; let's move on to the soul.

Lesser emphasizes that the *je ne sais quoi* we're talking about is something that exists within all of us—male *and* female. As opposed to the female brain Brizendine studies, what Lesser talks about is the feminine aspect—in a Jungian sense—that is a part of every human being, just as the masculine aspect is. The feminine isn't exclusive to women—though typically it's stronger. When we spoke with her, she told us that the issue, as she sees it, is that over the course of human history, "the feminine has been left out of what we consider to be the most important way of exerting power in the world, [and] it's not thriving in many women, and it's not thriving in men."

As cofounder of the Omega Institute, Lesser has firsthand experience with the pressure to play like the boys. "I was a woman in a leadership role from a very young age, and from a very young age I got that if I acted how I wanted to in the meeting, let's say, I would lose all cred with the men in the room. And it usually was all men in the room; I was usually the only woman."

Then she brought up something really interesting: In a meeting, when someone cries, it's perceived as a sign of weakness in a leader. But when someone yells or bullies or gets angry . . . well, not so much. But really, the responses represent two sides of the same coin: the feminine and masculine reactions to feeling diminished, or attacked, or frustrated . . . and neither reaction is especially productive. One just happens to be The Way Things Are Done Around Here. Unsurprising, when you consider who's been building and populating those boardrooms for the bulk of their history. And given that de facto culture, it's really no wonder that women feel forced to squash parts of themselves.

"If the rules of engagement in a meeting, let's say, are to kind of one-up each other, not to show your cards, not to speak from personal experience, not to cry, not to care too much—the kind of bravado boys' club that really still exists in many, many businesses and organizations— those are the unspoken rules, and you're having to really mold yourself into that way of being," she says. "You lose a whole part of yourself, and women don't even realize this is happening anymore, 'cause it's the water we've been swimming in forever," says Lesser.

But what do you lose when you're constantly operating in a way that's at odds with your instincts? A lot. "If you repress over and over and over your particular way of expressing your sense of being threatened or your discomfort, it really does a number on you, psychologically," Lesser says. "I think we lose an enormous amount of our life force

. . . this is a spiritual truth for anybody of any gender: that if you are not coming from your genuine self, you lose a good 50 percent of your power, because you are pretending to be someone else."

And doing so can come back to bite us.

Take, for example, Hillary Clinton.

We talked with Lesser about her disappointment when, in the run-up to the 2008 presidential election, Hillary Clinton opted not to give a "gender speech" on par with Obama's race speech. Where Obama took the opportunity to put it out there, says Lesser, and emerged "suddenly seen in the eyes of the public as a very vibrant, brilliant, alive, connected, brave human being, there was this sense of courage about him," Clinton, on the other hand, missed a golden opportunity.

"In New Hampshire, when Hillary cried she had this fantastic opportunity to say, 'Hey, look, I'm a woman, I do things a little differently, and when I cry it's a sign . . . that my heart is engaged, that I'm compassionate, that I feel the pain of others. And if you feel the pain of others, you're much more likely to make wise decisions about human beings.'"

Who can say what that sort of "gender speech" would have done for her campaign (and who among us can't understand why she opted not to go there)? But Lesser believes this is the sort of conversation we need to be having "all the time, everywhere."

Not least because it might help us integrate that feminine aspect into the way that power is wielded. In organizations, this might mean a reconsideration of what constitutes the "bottom line" to include not only the organization's financial health, but also the health and well-being of the staff. It might mean embracing a new paradigm of power, one that emphasizes "power with" (that is, empowering others so as to foster a real sense of ownership and caring) rather than "power over" (which leaves all but the most powerful to find an unempowered place within the system). And while the implications are important in the context of work, just think about what they might mean for the world.

Which leads us right back to Dr. Rosener's words about embracing a "women's way of leading," twenty years old, and still so much easier said than done. And she and Lesser are talking about change on the macro level. But we think it's relevant on the personal level as well. Because it's a choice. And maybe acknowledging who we really are is one way to make every decision we face just a little bit easier.

Granted, it can feel like we're still a long ways off—like the women who play like the boys are the ones who are getting ahead. We talked about it during our conversation, and Lesser offered a pleasantly positive spin. "They're more viable, at this stage of evolution, toward a more feminine structure of leadership and power. . . . Social evolution happens in stages, and it's always a lot slower than the people on the edge would like it to be, so I think that these are the least scary women within the paradigm of patriarchal leadership. The women [who] are truly in touch with their feminine—the women who are courageously speaking from an authentic voice, as opposed to trying to be like one of the boys—that's going to take a little longer, but I still think it's a really good step."

And, you know, any big journey begins with a single step.

Or some jump rope.

In a piece called "Girls, Women and Double Dutch" on *The Atlantic*'s website, Cristine Russell wrote, "'equality' is an elusive goal . . . the goal posts keep moving. They always will—and should. In fact, for most women, real progress is the journey, not the destination, in the experience of becoming a successful woman, regardless of your own definition of what constitutes success. It's an ongoing, complicated conversation."[32]

Ongoing, complicated conversation. We know a few women who are pretty good at that.

THIRTEEN

HAPPINESS, REROUTED

Just wait until now becomes then. You'll see how happy we were.
—Susan Sontag, "Unguided Tour," *The New Yorker*, October 1977

ON A HOT DAY IN JUNE, Penn economist Betsey Stevenson is the typically harried working mom. She's leaving work. Wrangling her baby into the carseat. Fighting traffic. Conducting, or trying to, a telephone interview.

Stevenson—lead author of the pivotal 2009 study on the paradox of women's declining happiness (covered in Chapter 10)—is talking to us about the media blowback, much of which implied that thirty years of women's expanded options was to blame for the study's findings. What she suggests—amid traffic, baby, and a bunch of dropped calls—is that maybe this happiness business is something that's actually more nuanced than, say, momentary bliss.

"It's possible there's something else that we're maximizing," she says. "We're sacrificing happiness in pursuit of something else, like, you know, fulfillment, or the sense of purpose. . . . We know we're sacrificing our happiness, but we think these other things are better."

She offers herself as example. "I have an infant and I don't go to yoga anymore, and it makes me less happy that I don't go to yoga. But I'm doing exactly what I want to be doing. If there were more hours in the day, I would go to yoga, and I would probably be *happier*. But that doesn't mean I think I'm making a mistake. I'm keeping my career at the level where I want it and spending all my free time with my kid."

For instance, she says, she's always puzzled by research that consistently points out that folks with kids rate themselves as less happy. And yet people keep having them. "That could be because we're all making big mistakes, and we shouldn't be having kids, or we should be spending less time with them," she says. "Or it could be that we're maximizing something else besides happiness . . . which leads me and others to wonder whether all people are doing is the best they can to maximize happiness. Or whether they're trying to maximize something else."

That *something else*. Happiness redefined? We vote yes. And so do other thinkers who have made the study of happiness their life's work. We'll get to them in a bit, but let's take one quick look at her parenthood example. (In 2010, journalist Jennifer Senior wrote a controversial cover story for *New York Magazine* entitled "All Joy and No Fun: Why Parents Hate Parenting." In the piece, she relays this exchange between Harvard psychologist Daniel Gilbert, who has written about parents' compromised well-being, and one of his colleagues: "Or, as a fellow psychologist told Gilbert when he finally got around to having a child: 'They're a huge source of joy, but they turn every other source of joy to shit.'"[1]) If you have kids, you get it. It's likely you're pissed off when they're naughty. Exhausted when they're teething. And bored stiff when you're stuck playing Chutes and Ladders.

You could substitute similar examples from your job, even if you happen to love it. But you get the picture: Negative emotions, one and all. At least in the short term. But does that necessarily mean you're not *happy*?

It's often about the *more*. The more our opportunities grow, the more our lives expand, and the more we juggle. More demands on our time. More responsibilities. More relationships. We reach, stretch, put ourselves out there in ways that mean others will judge us. We truly believe (but tell ourselves we don't) that we can have it all. And, you know, *do* it all perfectly. It doesn't take a rocket scientist—or a social scientist—to note that we feel pulled, stretched, and stressed. But truly unhappy?

No doubt, a life without options might be an easier one, but not necessarily worth the trade. After all, a life of PB&J for lunch every day is a reliable snooze. No sushi? No ceviche? No thank you. If we're truly in a funk because life has dealt us more options, maybe it's not the choices that have made us unhappy, but rather the fact that we haven't mastered the art of dealing with them. As Salon's Rebecca Traister writes in a piece aptly entitled "Screw Happiness," new opportunities bring women a range of both joys and anxieties. And yet, she writes, "It is this daily, varied reality that makes me wish we could stop using happiness, or perfection, as the yardstick by which we evaluate our lives, and that we could stop gravely shaking our heads at every instance that a woman fails to measure up."[2]

Lori Gottlieb tells us we'd be better off asking ourselves if we're *content*. The women who, by contrast, chase after constant happiness, she says, are "happy for a little while—but then there's something else that's going to make them start to feel empty. You know, I was perfectly happy but I wasn't happy *enough,* and I think that that's a really dangerous place to be in all aspects of life."

The problem with the short-term flavor of happy is not only that it's haywire, but also that when we buy into it, we find ourselves stuck. Choices become too important and weighty (our happiness depends on making the right one, right?), so we have trouble making them at all. And then, if we don't see ourselves as happy in the conventional sense, well, it's our fault, because somewhere along the line, we didn't choose right. *Get that better job. That cuter boyfriend. Have another kid. Wait, don't have any. And by all means get the bigger house. Bliss to follow.* Or so we think.

But as Harvard psychologist Daniel Gilbert tells us in *Stumbling on Happiness,* we have an uncanny ability to blow it when it comes to predicting what will make us happy. "With a little detective work, a pencil, and a good eraser, we can usually estimate—at least roughly—the probability that a choice will give us what we desire," he writes. "The problem is that we cannot easily estimate how we'll feel when we get it."[3]

Over the past year or so, we've read a lot of research, talked to a lot of women who zigged instead of zagged—and are pretty darned happy because of it—and reflected on what we mean by happiness. What we've figured out is that most of us have gotten it wrong, especially when it comes to media messages that define happiness as either perfection (everything in the universe is in its place) or brain-dead (as in, when life happens, you slap on a smile and tell yourself everything is peachy).

What gets us into trouble is a culture that is both acquisitional and aspirational, leaving us in a constant drool for the Next. Big. Thing. But once we get it, guess what? We're happy for five minutes, and then we're off on the chase. We're back to square one, lusting again over that greener grass. And here's an irony: Once we've jumped the fence, we sometimes wonder if what we had in the first place might have been what we really wanted after all.

Consumer culture doesn't help. We're constantly fed the message that we will be happy, sexy, thin, loved—pick one—if we buy the new and improved face cream, wheat bread, plastic wrap. Do we ever see the message that we have *enough*? Sure, we're smart enough to know that ads in glossy magazines do not promise happiness, but the subtext spills over: This *thing* will make you happy. Get the externals in order. Happiness to follow.

Ramani Durvasula calls it Pottery Barn psychosis. "Look at television, magazines, programming," she told us. "The opiate now is that Pottery Barn says, 'Look, you *can* have it all—your home office, your kids' organized rooms, everything into a basket—and isn't it grand?' There is a socialization from an early age that you are going to push for more, you're going to get more. We're socialized to an aspirational mindset, but what we're not socialized to do is consume that aspiration once we get it."

Siama is a wise life coach from Salida, Colorado. We'll hear more about her own story in the next chapter, but she would say that true happiness is completely internal, something that might take a lifetime to achieve. It shouldn't depend on what's outside of you—your job, your family, your *things*—because those change. "The point," she says, "is that when we reach into the silence of the heart, what happens is a certain kind of innate birthright, which is a choiceless, effortless, pure awareness of the joy and happiness: *life.*" She's been working on this for years and says she's learned to let go of whatever it is that comes between her and that inner sense. And she's, well, happy.

RESEARCH SHOWS THAT authentic happiness is about 10 percent dependent upon changed circumstances, like where you live, where you work, what you drive. (Which helps explain why lottery winners and accident victims report the same level of happiness a year or so after the event.) The rest breaks down like this: 50 percent genes and the remaining 40 percent, life itself and how you deal with it[4]—or what a cancer survivor we'll call Joanne says is a "process." She would never call her breast cancer "a gift," nor would she ever wear a pink-ribbon T-shirt, but what she has to say about happiness is this: "I definitely had a big wakeup call when I was sick. Before then I probably wouldn't have defined myself as happy, but after I got over the initial cancer shock, I did consider myself both happy and lucky. I think I just expected too much before then and felt I had the *right* to stuff. After having been sick, I am better able to be constructive. Somehow I figured out that happiness is something you can work on, and definitely [can] have, if you choose to." Her cancer spurred her to pursue a passion—photography—outside her day job, and what she discovered is that she's incredibly good at it.

In fact, a lot of what happiness is about has to do with finding purpose, passion, and meaning in our lives. (And finding ourselves, too, which is something we'll dive into in the next chapter.) As Po Bronson tells us in *What Should I Do with My Life?*, figuring it all out is our life's story, and there are several paths to that same destination, so long as we let the trip play out.[5] Often it's a second act.

Julie Metz, author of the best-selling *Perfection*, entered Act Two in 2003 when her husband of fifteen years died suddenly. She thought she had had the perfect life—beautiful house, adorable daughter, dozens of friends, solid career as a graphic designer—but found out that her husband had been leading a secret life that included affairs with at least five other women (one a good friend) and hefty credit card debts. To fight her way back—and to discover what had been real about her life—she wrote a memoir.[6] Along the way, she not only found herself, but also the meaning of happiness.

"Widowhood and its aftermath was a big lesson in imperma-nence," she told us. "These experiences helped me understand the truth that life is a series of present moments. My daughter, now a wise four-teen-year old, continues to remind me not to crumple in the face of change. I think that the writing process itself helped restore my sense of confidence in the world. And of course finding love and building a new relationship was part of my renewal. For me, this is an ongoing process, and I am always trying to grow in new ways. One idea of perfection gave way to something new."

Barrie Lynn's first act was a career in the top rungs of advertising in New York and Los Angeles. Then came cheese. True story. She had taken a client to a Slow Food fundraiser—a cheese-tasting event—and says she was hit by Cupid's arrow. "I literally fell in love with the amazing flavors and the whole concept of artisanal cheese—the family farmers and cheesemakers who take such pride in what they do," she told us. She quit her job, put her marketing skills to work, and reinvented herself as The Cheese Impressario, a media-savvy ambassador for small cheese-makers throughout the country. Her breakthrough came in 2006, when gift certificates for her "Artisanal Cheese & Wine Pairing Adventure" classes were included in the Academy Award goodie bags.

"Life is short," she says. "We have choices we can make that are broad strokes. I decided some years ago I wanted to use my skills to help more progressive businesses grow. I knew how to build brands, and us-ing these skills, all it took was my mission. And then I fell in love with cheese. Now I work longer and harder than I ever have and am happier than I've ever been."

And often, happiness is more about who you are, not what you do. Take Jill—the highly successful attorney we met back in Chapter 9—who says, "People today tend to see themselves as defined by their profession. I am a lawyer, and I consider myself a pretty decent one. But when I leave the office, I am a person with outside interests, friends, and family. My 'lawyer' hat comes off. I am not defined by my career choice, and I do not expect (or want) my work to be the most gratifying or interesting part of my life. I would rather be gratified by the personal relationships in my life, the nonwork experiences I have (some of which I can only afford because of my day job), and the values I hold dear.

"Fifty years ago, most of our parents or grandparents were doing manual labor, blue-collar work, or some other noncreative, noninteresting work. They, unlike us, did not believe that they were entitled to some sort of career nirvana. Having a job you love and that fulfills you is a luxury; you are very lucky (and in the minority) if that is your reality. But for most people, it's not. I'm not saying that we should stay in positions where we're miserable. But maybe set realistic expectations about how good your career can make you feel about yourself, and limits on how bad your job can make you feel about yourself. Focus on loving your nonwork life and finding your happiness outside of work." Jill, by the way, just made partner in her high-powered law firm.

The smart people say happiness is related to being part of a community, making good on our own values, and handling setbacks with a certain state of grace. In short, getting over ourselves and looking beyond our personal wants for satisfaction. What doesn't enter into the equation is instant gratification. And this chase for perfection? Having it all? Recipe for disaster.

What we should be shooting for is what Barry Schwartz might call the "good enough" life. Riffing on a surprising 2010 study that found that people get happier as they age,[7] he suggested to us that what's happening might have to do with the freedom that comes when we're able to let go of the notion that, because there are so many options out there, there *must* be one that's capital-P Perfect. And that it's our job to find it. That's what folks learn from experience, he says, and that's the secret: Let go of the search for the best, and you realize that good enough really is good enough.

GOOGLE "HAPPINESS," AND you're likely to get somewhere around 84 million hits. (Google "Jesus Christ," and you only get 32 million.) Search on Amazon, and you get some 36,000 results—over half of them books, and over a thousand of them published in the first half of 2010 alone. All of which points to an interest in, if not a hunger for, what our founding fathers considered one of our inalienable rights.

At the top of that Amazon list you find *The Happiness Project,* Gretchen Rubin's *New York Times* bestseller on how she spent a year trying to be more appreciative of her own life.[8] A former lawyer who clerked for Supreme Court Justice Sandra Day O'Connor after graduating from Yale Law School, she says she got the idea for her book while taking her daughter to school on a New York City bus. The bus wasn't something she particularly enjoyed, but one day, when her daughter pointed joyfully at a dog outside on the street, she says, it suddenly hit her: This bus ride, this moment, was *life*. And she didn't want to waste it. So over the course of a year, she taught herself to embrace it, to live in the moment, by teaching herself to be, well, happier. "Happiness," she tells us, "goes small and it goes big, and it looks different in different places. And a lot of the things that make you happy generally don't make you happy day-to-day."

Why does she think her book raced to the top of the bestseller list? "Part of it was that I was pretty happy when I started, and I think a lot of people identified with that. I wasn't in a place of deep despair, hadn't had a huge disaster in my life, and one of my goals for my happiness project was to appreciate my life more. I felt like I didn't appreciate that I *did* have the elements of happiness, and I wanted to live up to that better."

What she discovered is that happiness is somewhat malleable. Her prescription? It's a Zen-like sentiment, both simple and profound: "One of my truths is you're happy if you think you're happy, and you're not happy if you don't think you're happy. This gets into the idea of gratitude, and that's something that's so emphasized within happiness research—that you have to discipline yourself to be grateful, and to think about all the reasons you do have to be happy. It's very easy to be distracted by the petty annoyances and the passing grievances and let them pull you down and lose track of how you *do* have the basic elements of happiness."

Are we happier than we think we are? "I think maybe that's true," she says. "I wouldn't have put it that way, but I think there's something to that. It's interesting, this idea that 'I'll be happy when . . .'—when something else happens. 'When I lose forty pounds.' 'When I get a promotion.' Or, 'If I could only take that big trip or make that move. . . .' It's something called the 'arrival fallacy'—the idea that you will be happy once you arrive someplace. Because usually those arrivals do not bring the jump in happiness that people anticipate."

Scholars like Dan Ariely—author of *The Upside of Irrationality* and a professor of behavioral economics at Duke University—would call this the "hedonic treadmill," a theory that humans rapidly adapt to a new situation, whether good or bad.[9] It also suggests that one-shot bursts—buying a new sofa or a new car—are not nearly as conducive to increased well-being as, say, spending that money on a vacation—the memory of which can stay with you, change you, and up your happiness ante. The term was first coined in the early 1970s,[10] and the question of whether or not we can actually increase our sense of well-being has been plaguing us ever since: If we rapidly adapt to new cars, new jobs, even winning the lottery, can we ever make ourselves happier?

In a 2008 study, Ariely and others found that we can, but not necessarily the way we think. The study, which looked at activities like going to church or doing yoga, suggested that improvement in well-being doesn't come from single-shot events: "The key for long-lasting changes to well-being is to engage in activities that provide small and frequent boosts, which in the long run will lead to improved well-being, one small step at a time."[11]

That echoes what we found when we took our crash course on "happiness theory." Before we tell you what we learned, though, we have to point out that the attempt to scientifically define the elusive nature of happiness reminds us of that quote once attributed to the late jazz great Thelonious Monk: "Writing about music is like dancing about architecture." True, that. Nonetheless, here's the cheat sheet.

The Dalai Lama teaches that happiness has to do with embracing life and developing kindness and compassion; that it shouldn't be linked with life's ups and downs.[12] University of Pennsylvania psychologist Martin Seligman—who founded the field of "positive psychology" in 2000 and directs Penn's Positive Psychology Center—says that happiness can be broken down into three core components: positive emotion, engagement, and purpose. What sets his metric apart from what you might have heard from your grandma is the fact that it's all stuff that has been proven empirically. For example: Activities that make you happy in short bursts—shopping for stilettos, drinking the great malbecs—have quickly diminishing returns. On the other hand, losing yourself in an activity you love provides lasting gratification and increased well-being. And living a meaningful life—using your strengths and talents in the service of something larger than yourself—leads to authentic happiness.[13]

UC Berkeley psychologist Dacher Keltner is codirector of the Greater Good Science Center, and he agrees. In *Born to Be Good,* he suggests that we're wired for goodness.[14] He relies on research to show that, when it comes to the pursuit of happiness, we should look toward compassion and gratitude. UC Riverside Psychologist Sonja Lyubomirsky—whose happiness research was funded by a million-dollar grant from the National Institutes of Health—also agrees. She's the one who broke down the components of happiness into those percentages that were given earlier in this chapter. In her book *The How of Happiness,* she suggests we take that 40 percent chunk of happiness that depends on our own behavior, and that we use it wisely—the best use is to help someone else.[15] And psychologist Tal-Ben Shahar—who in 2006 drew a record 866 students to his Harvard class on positive psychology—says happiness lies at the intersection of pleasure and meaning. In his book *The Pursuit of Perfect,* he adds a new wrinkle, drawing a distinction between "perfectionists" and "optimalists," folks who not only make the best of what life dishes out, but who also are willing to accept the screwups.[16] First tip: Give yourself permission to be human.

Even the *New York Times* got in on this happiness action, running a Sunday trend piece in 2010 on the ways in which money *can* buy you "happy"—when you spend it on experiences (especially those that strengthen social bonds) rather than things.[17]

There's more, lots, but you get the picture. Rubin said that, starting with Aristotle, she discovered seventeen different definitions for happiness. And that each time she tried to define it for herself, it slipped through her fingers. She also discovered something else: "Even the idea of happiness can be intimidating, because the word "happiness" suggests a magical destination," she told us. "Where, if you could just get there, your life would be a perfect ten. Can you get there, how do you get there, what would it look like, and how do you stay there—is sort of intimidating and probably not even realistic. So I think that it's easier to think 'How can I be happier, today, tomorrow, or next month?' And if you think about 'What would make me happier,' then this issue of happiness versus pleasure falls into place. Because you can say to yourself, 'Sure it's fun to skip going to the gym, but over the course of my life, what's going to make me happier?'

"And then it's a good way to think about your choices. Somebody once was describing this job to me in these horrible terms. And I was like, why are you even applying for that job? You don't want to get that job. And it was like she had completely lost track of the fact that it mattered whether she wanted it or not. She just got locked into the idea of 'could she get it.' So if you think, 'Is this going to make me *happier?*' I think it sort of helps you see *you* more clearly."

RUBIN ONCE ASKED her former boss, Sandra Day O'Connor, what it took to have a happy life. The answer? Work worth doing. That's similar to advice that college graduates had for the class of 2009, according to a poll by the Adecco Group, an international human resources outfit. Almost three-quarters of the graduates advised the kids to choose passion, not paycheck, when figuring out what to do with their lives.[18] The late mythologist Joseph Campbell calls this "following your bliss," and others call it "listening to your heart." Sometimes it's risky business, and full of what can be serious cons: longer hours, less money. But yet are we too quick to dismiss the rewards, especially when we calculate the happiness quotient?

Take the case of a talented artist we'll call Brittany. At twenty-six, she's just quit her job of four years at a big-name investment bank to study graphic design, and she is jumping-out-of-her-skin excited. The job, she says, was never what she wanted to do. She had majored in painting, after all, and had been a fellow at a prestigious summer art program in upstate New York during her last year of college. And yet. After graduation, she felt she had to get a desk job in order to live on her own.

She was initially offered a job doing windows for Ralph Lauren for $25,000 a year, which meant she'd have to move back home. "So I ended up just going to a headhunter and being like, 'I need to make XYZ amount of money. Put me somewhere where I can do that.' So they put me in an investment bank, which was fine at the time. I was like, 'I'll do it for a year.' And then a year turned into four."

She says she felt she had to do the conventional thing first. "When you think of jobs, you think of 'doctor' or 'lawyer' or 'nurse'—you know, person in a suit. You don't think of 'artist' as a job, or 'writer' as a job. Those aren't the little picture books you see growing up. I think I kind of felt like, you know, Dad had a desk job, and it's what we're supposed to be doing."

But over the course of her four years in desk-job limbo, she thought constantly of something else. Maybe she should be a nurse. So she volunteered in a hospital pediatric ward—and ended up painting with the kids. Art was whispering in other ways, too: She sewed. She reupholstered. She painted. She made jewelry. She'd literally find stuff on the street, refinish it, and sell it on Craigslist. She got herself an Etsy store. "I kept thinking, I need to get this going as part of my real life. Like, it would be really nice if I didn't hate going to work every morn-ing. . . . Every other idea of a job came back to art, so I was like, I need to suck it up and do it, because this is what I love."

As of today, she's saved twenty months' worth rent, put together a studio in her apartment, and signed up for all the design classes she didn't take in college, just going with the flow. "I'm gonna kind of feel it out, which terrifies my father, but I think whatever I end up doing—I might even end up behind a desk again—I will be in a more creative area, and I feel like I'll have more room for growth than with [the investment company]. It's exciting to see myself that way."

Daniel Pink would approve. He tackled the idea of giving free rein to our right-brain selves—curiosity, empathy, inventiveness—in his bestseller *A Whole New Mind: Why Right Brainers Will Rule the Future*.[19] Pink makes the case that in our global, techno, increasingly outsourced economy, those who can embrace their inner artist will ultimately flourish. He drove his point home to new college grads in a 2005 *New York Times* op-ed suggesting that newbies ought to follow their hearts. "The abilities that matter more are turning out to be the abilities that are also fundamental sources of human gratification," he wrote. "To be sure, this new labor market is not a land in which every person will be able to pursue a passion and instantly arrive at a fat paycheck. Still, we may finally be at the point where we can tell freshly minted graduates: 'Look, it's a rough world out there. There's only one way to survive. Do what you love.'"[20]

Matthew Crawford offers somewhat similar advice in *Shop Class as Soulcraft*, his reflection on trading life in a think tank (he has his PhD in philosophy) for work with his hands in a motorcycle repair shop. His point: There is great value in "work that is meaningful because it is genuinely useful."[21]

That idea—that our education and social expectations should gear us up for more than work in a cube—has resonance, especially among women who long for work that *matters*. Chloe digs it. "I really think our generation is in the process of redefining this educational monoculture that Crawford talks about, which largely prepares us for the white-collar world of nebulous paper-pushing, ladder-climbing, and ultimately indefinable, dissatisfying work at a desk. It seems that younger generations are trying to get back to a 'work with your hands' culture," she says. "We need to embrace that contrarian notion that 'successful' work doesn't only exist behind a desk, but can also be found at a bakery, in a garden, at a boutique. . . . It's no wonder young vital cities like Portland and Austin are full of interesting, creative businesses. Younger generations have flocked there to pursue a different kind of American Dream—where life is a little more well rounded. You can own a small business that speaks to your interests—whether that be vinyl records or old letterpresses."

Or the dance studio. Tami was the first in her Latino family to go to college. An overachiever nominated for class valedictorian, she was ever the role model in her large, extended family, who fed her with 'Do well! Succeed! Study business! Go to law school! Make us proud!' The expectations—and the choices—were overwhelming. So much so that she compares the angst she felt to the latter-day version of Betty Freidan's "problem that has no name." "I didn't feel I had room to fail," she says.

She began her senior year in college with a corporate offer she couldn't refuse—though in her gut, she knew it wasn't right. Salvation arrived when the company declared bankruptcy. Freed from the responsibility of scoring the big paycheck, she decided to follow her heart, which led her to dance. "It caught me by surprise," she says, "how much I love it." She decided to move home after graduation, take a temp job to pay her bills—and take more dance classes. Her ultimate goal: start a nonprofit geared toward using dance as a catalyst for change for at-risk kids. A year later, her dream is taking off. She's in a professional dance company, she's a licensed Zumba instructor, and she's doing some choreography—all of which is starting to pay off. She says that even though money is tight, she's never been happier. "There's a difference between a job and a calling," she told us. "A calling is passionate. It fuels part of your identity. A job can't do that for you." When last we heard, she had just choreographed a Salsa FlashMob at the 2010 San Jose Jazz Fest in 2010—and had scored a full-time temp job to pay the bills.

The lesson? Listen to your heart, and trust it will not lead you astray—though it might send you on a circuitous route. Author Elizabeth Crawford has followed her passion ever since she began ballet at age four. She majored in dance and started her own dance company, only to give it up when she had a career-ending injury at twenty-seven. The logical step? Teaching Pilates, which she did for twelve years. She was good at it, but it left her lukewarm. So she went on a DIY discovery mission—via the self-help shelves and various seminars—and found herself drawn to a number of things she couldn't fit together: cooking, traveling, studying Italian. She also found she was drawn to the idea of making books. So she wrote one on Pilates. She took off for Italy. She tried travel writing but found it too difficult to pay the bills. But in the course of all this hit and miss, she realized that the real siren call was food, and it had been there all along. When she was in college, she read cookbooks for fun. At twenty-four, she entered the Pillsbury Bake-Off—and won $2,000. She also realized she loved photography—always had—and was good at it. The pieces of the puzzle came together in 2010 when her first cookbook, *Flavors of Friuli: A Culinary Journey through Northeastern Italy,* was published.

She says it was hard work—especially with a new baby—but she kept hearing the word "bliss." Now, she says, "'Follow your bliss' has become my motto. It's about discovering what things make you light up inside and make your eyes sparkle, the things that make time pass so quickly because you are so engrossed in the work. The hard part is finding a way to transform these passions into a source of income, but I'd like to believe there is always a way to do this."

Elizabeth's story brings to mind that 2009 movie *Julie and Julia.* Here's the trailer: In 2002, then twenty-nine-year-old office drone/

aspiring writer Julie Powell decided to cook her way through the 524 recipes in Julia Child's *Mastering the Art of French Cooking* in one year, and to blog about it. The blog turned into a book (and the book begot the movie), which charts the parallel lives of Powell and Child, who were both looking for something to do with their lives, and who stumbled upon their calling. What's most inspiring about both Child and Powell is, ironically, that their willingness to go forth *without* a recipe led them both to their bliss.

Which brings us to this: We all want to do something meaningful with our lives. But maybe the smarter recipe for this kind of fulfillment is to just set off toward something and see where it takes us.

Which brings us back to Sandra Day O'Connor and work worth doing. What's interesting is that "work worth doing" can mean anything—so long as it has purpose, that intangible *something* that gets us out of bed, that takes us outside ourselves. And the real truth is that purpose is where you find it.

Years ago, a family friend, Jock McCoy—a contractor by trade and a cook by avocation—rallied a crew of grownups to spend long nights building a sixty-square-foot gingerbread house, replete with lights, moving parts, a chocolate-coated amusement park, hundreds of individually sculpted candy people, and dozens of gumdrop trees. The biggest draw was that there was no real reason for the project, other than to rekindle the Christmas spirit—and to provide a centerpiece for a fundraiser later that month. But the magic was the soulcraft: the nightly stream of lawyers, doctors, engineers, chefs, writers —folks with "better things to do"—who rushed in after work, chucked their pumps and briefcases into the corner, and ditched their iconic selves to immerse themselves in something literally bigger than they were. As one member of the crew, a lawyer with a loosened tie, said at the time: "The best thing about the project is that it makes you feel that everything else you are doing is less important than this."

WHICH LEADS TO one last story. This one concerns Jenny, the twenty-nine-year old attorney we met back in Chapter 2 who considered ditching her job in favor of arranging flowers. Instead, she took a leap of faith and a leave of absence when Obama's presidential campaign was ramping up in the fall of 2008. She packed up and moved to a town in western Pennsylvania to work in a field office, recruiting and managing two teams of neighborhood volunteers. She worked seventeen-hour days, seven days a week, and lived in a strange family's spare bedroom. Back home, after the election, a friend asked her what she'd done all day. She listed her tasks: cold-calling volunteers, knocking on strangers' doors, entering data late into the night, daily conference calls. "Did you like knocking on doors?" the friend asked. "Well, no," Jenny answered. "What about calling volunteers?" the friend continued. "God, no! That was worse!" she howled. But over all? "I loved every minute of it," she said. And from the gleam in her eye, you knew it was true.

Later still, she reflected on what she'd learned. "The hard part is making the passion work as a career *or* accepting the fact that you may have passions you [will] follow, but your work may not be one of them. The hard part for me, when I came back, was to realize that for most people, that much passion is not a day-to-day reality, and that I should be grateful I was lucky enough to live it for two months. I also took away, after months of reflection, that the realities of doing something you are passionate about day in, day out for years on end feels very different from doing it for a short period. I never could have sustained what I was doing, and I'm glad it ended before the passion went away."

But what she also found was this: That sense of passion and purpose stayed with her. Changed her. Became part of that elusive *something else.*

Happiness, redefined.

FOURTEEN

WHEREVER YOU GO, THERE YOU ARE

The thing that is really hard, and really amazing, is giving up on being perfect and beginning the work of becoming yourself.
—Anna Quindlen

THERE'S A MOVEMENT AFOOT among the well-heeled, and those feet doing the moving? They're more likely to be bare than stiletto-clad. A 2009 *New York Times* article (which, not incidentally, appeared in the Style section) chronicled women in their late twenties to late thirties who've ditched the fabulous life in the fast lane in favor of something else.[1]

There's former PR scenester Gabrielle Bernstein, now leading classes as a "spiritual life coach." There's former actress Kris Carr, who—one month after appearing in two Super Bowl beer commercials—learned she had cancer and took the opportunity to get deep, chronicling her experience in the documentary *Crazy Sexy Cancer.* There's Elizabeth Gilbert and her phenomenon-spawning memoir, *Eat Pray Love.* There are many others like them, and there are the millions of us who gobble their offerings by the *om*-ful.

Women are hungry, seeking, desperate for guidance. We're in a state of transition. Wandering uncharted territory. And while the transition is collective, each of us feels it acutely, individually. With all the choices, all the paths before us, it's near impossible not to wonder "Am I going the right way? Am I making the right decisions to get me there?"

If it's a guide we're seeking, we'd do well to consider one bit of advice that came up in the interviews we did for this book, over and over and over again: Know yourself. It's the most ancient piece of advice, yet it remains the best compass around. Without it, you may find you're living your life on a path you're not even awake to, weak to the siren song of the road not traveled, easily seduced by your neighbor's grass. Or stuck, never really committing to any path, just idling. Undecided.

Know yourself. It's easier said than done, despite the fact that knowing oneself sounds easy enough—given that, you know, one *is* oneself. But with all the noise and expectations and judgments and messages about who we ought to be, it's difficult to find the space—not to mention the silence—to discover who we are outside all that.

And it can be slow going. Jane—who we last heard from in Chapter 10, when she was trying to decide whether to leave one awesome job for another awesome job (which, by the way, she did)—is still struggling with it all. Professionally, she's cranking. But personally, she's cracking. We talked late one July evening while she was on her way home from work. Bravely (and loudly) baring her soul over the noise on the bus, she said her new job—as a rapidly ascending manager at a green energy company in Seattle—gives her everything she ever thought she wanted: "my own office, to make big decisions, have lots of responsibility, have a hard job that I do really well and make the world a better place and work with young people who are interesting." But she's not happy.

"Maybe I'm someone that's just miserable and I'll never be

happy—it's like, isn't that what you thought was gonna make you happy? And that sucks, because you're sure it's gonna make you happy, and then you get it and you hate it. . . . It makes you feel like you're not doing it right, because you do everything you can, you passed every test, you pulled every string, you have taken every leap . . . yet what you think you wanted, if you aren't as happy as you [thought you would] be when you got there, it's disappointing."

It's an easy trap to fall into: seeking the answers externally, boarding that "hedonic treadmill" we heard about in the last chapter. Yeah, life is pretty awesome, but when I get married/promoted/laid/in shape/pregnant/a raise, *then* I'll be happy. But the trouble with a treadmill is, run as you might, you never really get anywhere.

Don't get us wrong. Without dreams and ambitions, what would be the point of life as a human being with a complex brain and opposable thumbs? It's part of the human condition to want.

But does fixating on external things allow us to ignore the harder issues? And is that why happiness, contentment, can be so elusive? Contentment, after all, is a rather deep feeling—likely too deep to be affected by externals. But compared to the internal stuff, the externals are easier to change. (They're certainly easier to see: The externals are right there, in your face. While the internals, well, they're somewhere *behind* your face.)

It's a big, brave shift. And often it only comes after a certain amount of chasing—and catching—the external stuff, only to discover that "stuff" isn't the answer at all. Jane says, "I think it was external for a while, and I did a lot of things to figure out what I wanted to be—switched jobs once, twice, three times; moved cities." All of which, she says, helped her learn more about herself. "Like I love Seattle. I don't want a job that's just medium, that doesn't challenge me . . . Okay, now do I take this job? Okay, I took it. So [I'm] putting myself in the place where all the external things were pretty much in order and it's like, Oh, so I got everything I asked for, so I either throw up my hands and realize I'm never happy, or I think 'Everything's wrong,' and I need to reevaluate my entire situation, or just say, 'I need to figure out what's going on for me, just *inside*.'"

Just like that, she's onto something.

When we're facing worldly dilemmas, it can seem beside the point to turn inward. But Elizabeth Lesser says that in fact, it's the opposite. Because whatever's going on deep inside, we'll likely find it replicated on the surface.[2]

"[For] women who are feeling just 'off' at work ('I can't get ahead.' 'People don't take me seriously.' 'When I speak, my voice gets lost.' 'I don't know how to follow these rules.' Or just a vague sense of dislocation at work), I would say it's probably showing up everywhere in your life," she told us, and suggested that women do the kind of work—even some therapy—to find their "own true voice."

"That's not an easy thing," she admits, "and some people say 'Oh that's so self-involved, that's psychobabble.' But unless you do that work, it's not gonna happen. And I can't say strongly enough that the first work at hand has nothing to do with workplace, it has to do with you. Your authentic self is lying in wait for you, but you gotta do some work to dig past the old tape loops you have going about who you think you are."

It's work that we, like Jane, often flirt with—only to retreat from, intimidated by its . . . monstrosity. External circumstances just seem more real. So we move, we quit, we cut our bangs, we go on diets. But this dance is a little melancholy, if only for its familiarity. We know how it ends. We catch whatever we're chasing—the proverbial carrot on the proverbial stick—only to find (as we suspected deep inside) that we weren't hungry for carrots after all. It's just so much easier to focus on the carrots, rather than working to discover what's in need of nourishment.

"Either I fucked up," says Jane (who, according to all conventional measures, did the precise opposite of fucking up), "or everything I completely thought to be a hundred percent true and busted my ass for is not actually true." (She lives in Seattle; it's okay that she's using this language at high decibels on a bus.) "In which case . . ." she pauses, "I don't want to believe that. Because then what do I do? I can't reset. I mean, I *can* reset, but, like, there's nothing scarier than *that* idea, right?"

Of course, she's right. And that fear—that were we to confront what's nagging us from within, we would have to engage in a full life-reset—well, it's enough to keep many of us chasing carrots for the rest of our lives.

AS LAUREN (WHOM you first met in Chapter 1) told us, "Change is scary to most people, and what's scarier is knowing you need change but not having a clue what to do or how to go about getting it. . . . Generally speaking, we wait for change to come to us instead. And holding onto the old patterns—whether they are friendships that are no longer working or career goals that haven't been met or revisited in years—these things are weight in our backpacks as we begin our journeys. Do we have to cut them loose to figure out who we are? Absolutely, at some point. But that point is different for everyone. Many of us probably slog on for miles with that extra weight because we don't even know it's holding us back. I think if we had the instinct to get rid of all the old stuff in our lives before moving on, we wouldn't need the journey in the first place."

But, heavy though they may be, those backpacks are full of precious cargo! They carry the load of the expectations, goals, and identities around which we've built our lives. Who wouldn't be terrified at the thought of cutting them loose?

But the things we fear most are often the things we most need to do.

And looking that fear in the face can be the first step toward breaking through and getting a clear glimpse of the person deep within. Growing up, making choices, getting on with our journeys, requires "having to look at the fear, and [realizing] that when we think we're stuck some place, the fear holds us there, and then we can't feel anything," says Siama, the life coach we met in the last chapter.

Holds us there and keeps us spinning. Looking for answers in all the wrong places. Gobbling carrots like a rabbit with the munchies. With a really, really heavy backpack.

Lauren recently made some huge changes (involving a move across the country and a new professional direction, which we'll get to soon), but not before staring down the spookiest of boogeymen. She characterizes the past several years of her life—marked by much professional success, or, less generously, "obsessive careerism"—as a time of "running, hiding, trying to outsmart my own psyche . . . afraid of what I might find."

Ultimately, what she did find wasn't so scary, but what she had to do to find it is pretty terrifying to any woman weaned on the idea that she can have it all: accepting that she can't.

In writing, we call this "killing your darlings." (Yes, it's dark. Haven't you heard? Writers are morbid.) The idea being that sometimes we come up with a clever turn of phrase, an anecdote, or some other word-heavy sentiment that's quite pleasing to our writerly soul. So pleasing that, when we're going over our too-long, mildly rambling story, looking for words to cut, we don't even think about axing *them*. But often, they're unnecessary, distracting, a waste of space. It can be heartbreaking, but the truth is, a story is usually much better after passing through the hands of a ruthless editor.

And maybe, when it comes to the many paths we face, we'd do well to wield the proverbial red pen. And even to take it to some of our darlings.

Maybe we've always wanted to move to Buenos Aires, write a novel, open a bakery. They're lovely dreams, so we refuse to let them go. It hurts to cross them off the bucket list—and in a way, such an idea amounts to blasphemy to anyone weaned on the idea that she can be anything she wants, that she can have it all. But, as with a well-edited story, might our lives be stronger if we could let them go?

Lauren would say so. In our first conversation, she described herself as "swimming in a sea of options"—restless, unable to resist indulging in fantasies about trying everything from cartography to conducting an orchestra. She had an anthology of short stories under her belt (the proceeds of which went to organizations working to rebuild the Gulf Coast after Hurricane Katrina) and a collection of half-written plays, stories, and novels atop her desk. But she recently came to a decision, and an enthused sense of peace. Her plan? A PhD in ecopsychology, part of a holistic psychology program she began in the fall of 2010.

"While I'll be able to see clients, in a therapist sense, I also want to integrate my interest in social work, helping people, helping our environment and world." Once she's done with the program, Lauren's plan is to donate a couple months each year to organizations such as Doctors Without Borders, offering psychological services to people who live in areas affected by natural disasters—thus satisfying her need for social work as well as for travel. Her writing will serve her practice—and there's little doubt her experiences will provide plenty of fodder for future written work. "It's a good way to start shaping my life in the direction I want to be going."

But this grand scheme didn't come without the pain of killing some of her most cherished darlings. "I've had to trim so much fat. . . .

I've literally had to let go of my ideas of publishing short stories, writing plays. . . . There simply were too many choices. I had to be honest with myself and cut about 75 percent of them . . . and lo and behold everything started falling into place. I feel more sane, because I admitted to myself that I'm a sucky freelance writer and I needed to . . . let that energy go. When I did, the floodgates opened in other areas; it was pretty amazing."

Lauren's story speaks to the power (not to mention the freedom) that comes with accepting that having it all—empowering as that message may once have been—is a myth. Period.

Elizabeth Lesser describes it as nothing less than a spiritual truth.

"You can't have everything in this life," Lesser says. "Every choice requires a sense of that sacrifice—so it was a mistake, that phase when we told women 'You can have everything.' You can't have everything. No one can have everything, so making a choice about what you want to do with your life first requires you to really accept and grasp that. . . . Everything is a trade-off; that's just a spiritual reality of life as a human being."

But that's a bitter pill to swallow. Just ask Jane. "Yeah, that's probably the most mature thing you could do. I don't even know how to sort of sift through all that, but I think it's like, we want too much. . . . [But] crossing things off your list," she says, can feel "like you suck at life for not making it happen."

As Siama said, just as fear can keep us stuck, stressing out over having the great unattainable—if promised—all can hold us back too. "Women today are so intent on trying to have everything. Have a great job . . . have a husband, have a family, have this, you know, have it all. And what happens is that there's a trying and a suffering rather than an allowing and a surrendering."

Easier said than done: Aspiration is the American way. But, she says, relaxing the grip of our expectations creates room for the good stuff to flow. "When we move on what we're passionate about, then that passion is expressed in our lives, [and] all that other stuff comes in its own timing, 'cause there's no anxiety behind it. No energy of frantic, 'Well, I better hurry up and do this now. I need to get my master's now so that blah blah blah, and if I have a baby now, then what's that going to mean for later?'"

As we saw, this idea played out in Lauren's life, when letting go of certain aspirations actually brought her to an expanse of promise. And, in turn, it made saying goodbye to certain dreams feel okay, if bittersweet. "When you grow, you lose something too," she says. "I still imagine my name in the *New Yorker,* but the reality is, it isn't going to happen on writing alone—not likely. But perhaps one day, my work in this field will reward my writing."

Buzzkill, yes. But also freeing, when you consider all the energy that's siphoned off into daydreams of the road not traveled and stress over trying to do, be, and have it all. Imagine you had all that energy to focus on the couple of things that matter *most*—the ones that get your juices flowing. Then where would you be?

SPEAKING OF FOCUS, Susan Butler (she who is not "a man in a skirt" and whom you met in Chapter 12) insists one of the best tools in your decision-making arsenal is a clearly articulated vision. "Write it down," she says. What do you want to do in this life? What do you have to offer this world? Really think about it. And, she says, "Be specific."

It worked for Erin, the radio-show producer turned bid consultant we met in Chapter 6. She was struggling with how to reconcile her creative self with her hungry self—you know, the one who requires food on the table. We caught up with her several months after that first conversation and found she'd become a serious proponent of the power of the pen. As in "writing it down." She was in her car again, this time driving home from her new job as a brand manager at a stone company. Yes, a stone company. But her CEO describes her job as the "sexy" one in the operation, and she kinda agrees. She'd been brought on to manage a cool, recycled-glass surface brand the company acquired, and so far, she's loving it. "I always knew that there was some reason why I had this completely whacked-out résumé!" She's discovered there's a lot of creativity to be found in the new gig. "I feel like, yes, you can find satisfaction in working for a real company," and, she says, it comes from finding a great fit. A great fit she was able to recognize because she'd consciously thought about what she wanted. And wrote it down.

"I made this . . . it's called a butterfly graph. . . . People do it when they're trying to figure out their career path or whatever, and I thought it would be fun to do before I went to Atlanta, so that when I got there, I knew these were the things I wanted out of a career and a job," she says. (She couldn't remember the name of the find-your-calling book from which she'd plucked the idea—only that she'd bought it while in the throes of crisis, found the exercise in the back—and promptly exchanged it for a novel. But back to the butterfly.) "I pasted the graph on my wall and would look at it like, 'When is this gonna happen? Is this just a pipe dream?' And the day I got the job, I sat down with the graph and highlighted everything the job would satisfy, and the whole thing was highlighted!"

Magic? Nah. "You still have to set goals for yourself, even if they seem really unrealistic. Then write them down, because if you at least make them concrete, you have a goal to look forward to, and you'll be surprised that you can achieve those goals. . . . But you have to write them down. You have to believe in them."

Whatever your feelings about vision boards and butterfly graphs, we think there might be something to this business about articulating your goals. Which is something Butler hinted at. When she retired, she says, someone asked her where she saw herself in the next couple of years, what did she want to say she'd accomplished. Butler says it took her awhile to come up with an answer, but once she did ("I want to have impacted billions of women and girls to be all they could be"), she found herself firmly on a path.

And therein lies the magic juju: At least part of the power of articulating what you want is the fact that doing so makes your decisions easier. And—not incidentally—makes saying 'no' easier too. "It identified things right away that I was spending my time on that [weren't] gonna get me to my vision," Butler says.

"No" is important, but Butler's vision helped her identify the yeses too. "It has guided me—and everything that I'm doing and have done—since I retired." That includes writing books for women in business. And being selected as a delegate for the upcoming Vision 2020 conference, which will take place in Philadelphia on August 26, 2020 (the 100th anniversary of women's right to vote) with the goal of achieving gender equality. Pretty darn in line with that vision of hers. Maybe it sounds silly. Or impossible. But even a general intention can serve as a compass. If you know where you want to go, the detours start to lose their appeal.

Or, as Butler says, "If you don't know where you're going, any road's gonna take you there." But "once you think about it . . . once you, as I say, throw it out to the universe, it happens. I mean, you just gotta let it happen. But it's like the people with their iPhones and iPods in their ears a hundred percent of the time—how can they hear what's going on in their heads?"

AH, YES, THE noise. Another thing everyone seems to agree on is that one of the best ways to get to know ourselves is to disconnect. Get quiet. Look inward.

"Look at 'who am I' beyond the roles that were assigned me by my family and my culture," Lesser suggests. "There's the voice of your essential core self. It's a very quiet voice. And if you've never tried to get in touch with it, it's hiding behind much louder voices: who you were told you were in your family system, and who you've been told you are—subtly, and not so subtly—in our culture. It's excavating work, excavating your core sense of strength and original self from the voices that have been dominating your sense of self your whole life."

Siama spent several years doing just that. After her marriage came to an end and her youngest child moved out, she went on an *Eat Pray Love*–variety quest to discover who she was outside of those roles. (Of course, she did this in 1990—many moons before such an adventure was but a twinkle in Ms. Gilbert's eye.) She spent three years trucking around North America in an RV, frequently hanging out in the mountains, where she wouldn't see another person for weeks at a time. Then she set out with a round-the-world ticket west, and no plan. Or, let us rephrase: She had a very explicit plan, and that was to have no plan. To go by "omens and dreams and messages" in order to discover "if I didn't have a plan, what would my life be like?"

And what she found was this: "I was *always* in the right place . . . . When you're connected to a source other than your mind, and you're open to allowing, that creates life as being way more magical than anything I could think of. . . . When you're willing to live like that, to make choices like that, to not know—it's very empowering to not know. People really don't understand that."

The other thing she discovered out there was, of course, herself.

"We can't know anything unless we get quiet, because it's not outside of ourselves. It's, you know, we are what we're looking for. . . . What I learned from getting quiet was that *I am* what I'm looking for."

And she got *seriously* quiet. More than a year into her worldwide adventure, she had an explicit dream: She saw herself standing on the side of the road with a sign around her neck that read GO TO INDIA Now. (If only all intuition took such literal form!) The dream had her abandoning her beautiful Balinese home—and giving up the friends she'd made and the things she was learning, the language, the cooking—for India, the last place she wanted to go.

One synchronicity after another led her to a twelve-day vipas-sana meditation retreat—another thing she didn't want to do. "They take your books, your pens—they take every single thing—your pass-port, your money, everything away from you. And there's no talking, no eye contact, nothing except sitting eight hours a day. . . . And what happens is you're really forced to face yourself. You're forced to pay at-tention to all the chatter that is ceaseless. . . . We all have that chatter going on and on."

And it's not only the internal chatter that does us in—it's the noise of the modern world itself. And for most of us—the multitasking mil-lions—getting quiet and mindful is easier said than done. No matter how simple it sounds.

There's this story, about a Zen teacher trying to impart the lesson of mindfulness to a student: "When drinking tea," the teacher tells his student, "just drink tea."

How often do you just drink tea?

Such a beautiful idea. Be here now. Focus. Breathe. So simple . . . and yet, so impossible. We spend our days assaulted by information, stimulation, texts, tweets, pings and rings, bouncing from one thing to the other and back again, while also trying to work—and to determine what to make for dinner. Maybe we're simultaneously drinking tea.

It reminds us of that old Enjolie ad, the one that celebrated women's success by singing that we can bring home the bacon and fry it up in a pan. Well, yes. We can. But between all that's required to bring it home and fry it up, do we ever get a second to stop and think? Or, more to the point, to stop and feel: Are we *enjoying* bringing it home? Are we *enjoying* frying it up? Do we have enough psychic space available to notice how it smells as it's cookin', let alone how it tastes?

There's a lot of lip service paid to the importance of finding our passion. But when our attention is so splintered, how can we even know whether we're actually enjoying something? And might this fractured consciousness have something to do with why we're so damn angsty in the face of big decisions? It's hard enough to make an informed decision. But how can we feel adequately informed if we can't focus, if we can't just drink the tea?

(Oh, that tea? The end of the story might make you feel a bit better. One day, that Zen student busted his teacher drinking tea *and* reading the paper. When confronted, the teacher said, "When drinking tea and reading the paper, just drink tea and read the paper!")

But just imagine what whispers we might hear were we able to just drink the tea, to tune it all out, to get quiet.

OF COURSE, NOT everyone can take off like Siama. Or get Siama-level quiet. But Gretchen Rubin (whom we met in the last chapter) got to know herself—and found bestseller-variety happiness—while living in New York City, one of the least-quiet places on earth. "A lot of people do radical happiness projects," she says, "I love . . . hearing about those where people move to a different country or make a complete career change or do some[thing] crazy . . . climb Mount Kilimanjaro or whatever. But I didn't do that kind of happiness project, and couldn't have even if I wanted to. I was pretty locked into my life."

Locked in though she was, Rubin also emphasizes the value of self-discovery. Of knowing—and accepting—herself for exactly who she is. And, equally important, exactly who she is not. She calls this "being Gretchen."

"You really need to know yourself—which is the most ancient of all happiness pointers, but still true and surprisingly difficult to follow. I remind myself constantly to be Gretchen. I think what happens to a lot of people is they drift into decisions and sort of think happiness is going to evolve. I went to law school, which is the classic drift decision. And I drifted into it for sure; I'm a poster child for that. And I'm no longer a lawyer; I'm a poster child for that too. The thing is, you can only build a happy life on the foundation of your own nature. And you really can't get out of that examination, and you have to really think about what would make you happy—not what would make the people around you happy, or what you think ought to make you feel happy, but what truly makes you feel happy. So it's really about self-knowledge. . . . You are who you are. I think it's really important to think about that very hard and not just make decisions because it's the obvious thing to do."

She described her motivation to go the high-flying legal route (clerking for Sandra Day O'Connor) as having more to do with assumptions and aspirations than passion or self-expression—and contrasted that with her second act.

"When I looked back on my life, I realized all these clues that I wanted to be a writer, but I was resisting them, again because I didn't want that to be who I was at that time. I was like, 'No, I want to be legitimate. I want to have this serious career, to be taken seriously. I don't want to have to cast about and make my own way. I want somebody to tell me what to do to be successful. Just tell me what to do, and I'll do it.' And that's what I did. And I did it very well. But there were all these clues that I wanted to be a writer."

Among those clues were her college career as an English major, her passion for reading, the book-length legal briefs, the three ("terrible") novels she wrote in her spare time. "I was writing and doing writerly things all the time," she says. "And this is a really important point. I would say, to anybody who doesn't know what they want to do, ask yourself: What do you *do*? Not what you wish you did, or what you think you ought to do, or what sounds cool, but what do you literally do. . . . Sometimes you just don't realize what you really want to do because you're blinded by what you think you ought to do."

Of course, it's difficult not to get caught up in the oughts.

Which brings us to an update from Lisa, the belly dancer you met in Chapter 6 who was debating hanging up her tassels in favor of getting her teaching credential. A couple months after that, we checked in and found she'd done an about face. (Or whatever such a maneuver is called in belly dance.) And we were lucky to catch her: She was in between sold-out workshops and filming two DVDs—and recommitted enough to the dancing life to have booked a workshop for the following summer in Mexico.

What inspired the change of heart? An artist cousin "lit a fire under my butt," she says. That helped—as did getting a closer look at that grass that had looked green enough to warrant exchanging her passion for a nice patch to call her own. She visited her hometown and "spent time with old friends [who] stayed home. Most of them are still undecided about what their calling or passion is. They are working jobs but haven't discovered or gone for their dream career," she wrote. "I figure that, since I found my dream, and though it is rough sometimes, I am making progress. I should stick to it. . . . I am pretty happy right now, and excited to be doing what I'd always dreamed of."

For Rubin, forgoing the "oughts" meant accepting that, despite living in Manhattan, she would never be a foodie, would never enjoy going to restaurants—never mind that, as a self-respecting New Yorker, she really ought to. (Yeah, we don't relate to that one either.) This also meant indulging a guilty pleasure: children's literature. "This was a passion I was shoving to the side because it didn't fit with my idea of who I was. I felt I was sophisticated and intellectual but I had this illegitimate and childish passion. So I never did anything with it."

Until she did. She confessed this secret passion to an acquaintance, who confessed she felt the same. They started a book club. When it got too big, they started another. And when that one got too big, they started another.

"This passion has come from the shadows into the center. But it was because I was willing to accept this about myself," she says. "You ask around, and you're going to find your people; they're there. They're just in hiding, like you are. Why not? Who cares if you're not supposed to? Let your freak flag fly."

This sort of self-acceptance is what Wavy Gravy (of Woodstock and ice-cream fame) was getting at when he said, "We're all just bozos on the bus, so we might as well sit back and enjoy the ride."[2]

Of course, that's well and good in theory, but who wants to admit to being a bozo? We have images to uphold! Whether the indie artist with no interest in the mainstream, or the intellectual with no time for kids' books, or the superwoman who has it all and has it all together—whatever our role, the performance is remarkably similar. We put on our mask and keep up the charade.

But what a shame. We deny ourselves—and in doing so, we implicitly encourage our friends and neighbors to deny themselves too. But maybe, as Rubin found, a willingness to own our idiosyncratic, oddball, not-always-delightful but utterly human nature can make our choices clearer. With no one to impress, no images to uphold, there's less to factor in. There's a freedom there. (We can be an indie artist *and* a *Hills* junkie. A serious writer *and* a Harry Potter freak.) And there's power in it too. Because when we are willing to come out of the closet, maybe our friends will join us. Maybe so many friends will join us, we'll have to start three kiddie-lit book clubs to contain them all.

BUT WHAT ABOUT our pint-sized blond Hannah, the chronically undecided ex-dresser of George Clooney you met in Chapter 1?

We talked to Hannah (who is, incidentally, now a brunette) one Thursday night after a long day at work. She's now a year into a gig as senior art buyer/producer for an advertising agency. And despite dropping the phrase "one foot out the door" approximately ten times, she seemed to have come to a certain Hannah-style peace. Tossing bikinis into a bag for a last-minute trip to Nicaragua with a college friend, she recounted the conversation she had with her boyfriend on their walk home after dinner. They'd been talking about how he came to New York with a firm five-year plan, which he'd been studiously executing since his arrival three years prior. She mentioned the pal she'd moved to New York with ten years ago, who has been in the same job, at the same company, ever since.

"I do not understand this philosophy. I'm bored out of my mind in six to eight months. I'm like, 'I want to do something new!'" she said. "This jumping around from job to job simply to satiate a curiosity about what it would be like to do this and that? I don't know if it will ever be satiated, or if this is what you get with me."

But in a strange way she's content. And a certain amount of that content has to do with some insights about her own nature. "In my world, like, I still want to change so much and learn so much and do so much. . . . I leap a lot without looking. Sometimes it works and sometimes it doesn't, but I never—I mean, of course I have regrets—but I don't let it kill me on the inside. . . . I'm in a place now where I would never have come to had it not been for my ride up until now, that's the way I see things. . . . I'm satisfied," she said.

And then, true to form, added, "I just want to see what *else* I might like. I'm still searching, looking at schools." On that walk home from dinner, she told us, she wondered aloud to her boyfriend, "'What if we move to Colorado, and I run my own spa-cum-yoga-cum-running company?' I feel like I'll end up in some sort of health lifestyle job. What that is, god knows, but I feel like I'm moving there, strategically or not."

Currently, she and her boyfriend have a one-year-and-four-month plan, at which point six months of travel is on the itinerary. And then a move. To where? That remains to be seen. Somewhere slower-paced, where she can live a life less focused on work. Maybe California, maybe Colorado.

Or maybe back to school. Remember that NYU program she was accepted to? She deferred her acceptance, but the day after she returned from Nicaragua, she sent us an email: "I hate being at work. I realize a bit of that is 'vacation nostalgia,' but the majority is definitely that I'm in the wrong industry. I could care less what the next Lord and Taylor campaign looks like. I feel like I have tried every possible angle in this industry, and it just doesn't want to stick—no one can fault me for not trying. I think I want to do that program at NYU after all. I will have to try to beg my way in. . . . What other choice do I have?"

But wherever she goes, she harbors no illusions that she'll find anyone there but Hannah. "Or we'll move our asses somewhere else, and then—well, okay, I feel like I'll be the same way," she laughed.

Maybe she will, and maybe she won't. It's a never-ending job, this business of becoming ourselves. This search can be tough, but take comfort: Wherever you go, there you are.

DISCUSSION QUESTIONS

1. Are you "undecided" too? What parts of the book resonate most with you?

2. Do you find decision-making stressful? Are you plagued by buyer's remorse? Or nonbuyer's remorse? Have you ever made a decision you thought was monumental but turned out to mean nothing?

3. Which woman do you relate to the most? Which one pisses you off? Is there someone you don't understand at all? Do you think this is all just a question of privilege?

4. Why doesn't this phenomenon apply to men? Do you believe men and women are fundamentally different? Do men have it easier than women?

5. What does "settling" mean to you? Have you ever settled—and if so, how has it played out? What's the difference between "settling" and "good enough"? Do you believe "good enough" is actually good enough? Why or why not? What trade-offs are worth it?

6. What is happiness for you? Do you consider yourself happy? Do you believe you will be? What will it take for you to be happy?

7. Who has determined your goals? Do you feel like you had to try all the approved things first? To fulfill others' expectations before your own?

8. What do you daydream about at your job? What did you want to be when you were five years old? Are you doing that now? Why or why not?

9. Do you consider yourself a feminist? Why or why not?

10. Whose life is perfect? Do you think yours should be? Is the grass always greener? How have your friends' decisions affected your relationships? Does it make you less satisfied with your life when you hear of friends' decisions?

11. Can you have it all? Are you trying to have it all?

ENDNOTES

ONE **YOU ARE HERE**

1. Malcolm Gladwell, *Blink: The Power of Thinking without Thinking* (Little, Brown, 2005), 142.

2. George Miller, "The Magical Number Seven, Plus or Minus Two: Some Limits on Our Capacity for Processing Information," *The Psychological Review* 63 (1956): 81–97.

3. B. Shiv and A. Fedorikhin, "Heart and Mind in Conflict: Interplay of Affect and Cognition in Consumer Decision Making," *Journal of Consumer Research* 26 (1999): 278–82.

4. International Museum of Women, the *Imagining Ourselves* project, subtheme: "Too Many Choices," http://imaginingourselves.imow.org/pb/SubTheme.aspx?id=46&lang=1 (accessed October 4, 2010).

5. Amy Benfer, "Freeze Your Eggs for Feminism!" *Salon Broadsheet,* May 5, 2009, http://www.salon.com/life/broadsheet/feature/2009/05/05/frozen_eggs.

6. J. Courtney Sullivan, *Commencement* (Alfred Knopf, 2009), 182.

7. U.S. Department of Labor, Bureau of Labor Statistics, "Employee Tenure in 2008," September 26, 2008, http://www.bls.gov/news.release/archives/tenure_09262008.htm (accessed October 4, 2010).

8. Pew Research Center, "American Mobility: Who Moves? Who Stays Put? Where's Home?" December 17, 2008, http://pewsocialtrends.org/assets/pdf/Movers-and-Stayers.pdf (accessed October 4, 2010).

9. Ellen Goodman, "A New Day at Harvard," *The Boston Globe,* February 16, 2007.

10. Germaine Greer, interview by Tom Ashbrook, *On Point with Tom Ashbrook,* NPR/WBUR, March 25, 2009, http://www.onpointradio.org/2009/03/germaine-greer (accessed October 4, 2010).

11. Dacher Keltner, *Born to Be Good: The Science of a Meaningful Life* (W. W. Norton, 2009).

12. Daniel Gilbert, *Stumbling on Happiness* (Alfred Knopf, 2007).

13. Po Bronson, *What Should I Do with My Life? The True Story of People Who Answered the Ultimate Question* (Random House Trade Paperbacks, 2003), 389, 392.

14. Craig Lambert, "The Marketplace of Perceptions," *Harvard Magazine* (March/April 2006).

15. Barry Schwartz, *The Paradox of Choice: Why More Is Less* (Harper Perennial, 2004).

16. Sheena S. Iyengar, Rachael E. Wells, and Barry Schwartz, "Doing Better But Feeling Worse: Looking for the 'Best' Job Undermines Satisfaction," *Psychological Science* 17, no. 2 (2006): 143–50.

17. Sheena S. Iyengar and Mark R. Lepper, "When Choice Is Demotivating: Can One Desire Too Much of a Good Thing?" *Journal of Personality and Social Psychology* 79, no. 6 (December 2000): 995–1006.

18. "Choice," *Radiolab,* no. 501, WNYC/PRX, http://www.prx.org/pieces/30643 (accessed October 4, 2010).

19. Jonah Lehrer, interview by Terry Gross, "Jonah Lehrer: Passions of the Brain," *Fresh Air*, NPR/ WHYY, March 2, 2009, http://www.npr.org/templates/story/story.php?storyId=101334645 (accessed October 4, 2010).

TWO **OH, THE PLACES YOU'LL GO**

1. New Strategist Publications, "The Millennial Generation: Another Baby Boom," American Generations Series, p. 1, *http:// www.newstrategist.com/store/files/AmGen6SamplePgs.pdf (accessed October 4, 2010).*
2. Morley Safer, "The 'Millennials' Are Coming: Morley Safer on the New Generation of American Workers," *60 Minutes,* November 11, 2007, http://www.cbsnews.com/stories/2007/11/08/60minutes/main3475200.shtml (accessed October 4, 2010).
3. Jenny Norenberg, "I Can Do Anything, So How Do I Choose?" *Newsweek,* December 6, 2004.
4. Hana R. Alberts, "The Economics of Quarterlife," Forbes.com, June 24, 2009, http://www.forbes.com/2009/06/23/young-adult-income-employment-health-opinions-columnists-quarterlife.html (accessed October 4, 2010).
5. Pew Research Center, "Millennials: A Portrait of Generation Next," February 24, 2010, http://pewresearch.org/millennials (accessed October 4, 2010).
6. London Business School, "The Reflexive Generation: Young Professionals' Perspectives on Work, Career, and Gender," 2009, p. 4, http://www.london.edu/assets/documents/facultyandresearch/Gen_Y_The_Reflexive_Generation_The_Report.pdf (accessed October 4, 2010).
7. Benedict Carey, "A Snapshot of a Generation May Come Out Blurry," *The New York Times,* August 2, 2010.
8. Lindsay Minnema, "Hard Times Can Be Troubling Even for Those Too Young for a Midlife Crisis," *The Washington Post,* August 11, 2009.
9. Robin Marantz Henig, "What Is It about 20-Somethings?" *The New York Times Magazine,* August 18, 2010.
10. "What's the Matter with Twentysomething Kids Today?" a Slate online discussion, August 20, 2010, http://www.slate.com/id/2264542 (accessed October 4, 2010).
11. Transitions2Adulthood, "Becoming Adult Is a Different World Today," May 24, 2010, http://transitions2adulthood.com/2010/05/24/becoming-adult-is-a-different-world-today-too-bad-the-social-supports-havent-kept-pace (accessed October 4, 2010).
12. Adecco, "Hoping for Stabilization . . . Better Plan for Resignations," press release, June 25, 2009.

THREE **THE ROAD NOT TRAVELED**

1. Erica Kennedy, *Feminista* (St. Martin's Press, 2009), 106.
2. Kate Torgovnick, "Renee Zellweger Supposedly Pushing to Make Bridget Jones Skinny in the Next Flick," The Frisky, February 19, 2010, http://www.thefrisky.com/post/246-renee-zellweger-supposedly-pushing-to-make-bridget-jones-skinny-in-the- (accessed October 4, 2010).
3. Erica Kennedy, "FEM Real Talk: Marrying Rich and Being Renee Zellweger," *The Feminista Files,* February 21, 2010, http://thefeministafiles.blogspot.com/2010/02/fem-real-talk-marrying-rich-and-being.html (accessed October 4, 2010).
4. Elizabeth Wurtzel, "Failure to Launch: When Beauty Fades," *Elle,* May 20, 2009.
5. Hannah Seligson, "Why We're Not Getting Married," The Daily Beast, January 17, 2010, http://www.thedailybeast.com/blogs-and-stories/2010-01-17/why-were-not-getting-married (accessed October 4, 2010).
6. Wesley Yang, "A Critical (But Highly Sympathetic) Reading of New Yorkers' Sexual Habits and Anxieties," *New York Magazine,* November 2, 2009.

7. Ibid.

8. Sophia Karathanasis, "Generation Y: Most Depressed Generation," *The Ticker,* February 6, 2010, http://www.theticker.org/about/2.8219/generation-y-most-depressed-generation-1.2140234 (accessed October 4, 2010).

9. David Brooks, "Cellphones, Texts, and Lovers," *The New York Times,* November 2, 2009.

10. Dan Ariely, *Predictably Irrational: The Hidden Forces That Shape Our Decisions* (Harper Collins, 2010).

11. Naomi Wolf, "The Achievement Myth," *Project Syndicate,* November 30, 2009, http://www.project-syndicate.org/contributor/1328/2?nipp=10 (accessed October 4, 2010).

FOUR CHASING THE MIRAGE

1. Peggy Orenstein, "I Tweet Therefore I Am," *New York Times Magazine,* July 30, 2010.

2. Soraya Mehdizadeh, "Self-Presentation 2.0: Narcissism and Self-Esteem on Facebook," *Cyberpsychology, Behavior, and Social Networking* 13, no. 4 (August 2010): 357–64.

3. Erving Goffman, *The Presentation of Self in Everyday Life* (Anchor Books, 1959).

4. Rachel Shukert. *Everything is Going to Be Great: An Underfunded and Overexposed European Grand Tour* (Harper Perennial, 2010).

5. Anna North, "Scary Italians, Bad Sex, and Other Worthwhile Mistakes," Jezebel, July 20, 2010, http://jezebel.com/5590971/scary-italians-bad-sex-and-other-worthwhile-mistakes (accessed October 4, 2010).

6. Rachel Shukert, "Memoirist Rachel Shukert on 'Eat Pray Love,' Self-Censoring Authors, and Embracing Mistakes," *The Wall Street Journal Speakeasy,* August 2, 2010, http://blogs.wsj.com/speakeasy/2010/08/02/memoirist-rachel-shukert-on-eat-pray-love-self-censoring-authors-and-embracing-mistakes (accessed October 4, 2010).

7. A. O. Scott, "The John Hughes Touch," *The New York Times,* August 7, 2009.

8. Gloria Steinem, "Reflections on Feminism: A Voyage of Discovery with Gloria Steinem," The Thomas Harriot College of Arts and Sciences 2009-2010 Voyages of Discovery Lecture Series, East Carolina University, November 6, 2009, http://www.ecu.edu/cs-cas/voyages/0910/premier0910.cfm.

9. Peggy Orenstein, "The Femivore's Dilemma," *New York Times Magazine,* March 11, 2010.

10. Diana Appleyard, "The New Feminist Housewives," *The Mail Online,* July 14, 2010, http://www.dailymail.co.uk/femail/article-1294231/How-latest-generation-graduates-choosing-time-motherhood-high-flying-careers.html (accessed October 4, 2010).

FIVE SYNAPSE TRAFFIC JAM

1. Gladwell, *Blink,* 142 (see chap. 1, no. 1).

2. Miller, "The Magical Number Seven" (see chap. 1, no. 2).

3. Shiv and Fedorikhin, "Heart and Mind in Conflict" (see chap. 1, no. 3).

4. Andy Raskin, "How to Lead Your Customer into Temptation," CNNMoney.com *Business 2.0 Magazine,* May 1, 2006, http://money.cnn.com/magazines/business2/business2_archive/2006/05/01/8375932/index.htm (accessed October 4, 2010).

5. "Choice," *Radiolab* (see chap. 1, no. 18).

6. Kathleen D. Vohs et al., "Making Choices Impairs Subsequent Self-Control: A Limited-Resource Account of Decision Making, Self-Regulation, and Active Initiative," *Journal of Personality and Social Psychology* 94, no. 5 (2008): 883–98.

7. Christopher F. Chabris et al., "The Allocation of Time in Decision-Making," *Journal of the European Economic Association* 7, no. 2–3 (2009): 628–37.

8. Sheena Iyengar, *The Art of Choosing: The Hidden Science of Choice* (Twelve, Hachette Book Group, 2010).

9. Iyengar and Lepper, "When Choice Is Demotivating" (see chap 1., no. 17).

10. Iyengar and Lepper, "When Choice Is Demotivating," 1004 (see chap 1., no. 17).

11. Pai-Lu Wu and Wen-Bin Chiou, "More Options Lead to More Searching and Worse Choices in Finding Partners for Romantic Relationships Online: An Experimental Study," *CyberPsychology & Behavior* 12, no. 3 (June 2009): 315–8.

12. Jeana H. Frost et al., "People Are Experience Goods: Improving Online Dating with Virtual Dates," *Journal of Interactive Marketing* 22, no. 1 (Winter 2008): 51–61.

13. Andrew Schrock, "Data Overload on Dating Sites," *Technology Review,* published by MIT, July 17, 2009, http://www.technologyreview.com/web/23016/page1 (accessed October 4, 2010).

14. Lori Gottlieb, *Marry Him: The Case for Settling for Mr. Good Enough* (Penguin Group, 2010), 113.

15. Schwartz, *The Paradox of Choice* (see chap. 1, no. 15).

16. "Barry Schwartz on the Paradox of Choice," TEDtalk online video, http://www.ted.com/talks/lang/eng/barry_schwartz_on the paradox_of_choice.html (accessed October 4, 2010).

17. Barry Schwartz, "The Tyranny of Choice," *Scientific American* (April 2004): 74.

18. D. Kahneman and A. Tversky, "Prospect Theory: An Analysis of Decision under Risk," *Econometrica* 47 (1979): 263–92.

19. A. Tversky and E. Shafir, "Choice under Conflict: The Dynamics of Deferred Decision," *Psychological Science* 3 (1992): 359–61.

20. Ben Irons and Cameron Hepburn, "Regret Theory and the Tyranny of Choice," *Economic Record* 83, no. 261 (June 2007): 191–203.

21. Iyengar, Wells, and Schwartz, "Doing Better But Feeling Worse" (see chap. 1, no. 16).

22. Ibid., 149.

23. Ariely, *Predictably Irrational,* 4 (see chap. 3, no. 10).

24. Michael Norton, Jeana Frost, and Dan Ariely, "Less Is More: The Lure of Ambiguity, or Why Familiarity Breeds Contempt," *Journal of Personality and Social Psychology* 92 (2007): 97–105.

25. Ibid., 103.

26. Lambert, "The Marketplace of Perceptions," 53 (see chap. 1, no. 14).

27. Eduardo Dias-Ferreira et al., "Chronic Stress Causes Frontostriatal Reorganization and Affects Decision-Making," *Science* 325, no. 5940 (July 2009): 621–5.

28. Louisa Kamps, "Analyze This: Should You Go with Your Head or Your Heart?" *Elle,* July 16, 2009, http://www.elle.com/Life-Love/Society-Career-Power/Analyze-This (accessed October 4, 2010).

29. Ibid., 4.

30. J. J. Bauer, D. P. McAdams, and A. R. Sakaeda, "Crystallization of Desire versus Crystallization of Discontent in Life-Changing Decisions," *Journal of Personality* 73 (2005): 1181–1213.

31. Gladwell, *Blink,* 141 (see chap. 1, no. 1).

32. Pico Iyer, "The Journey of Sitting Still: A Conversation with Pico Iyer" (lecture, Sun Valley Writers' Conference, Ketchum, ID, August 2010).

33. Eyal Ophira, Clifford Nass, and Anthony D. Wagner, "Cognitive Control in Media Multitaskers," *PNAS* 106, no. 37 (September 15, 2009): 15583–7.

34. Adam Gorlick, "Media Multitaskers Pay Mental Price, Stanford Study Shows," *Stanford Report,* August 24, 2009, http://news.stanford.edu/news/2009/august24/multitask-research-study-082409.html (accessed October 4, 2010).

35. E. Aboujaoude et al., "Potential Markers for Problematic Internet Use: A Telephone Survey of 2,513 Adults," *CNS Spectrums* 11, no. 10 (October 2006): 750–5.

36. Benny Evangelista, "Attention Loss Feared as High-Tech Rewires Brain," SFGate, November 15, 2009, http://articles.sfgate.com/2009-11-15/business/17179391_1_texting-tweets-attention (accessed October 4, 2010).

37. Ibid.

38. Joint study between HP in the United Kingdom and the University of London, "Abuse of Technology Can Reduce UK Workers' Intelligence," http://www.scribd.com/doc/6910385/Abuse-of-technology-can-reduce-UK-workers-intelligence (accessed October 4, 2010).

39. Jan Van Der Veken, "Top of the World," *The New Yorker* cover image, January 11, 2010.

40. Douglas Merrill, interviewed by Renee Montagne, "Former Google Executive on Getting Organized," NPR's *Morning Edition,* March 22, 2010, http://www.npr.org/templates/story/story.php?storyId=125005439 (accessed October 4, 2010).

41. Rob Walker, "This Year's Model," *New York Times Magazine,* July 9, 2009.

SIX **SETTLING FOR THE DETOURS**

1. Maureen Dowd, "Questions for Maureen Dowd," *The New York Times,* Readers' Opinions, November 4, 2005, http://select.nytimes.com/2005/11/04/readersopinions/dowd-questions.html?_r=1(accessed October 4, 2010).

2. Gottlieb, *Marry Him,* 44 (see chap. 5, no. 14).

3. Ibid., 45.

4. Jessica Ravitz, "'Marry Him' Author Answers Outrage about 'Settling,'" "CNNLiving, "February 24, 2010, http://www.cnn.com/2010/LIVING/02/24/lori.gottlieb.marry.him/index.html (accessed October 4, 2010).

5. Schwartz, *The Paradox of Choice* (see chap. 1, no. 15).

6. John Tierney, "Carpe Diem? Maybe Tomorrow," *The New York Times,* December 28, 2009.

7. Ibid.

SEVEN **CONVERSATIONS WITH THE ROAD WARRIORS**

1. Garey Ramey and Valerie A. Ramey, "The Rug Rat Race," National Bureau of Economic Research (NBER) Working Paper no. 15284, August 2009.

2. Ibid., 2.

3. Ibid., 37.

4. Stephanie Chen, "Moms Quit Jobs for the Child's College Dreams," CNN, April 27, 2009, http://www.cnn.com/2010/living/04/27/moms.quit.job.college.admissions (accessed October 4, 2010).

5. Barry Schwartz, "Top Colleges Should Select Randomly from a Pool of 'Good Enough,' *The Chronicle of Higher Education,* February 25, 2005, http://www.swarthmore.edu/SocSci/bschwar1/srp.html, scroll to 2005 publications (accessed October 4, 2010).

6. Juliette Mullin, "Fine with Not Having a Job Yet," In Case You Missed Me, *The Daily Pennsylvanian,* March 2, 2010, http://www.dailypennsylvanian.com/article/case-you-missed-me-fine-not-having-job-yet (accessed October 4, 2010).

7. "Plastics" is a reference to *The Graduate,* a 1967 Mike Nichols film starring Dustin Hoffman and Anne Bancroft. In the scene referenced, Benjamin—a new college grad played by Hoffman—is on the receiving end of career advice from a family friend (who thinks the plastics industry is a good choice).

8. Elizabeth Gilbert, "The Key to a Well-Lived Life: Lighten Up!" *O* (the Oprah Magazine), April 13, 2010.

9. Aarons-Mele refers to the iconic TV commercial for Enjolie perfume that billed itself as the "eight-hour perfume for the 24-hour woman." The classic 1970s television commercial (http://www.you-

tube.com/watch?v=4X4MwbVf5OA) featured a woman who morphed from housewife to business-woman to sex kitten wife, all the while singing: "I can bring home the bacon, fry it up in a pan, and never, ever let you forget you're a man, cause I'm a woman."

EIGHT **THE REARVIEW MIRROR**

1. "Pill Talk with Hilary Swank and Gloria Steinem," CNN's *The Joy Behar Show*, May 6, 2010, http://joybehar.blogs.cnn.com/2010/05/06/pill-talk-with-hilary-swank-and-gloria-steinem (accessed October 4, 2010).

2. "No Slacks in the Office: Gail Collins and Lesley Stahl Relive the Birth of Feminism," a conversation between Gail Collins and Lesley Stahl, WowOWow, October 21, 2009, http://www.wowowow.com/culture/gail-collins-lesley-stahl-interview-feminism-sarah-palin-gloria-steinem397308?page=0%252C6 (accessed October 4, 2010).

3. Joan Walsh, "Feminism after Friedan," Salon, February 6, 2008, http://www.salon.com/life/feature/2006/02/06/friedan/index.html (accessed October 4, 2010).

4. Dorothy Sue Cobble, "It's Time for New Deal Feminism," *The Washington Post*, December 13, 2009.

5. Ibid.

6. Susie Orbach and Shahesta Shaitly, "The New Feminists: Still Fighting," *The Observer*, August 15, 2010.

7. Joan Walsh, "Has Everything Changed for Women?" Salon, December 1, 2009, http://www.salon.com/news/opinion/joan_walsh/feminism/2009/12/01/gail_collins/index.html?source=newsletter (accessed October 4, 2010).

8. Nancy Folbre, "Feminists at Fault?" Economix, *The New York Times*, August 9, 2010, http://economix.blogs.nytimes.com/2010/08/09/feminists-at-fault (accessed October 4, 2010).

9. Joan Walsh, "Feminism after Friedan," Salon, February 6, 2008, http://www.salon.com/life/feature/2006/02/06/friedan/index.html (accessed October 4, 2010).

10. Ibid.

11. Ariel Levy, "Lift and Separate: Why Is Feminism Still So Divisive?" Books, *The New Yorker*, November 16, 2009.

12. "No More Miss America!" jofreeman.com, http://www.cwluherstory.org/no-more-miss-america.html.

NINE **YOU'VE COME A LONG WAY, BABY . . . MAYBE**

1. Germaine Greer, "I Admire Women Who Divorce," *The Times Online*, March 22, 2010, http://women.timesonline.co.uk/tol/life_and_style/women/article7070174.ece (accessed October 4, 2010).

2. Ellen Goodman, "Women," *The Washington Post* Writer's Group, December 24, 2009, http://www.postwritersgroup.com/archives/good091224.htm (accessed October 4, 2010).

3. Maria Shriver, "The Unfinished Revolution," *Time*, October 14, 2009.

4. J. E. Arnold, "Economic Ecology of the Contemporary American House," paper presented at the CELF Conference "Reconsidering the American Dream: Middle-Class Families Experience the 21st Century," Los Angeles, April 28–29, 2010.

5. Benedict Carey, "Families' Every Fuss, Archived and Analyzed," *The New York Times*, May 22, 2010, http://www.nytimes.com/2010/05/23/science/23family.html (accessed October 4, 2010).

6. Ibid.

7. Heather Boushey, Jessica Arons, and Lauren Smith, "Families Can't Afford the Gender Wage Gap," Center for American Progress, April 20, 2010, http://www.americanprogress.org/issues/2010/04/equal_pay.html (accessed October 4, 2010).

8. Ibid.

9. Michael J. Silverstein and Kate Sayre, *Women Want More: How to Capture Your Share of the World's Largest, Fastest-Growing Market* (HarperBusiness, September 2009), 3.

10. Maria Shriver and the Center for American Progress, "The Shriver Report: A Woman's Nation Changes Everything," ed. Heather Boushey and Ann O'Leary, October 16, 2009, http://www.americanprogress.org/issues/2009/10/womans_nation.html/#introduction (accessed October 4, 2010).

11. Nancy Gibbs, "What Women Want Now," *Time,* October 14, 2009. (Ms. Gibbs's statement was based on data from a Rockefeller Foundation/Time collaboration.)

12. Ibid.

13. Ibid.

14. "No Slacks in the Office," WowOWow (see chap. 8, no. 2).

15. Gail Collins, *When Everything Changed: The Amazing Journey of Women from 1960 to the Present* (Little, Brown, 2009).

16. Ibid.

17. In case you didn't catch the reference, the classic 1970s "empowerment" message ("You've come a long way, baby") was a jingle for Virginia Slims cigarettes.

18. Goodman, "Women" (see no. 2).

19. Boushey, Arons, and Smith, "Families Can't Afford the Gender Wage Gap" (see no. 7).

20. Jenny M. Hoobler, Sandy J. Wayne, and Grace Lemmon, "Bosses' Perceptions of Family–Work Conflict and Women's Promotability: Glass Ceiling Effects," *Academy of Management Journal* 52, no. 5 (October 2009): 939–57.

21. Laura Clark, "Childless Women 'Vilified by Bosses,'": Why *Not* Having a Family Could Ruin Your Career," *The Mail Online,* May 18, 2009, http://www.dailymail.co.uk/femail/article-1183895/Childless-women-vilified-bosses-Why-not-having-family-ruin-career.html (accessed October 4, 2010).

22. Gibbs, "What Women Want Now" (see no. 11).

23. Katha Pollitt, "Working Women: Strength in Numbers," *The Nation,* November 16, 2009, http://www.thenation.com/article/working-women-strength-numbers (accessed October 4, 2010).

24. Jacqueline A Berrien, "Statement to Commemorate Equal Pay Day," the U.S. Equal Employment Opportunity Commission, April 20, 2010, http://www.eeoc.gov/eeoc/newsroom/equalpayday2010.cfm.

25. Richard Fry and D'Vera Cohn, "Women, Men, and the New Economics of Marriage," Pew Research Center, January 19, 2010, http://pewsocialtrends.org/pubs/750/new-economics-of-marriage (accessed October 4, 2010).

26. Boushey, Arons, and Smith, "Families Can't Afford the Gender Wage Gap" (see no. 7).

27. Jennifer Ludden, "Despite New Law, Gender Salary Gap Persists," *Morning Edition,* National Public Radio, April 19, 2010.

28. Ibid.

29. Ibid.

30. Boushey, Arons, and Smith, "Families Can't Afford the Gender Wage Gap" (see no. 7).

31. "Facts about Pay Equity," National Organization for Women, http://www.now.org/issues/economic/factsheet.html (accessed October 4, 2010).

32. "What Are the Costs of the Wage Gap?" WAGE (Women Are Getting Even), http://www.wageproject.org/files/costs.php (accessed October 4, 2010).

33. Institute for Women's Policy Research, "Still A Man's Labor Market: The Long-Term Earnings Gap," Research-in-Brief (February 2008), p. 1, http://www.iwpr.org/pdf/C366_RIB.pdf (accessed October 4, 2010).

34. Marianne Bertrand, Claudia Goldin, and Lawrence F. Katz, "Dynamics of the Gender Gap for Young Professionals in the Financial and Corporate Sectors," *American Economic Journal: Applied Economics* no. 2 (July 2010): 228-55.

35. Stephen J. Dubner, "SuperFreakonomics Book Club: Goldin and Katz on the Male–Female Wage Gap," *The New York Times*, January 28, 2010, http://freakonomics.blogs.nytimes.com/2010/01/28/super-freakonomics-book-club-goldin-and-katz-on-the-male-female-wage-gap (accessed October 4, 2010).

36. Jessica Bennett, Jesse Ellison, and Sarah Ball, "Are We There Yet?" *Newsweek*, March 19, 2010.

37. Ibid.

38. Ibid.

39. "Rewriting an All-Too-Familiar Story?" The 2009 Hollywood Writers Report (May 2009), 1–2.

40. Ibid., 2–3.

41. Mary C. Murchy, Claude M. Steele, and James J. Gross, "Signaling Threat: How Situational Cues Affect Women in Math, Science, and Engineering Settings," *Psychological Science* 18, no. 10 (2007): 879–85.

42. Marcella Bombardieri, "Summers' Remarks on Women Draw Fire," *The Boston Globe*, January 17, 2005.

43. Claire Cain Miller, "Out of the Loop in Silicon Valley," *The New York Times*, April 16, 2010.

44. Bennett, Ellison, and Ball, "Are We There Yet?" (see no. 34).

45. "Women, Ambition, and (Still) the Pay Gap," a video interview with Rosabeth Moss Kanter, *Harvard Business Review*, April 2, 2010, http://blogs.hbr.org/video/2010/04/women-ambition-and-still-the-p.html (accessed October 4, 2010).

46. Karen Heller, "Commentary: Diane Sawyer's Promotion No Watershed Moment," *The Philadelphia Inquirer*, September 17, 2009, http://readingeagle.com/article.aspx?id=157271c (accessed October 4, 2010).

47. Mary Jordan, "'Hillary Effect' Cited for Increase in Female Ambassadors to U.S.," *The Washington Post*, January 11, 2010.

48. Ibid.

49. Susan J Douglas, *Enlightened Sexism: The Seductive Message That Feminism's Work Is Done* (Henry Holt, 2010).

50. Barbara Bailey Kelley, "Feminism's Third Wave: If Only There Were One," *San Francisco Chronicle Magazine*, September 14, 2003, http://articles.sfgate.com/2003-09-14/living/17508732_1_feminists-student-piece (accessed October 4, 2010).

51. Patt Morrison, "Feminism's Freedom Fighter," *Los Angeles Times*, October 17, 2009.

52. Laura Ling and Euna Lee, "Hostages of the Hermit Kingdom," *Los Angeles Times*, September 1, 2009.

53. Cover of special issue "Saving the World's Women," *New York Times Magazine*, August 18, 2009.

54. Hillary Rodham Clinton, "A New Gender Agenda," interview by Mark Landler, *New York Times Magazine*, special issue "Saving the World's Women," August 18, 2009.

55. Laura Liswood, "Global Gender Gap Report: Some Gains in Africa," The Women's Media Center, November 18, 2009, http://womensmediacenter.com/blog/2009/11/global-gender-gap-report-some-gains-in-africa-2 (accessed October 4, 2010).

56. Latoya Peterson, "Closing the Gender Gap Requires Effort at Every Level," Jezebel, November 18, 2009, http://jezebel.com/5407636/closing-the-global-gender-gap-requires-effort-every-level (accessed October 4, 2010).

57. Liswood, "Global Gender Gap Report" (see no. 53).

58. Charlotta Kratz, "Taking It Public," a guest post, Undecidedthebook.wordpress.com, September 1, 2009, http://undecidedthebook.wordpress.com/2009/09/01/taking-it-public-a-guest-post-by-charlotta-kratz (accessed October 4, 2010).

59. Goodman, "Women" (see chap. 2, no. 9).

60. "SF Gender Equity Principles Initiative," San Francisco Department on the Status of Women, http://www.sfgov3.org/index.aspx?page=132 (accessed October 4, 2010).

61. Londa Schiebinger and Shannon K. Gilmartin, "Housework Is an Academic Issue," *Adademe,* January/February 2010, http://www.aaup.org/AAUP/pubsres/academe/2010/JF/feat/schie.htm (accessed October 4, 2010).

62. Adam Gorlick, "Stanford Researcher Urges Universities, Businesses to Offer Benefit to Pay for Housework," *Stanford Report,* January 19, 2010.

63. Cora Lewis, "Steinem Headlines Talk about Feminism," *Yale Daily News,* February 1, 2010.

TEN **WHAT A LONG, STRANGE TRIP IT IS**

1. Betsey Stevenson and Justin Wolfers, "The Paradox of Declining Female Happiness," National Bureau of Economic Research (NBER) Working Paper no. w14969 (May 2009).

2. Richard Woods, "Women Less Happy after 40 Years of Feminism," *The Sunday Times,* May 31, 2009.

3. Arianna Huffington, "The Sad, Shocking Truth about How Women Are Feeling," The Huffington Post, September 17, 2009, http://www.huffingtonpost.com/arianna-huffington/the-sad-shocking-truth-ab_b_290021.html (accessed October 4, 2010).

4. Michelle Conlin, "Career Women at Midlife: Sadder and Sicker," *BusinessWeek,* March 27, 2009.

5. Marcus Buckingham, "What the Happiest and Most Successful Women Do Differently," The Huffington Post, September 28, 2009, http://www.huffingtonpost.com/marcus-buckingham/what-the-happiest-and-mos_b_301406.html (accessed October 4, 2010).

6. Greer, *On Point with Tom Ashbrook* (see chap. 1, no. 10).

7. Maureen Dowd, "Blue Is the New Black," *The New York Times,* September 19, 2009.

8. "Values Change the World," World Values Survey, January 2009, http://www.worldvaluessurvey.org/wvs/articles/folder_published/article_base_111.

9. Charlotta Kratz, "There's Nothing Wrong with Women," a guest post, Undecidedthebook.wordpress.com, September 29, 2009, http://undecidedthebook.wordpress.com/2009/09/29/theres-nothing-wrong-with-women-a-guest-post-by-charlotta-kratz (accessed October 4, 2010).

10. Dowd, "Blue Is the New Black" (see no. 7).

11. Marcus Buckingham, "What's Happening to Women's Happiness?" The Huffington Post, September 17, 2009, http://www.huffingtonpost.com/marcus-buckingham/whats-happening-to-womens_b_289511.html (accessed October 4, 2010).

12. Dowd, "Blue Is the New Black" (see no. 7).

13. Kratz, "Taking It Public" (see chap. 9, no. 56).

14. Aaron Traister, "And May Your First Child Be a Feminine Child," Salon, November 15, 2009, http://www.salon.com/life/feature/2009/11/15/feminine_child (accessed October 4, 2010).

15. Ibid.

16. Mary Elizabeth Williams, "Did You Mean That, Google?" *Salon Broadsheet,* October 23, 2009, http://www.salon.com/life/broadsheet/feature/2009/10/23/google_fail (accessed October 4, 2010).

17. Ibid.

18. Amanda Marcotte, "Devaluing Daughters," *Double X,* November 16, 2009, http://www.doublex.com/blog/xxfactor/devaluing-daughters (accessed October 4, 2010).

19. "Women are Sort of More Tentative Than Men, Aren't They?" Eurekalert.org. August 24, 2009, http://www.eurekalert.org/pub_releases/2009-08/uoc--was082409.php (accessed October 4, 2010).

20. Ibid.

21. Ibid.

22. Stevenson and Wolfers, "The Paradox of Declining Female Happiness" (see no. 1).

23. Buckingham, "What's Happening to Women's Happiness?" (see no. 11).

24. Leslie Bennetts, "Something About Meryl," *Vanity Fair,* January 2010.

25. Judith Warner, "The Real Cougar Fans," Opinionator, *The New York Times* September 24, 2009, http://opinionator.blogs.nytimes.com/2009/09/24/the-real-cougar-fans (accessed October 4, 2010).

26. Fawn Germer, "Work–Life Balance? The Mantra That Balances What Matters," The Huffington Post, October 28, 2009, http://www.huffingtonpost.com/fawn-germer/work-life-balance-the-man_b_335407.html (accessed October 4, 2010).

27. Cindy Krischer Goodman, "Madeleine Albright on Work/Life Balance," *The Miami Herald Blog,* October 7, 2009, http://miamiherald.typepad.com/worklifebalancingact/2009/10/madeleine-albright-on-worklife-balance.html (accessed October 4, 2010).

28. Arianna Huffington and Cindi Leive, "Sleep Challenge 2010: Women, It's Time to Sleep Our Way to the Top. Literally," The Huffington Post, January 4, 2010, http://www.huffingtonpost.com/arianna-huffington/sleep-challenge-2010-wome_b_409973.html (accessed October 4, 2010).

29. Jessica Valenti, "Is Sleep a Feminist Issue?" *Feministing,* January 6, 2010, http://feministing.com/2010/01/06/is-sleep-a-feminist-issue (accessed October 4, 2010).

30. Huffington and Leive, "Sleep Challenge 2010" (see no. 28).

31. Ibid.

32. Lisa Belkin, "Why Women Don't Get Enough Sleep," *The New York Times Magazine,* January 5, 2010, http://parenting.blogs.nytimes.com/2010/01/05/why-parents-dont-get-enough-sleep (accessed October 4, 2010).

33. Marta Mossburg, "Freedom Is Not Always Fun," Marta Mossburg, *The Washington Examiner,* May 29, 2009, http://www.washingtonexaminer.com/opinion/columns/marta-mossburg/Freedom-is-not-always-fun-46455502.html (accessed October 4, 2010).

ELEVEN **LIFE IN THE CARPOOL LANE**

1. Martha Irvine, "Gen Xers Lament Lack of Upward Mobility," Associated Press, November 29, 2009, http://articles.sfgate.com/2009-11-29/news/17180227_1_gen-xers-gen-yers-boomers (accessed October 4, 2010).

2. "Women in their 20s and 30s," Catalyst, March 2009, http://www.catalyst.org/publication/237/women-in-their-20s-30s (accessed October 4, 2010).

3. Alex Jung, "Were You Born on the Wrong Continent? America's Misguided Culture of Overwork," Salon, August 25, 2010, http://www.salon.com/books/feature/2010/08/25/german_usa_working_life_ext2010/index.html (accessed October 4, 2010).

4. Judith Warner, "The Choice Myth," Opinionator, *The New York Times* October 8, 2009, http://warner.blogs.nytimes.com/2009/10/08/the-opt-out-myth (accessed October 4, 2010).

5. Ellen Goodman, "Just Grateful to Have a Job," *The Boston Globe,* September 11, 2009.

6. A. Nolan, in response to the question, "Have you ever used the Family Medical Leave Act?" Sloan Work and Family Research Network, Boston College, http://wfnetwork.bc.edu/template.php?name=news_polls (accessed October 4, 2010).

7. Kim Parker, "The Harried Life of the Working Mother," Pew Research Center Publications, October 1, 2009, http://pewresearch.org/pubs/1360/working-women-conflicted-but-few-favor-return-to-traditional-roles (accessed October 4, 2010).

8. Ibid.

9. U.S. Department of Labor, Bureau of Labor Statistics, "Married Parents' Use of Time Summary," May 8, 2008, http://www.bls.gov/news.release/atus2.nr0.htm (accessed October 4, 2010).

10. Cari Tuna and Joann S. Lublin, "Jack Welch: No Such Thing as Work–Life Balance," *The Wall Street Journal* Blogs, July 14, 2009, http://blogs.wsj.com/juggle/2009/07/13/jack-welch-no-such-thing-as-work-life-balance (accessed October 4, 2010).

11. Hoobler, Wayne, and Lemmon, "Bosses' Perceptions of Family–Work Conflict and Women's Promotability" (see chap. 9, no. 20).

12. Brad Harrington, Fred Van Deusen, and Jamie Ladge, "The New Dad. Exploring Fatherhood within a Career Context," June 2010, http://www.bc.edu/centers/cwf/meta-elements/pdf/BC-CWF_Fatherhood_Study_The_New_Dad.pdf (accessed October 4, 2010).

13. Joan Williams, *Unbending Gender: Why Family and Work Conflict and What to Do about It* (Oxford University Press, 2000), 6.

14. Joan C. Williams and Heather Boushey, "The Three Faces of Work–Family Conflict: The Poor, the Professionals and the Missing Middle," combined report from Center for American Progress and the Center for WorkLife Law at University of California, Hastings College of the Law (January 2010), 3–4. http://www.americanprogress.org/issues/2010/01/three_faces_report.html (accessed October 4, 2010).

15. Felice Schwartz, "Management Women and the New Facts of Life," *Harvard Business Review,* January/February 1989, http://hbr.org/1989/01/management-women-and-the-new-facts-of-life/ar/1 (accessed October 4, 2010).

16. "The Earnings Penalty for Part-Time Work: An Obstacle to Equal Pay," a report by the Joint Economic Committee, United States Congress, April 20, 2010, http://jec.senate.gov/public/index.cfm?p=Reports1&ContentRecord_id=d6034bc5-9247-4b08-91f3-a41e86b3a0d0 (accessed October 4, 2010).

17. "National Women's Business Council Fact Sheet," National Women's Business Center, January 2010, available at http://www.nwbc.gov/research/FACTS_ISSUES.html (accessed October 4, 2010).

18. Morra Arrons-Mele, "Where Did Mommytracking Come From?" *BlogHer,* May 2, 2010, http://www.blogher.com/where-did-mommytracking-come?from=top (accessed October 4, 2010).

19. Lisa Belkin, "The Opt-Out Revolution," *The New York Times Magazine,* October 26, 2003.

20. Donna St. George, "Most Stay-at-Home Moms Start That Way, Study Finds," *The Washington Post,* October 1, 2009.

21. Elizabeth Gudrais, "Family or Fortune," *Harvard Magazine,* January/February 2010.

22. A reader post by Erin Beaumont in response to "Your Take: Work–Life Balance," *Harvard Magazine* online, December 22, 2009, http://harvardmagazine.com/extras/reader-discussion-work-life-balance?page=1#comments (accessed October 4, 2010).

23. Australian Government, "Australia's Paid Parental Leave Scheme," http://*www.familydaycare.com.au/forms/Aust_paid_parental_leave_scheme.pdf* (accessed October 4, 2010).

24. Jennifer Ludden, "U.S. Only Industrialized Nation with No Paid Leave for New Parents," *The Two-Way,* NPR's News Blog, June 17, 2010, http://www.npr.org/blogs/thetwoway/2010/06/17/127904924/u-s-now-only-industrialized-nation-without-paid-leave-for-new-parents (accessed October 4, 2010).

25. Williams and Boushey, "The Three Faces of Work-Family Conflict" (see no. 14).

26. Katrin Bennhold, "In Sweden, Men Can Have It All," *The New York Times,* June 9, 2010.

27. Kratz, "Taking It Public" (see chap. 9, no. 56).

28. Ilyse Schuman, "Work–Life Balance Award Act Fails," Washington DC Employment Law Update, June 17, 2010, http://www.dcemploymentlawupdate.com/tags/hr-4855 (accessed October 4, 2010).

29. Ellen Galinsky, Kerstin Aumann, and James T. Bond, "Times Are Changing: Gender and Generation at Work and at Home," Families and Work Institute, http://familiesandwork.org/site/research/reports/Times_Are_Changing.pdf (accessed October 4, 2010).

30. Heather Boushey and Joan C.Williams, "Resolving Work–Life Conflicts: Progressives Have Answers," Center for American Progress, March 29, 2010, http://www.americanprogress.org/issues/2010/03/work_life_conflict.html (accessed October 4, 2010).

31. "Michelle Obama's remarks at Workplace Flexibility Conference," *The Washington Post,* March 31, 2010, http://www.washingtonpost.com/wp-dyn/content/article/2010/03/31/AR2010033103642.html (accessed October 4, 2010).

32. "Remarks by the President at Workplace Flexibility Forum," White House press release, March 31, 2010, http://www.whitehouse.gov/the-press-office/remarks-president-workplace-flexibility-forum (accessed October 4, 2010).

33. "52%: Parenting a Priority," Pew Research Center, The Databank, http://pewresearch.org/databank/dailynumber/?NumberID=976 (accessed October 4, 2010).

34. Leslie Gevirtz, "U.S. 'Millennial' Women Believe They Can Have It All," Reuters, January 16, 2010.

35. Richard Fry and D'Vera Cohn, "The New Economics of Marriage: The Rise of Wives," Pew Research Center Publications, January 19, 2010, http://pewresearch.org/pubs/1466/economics-marriage-rise-of-wives (accessed October 4, 2010).

TWELVE **TRAVELING THE REVOLUTIONARY ROAD**

1. Lynn Harris, "Late-Night's Real Problem," Salon, January 10, 2010, http://www.salon.com/life/feature/2010/01/10/women_writers_late_night/index.html (accessed October 4, 2010).

2. Ibid.

3. Gloria Steinem, *Outrageous Acts and Everyday Rebellions* (Holt, Rinehart and Winston, 1983), 19.

4. Harris, "Late-Night's Real Problem" (see no. 1).

5. Clay Shirky, "A Rant about Women," Shirky.com, January 15, 2010, http://www.shirky.com/weblog/2010/01/a-rant-about-women (accessed October 4, 2010).

6. Anna North, "3 Reasons Why Women Can't Be More Like Men," Jezebel, January 18, 2010, http://jezebel.com/5450891/3-reasons-why-women-cant-be-more-like-men (accessed October 4, 2010).

7. Naomi Wolf, "What Price Happiness?" *More,* April 20, 2010, http://www.more.com/2050/13167-what-price-happiness/5 (accessed October 4, 2010).

8. Judy B. Rosener, "Ways Women Lead," *Harvard Business Review* 68, no. 6 (November/December 1990): 119–25.

9. Louann Brizendine, *The Female Brain* (Doubleday Broadway, 2006), 36.

10. Peg Tyre and Julie Scelfo, "Why Girls Will Be Girls," *Newsweek,* July 31, 2006, http://www.msnbc.msn.com/id/13989048/site/newsweek (accessed October 4, 2010).

11. Ibid.

12. Brizendine, *The Female Brain,* 14 (see no. 9).

13. Brizendine, *The Female Brain,* 12 (see no. 9).

14. Brizendine, *The Female Brain,* 13 (see no. 9).

15. Brizendine, *The Female Brain,* 16 (see no. 9).

16. Brizendine, *The Female Brain,* 17 (see no. 9).

17. "The Bottom Line: Connecting Corporate Performance and Gender Diversity." Catalyst, January 2004, http://www.catalyst.org/publication/82/the-bottom-line-connecting-corporate-performance-and-gender-diversity (accessed October 4, 2010).

18. "Innovative Potential: Men and Women in Teams," London Business School: The Lehman Brothers Centre for Women in Business, November 2007, http://www.london.edu/assets/documents/facultyandresearch/Innovative_Potential_NOV_2007.pdf (accessed October 4, 2010).

19. Ylan Q. Mui, "Women a Big Force in Business, Study Finds," *The Washington Post,* October 3, 2009, http://www.washingtonpost.com/wp-dyn/content/article/2009/10/02/AR2009100205317.html (accessed October 4, 2010).

20. Kate Whittle, "Women Clean Up After BP's 'Man-Made' Oil Spill," *Ms.* Magazine Blog, June 2, 2010, http://msmagazine.com/blog/blog/2010/06/02/women-clean-up-after-bps-man-made-oil-spill (accessed October 4, 2010).

21. Ibid.

22. Maureen Tkacik, "Why Corporate Women Are More Likely to Blow the Whistle," *Slate Double X,* July 27, 2009, http://www.doublex.com/section/work/why-corporate-women-are-more-likely-blow-whistle (accessed October 4, 2010).

23. "Persons of the Year," *Time,* December 30, 2002.

24. Tkacik, "Why Corporate Women Are More Likely to Blow the Whistle" (see no. 22).

25. Sylvia Ann Hewlett, "Are Your Best Female Employees a Flight Risk?" *Harvard Business Review* Blogs, October 5, 2009, http://blogs.hbr.org/hbr/hewlett/2009/10/smart_women_stronger_companies.html (accessed October 4, 2010).

26. Sean Silverthorne, "Why Are Women So Unhappy At Work?" *Harvard Business Review* Blogs, October 7, 2009, http://blogs.bnet.com/harvard/?p=3972&tag=nl.e713 (accessed October 4, 2010).

27. Ibid.

28. Ibid.

29. Naomi Wolf, "What Price Happiness?" (see no. 7).

30. Joanne Lipman, "The Mismeasure of a Woman," *The New York Times,* October 23, 2009.

31. Deborah Solomon, "Madame President," *The New York Times Magazine,* August 23, 2009.

32. Cristine Russell, "Girls, Women, and Double Dutch," *The Atlantic,* October 26, 2009, http://www.theatlantic.com/science/archive/2009/10/girls-women-and-double-dutch/29056 (accessed October 4, 2010).

THIRTEEN **HAPPINESS, REROUTED**

1. Jennifer Senior, "All Joy and No Fun: Why Parents Hate Parenting," *New York Magazine,* July 4, 2010.

2. Rebecca Traister, "Screw Happiness," Salon, May 10, 2010, http://www.salon.com/life/feature/2010/05/10/screw_happiness/index.html?source=newsletter (accessed October 4, 2010).

3. Gilbert, *Stumbling on Happiness,* 236 (see chap. 1, no. 12).

4. Sonja Lyubomirsky, *The How of Happiness: A Scientific Approach to Getting the Life You Want* (Penguin, 2008), 64.

5. Po Bronson, *What Should I Do with My Life?,* 434 (see chap. 1, no. 13).

6. Julie Metz, *Perfection: A Memoir of Betrayal and Renewal* (Hyperion, 2009).

7. Arthur A. Stone et al., "A Snapshot of the Age Distribution of Psychological Well-Being in the United States," *PNAS* 107, no. 22 (June 2010): 9985–90.

8. Gretchen Rubin, *The Happiness Project: Or, Why I Spent a Year Trying to Sing in the Morning, Clean My Closets, Fight Right, Read Aristotle, and Generally Have More Fun* (HarperCollins, 2009).

9. Dan Ariely, *The Upside of Irrationality: The Unexpected Benefits of Defying Logic at Work and at Home* (HarperCollins, 2010).

10. P. Brickman and D. T. Campbell, "Hedonic Relativism and Planning the Good Society," in *Adaptation-Level Theory: A Symposium,* ed. M. H. Appley (Academic Press, 1971) 287–302.

11. Daniel Mochon, Michael I. Norton, and Dan Ariely, "Getting Off the Hedonic Treadmill, One Step at a Time: The Impact of Regular Religious Practice and Exercise on Well-Being," *Journal of Economic Psychology* 29 (2008): 632–42.

12. His Holiness the Dalai Lama and Howard C. Cutler, *The Art of Happiness: A Handbook for Living* (Riverhead Books, 1998).

13. Martin E. P. Seligman, *Authentic Happiness: Using the New Positive Psychology to Realize Your Potential for Lasting Fulfillment,* (Free Press, 2002).

14. Dacher Keltner, *Born to Be Good* (see chap. 1, no. 11).

15. Lyubomirsky, *The How of Happiness* (see no. 4).

16. Tal Ben-Shahar, *The Pursuit of Perfect: How to Stop Chasing Perfection and Start Living a Richer, Happier Life* (McGraw Hill, 2009).

17. Stephanie Rosenbloom, "But Will It Make You Happy?" *The New York Times,* August 7, 2010.

18. Adecco, "Top Piece of Advice from Previous College Grads to Class of 2009: Pursue Passion over Money and Job Security," press release, no date, http://adeccousa.com/articles/Top-Piece-of-Advice-from-Previous-College-Grads-to-Class-of-2009:-Pursue-Passion-over-Money-&-Job-Security.html?id=105&url=/pressroom/pressreleases/pages/forms/allitems.aspx&templateurl=/AboutUs/pressroom/Pages/Press-release.aspx (accessed October 4, 2010).

19. Daniel Pink, *A Whole New Mind: Why Right Brainers Will Rule the Future* (Riverhead Books, 2005), 3.

20. Daniel Pink, "Pomp and Circumspect," *The New York Times,* June 4, 2005.

21. Michael Crawford, *Shop Class as Soulcraft* (Penguin Group, 2009), 6.

FOURTEEN **WHEREVER YOU GO, THERE YOU ARE**

1. Allen Salkin, "Seeing Yourself in Their Light," *The New York Times,* September 18, 2009.

2. Elizabeth Lesser, *Broken Open: How Difficult Times Can Help Us Grow* (Villard, 2008), 27.

INDEX

ACKNOWLEDGMENTS

HAVING JUST WRITTEN A BOOK about how to make decisions, one might think we'd be pretty skilled at making them by now. Yeah, not so much. Which made putting together the Who We'd Like to Thank section a little tough. But here we go.

First off, a huge thank you to those people who helped us decide how to turn a good idea into *Undecided*. To our agent, Jessica Papin, at Dystel & Goderich Literary Management; and our editor and publisher, Krista Lyons, at Seal Press: a thousand thank-yous for your faith, encouragement, support, and all of your guidance in developing this project.

We'd also like to thank the legions of undecided women who so freely and honestly shared their stories with us, our colleagues and friends who not only provided insight but pointed us in the direction of relevant research and studies, and every person we spoke to: Whether the conversations took place over email, tape recorder, cocktails, or hike, your assistance was invaluable. And to the many experts we've quoted in this book (including Barry Schwartz, Elizabeth Lesser, Gretchen Rubin, Lori Gottlieb, Judy Rosener, Ellen Galinsky, Susan Bulkeley Butler, Myra Strober, and Ramani Durvasula among others), and who so graciously shared their time and knowledge with us— We can't thank you enough.

We want to thank Tom, Ryan, and Colleen—our family, our enablers—who have been in it with us from the start, and have put up with us rather well.

Most of the time.

Sometimes.

Usually.

Whatever.

And all of our dear friends, who have been so supportive—whether in offering their words, listening to ours, or just realizing (and accepting) that we were kind of crazy for a while there. Or really crazy. To everyone who took the time to ask, "Aren't you writing a book? How's it going?" We noticed. And thanks.

Also, so many—too many to name, but you know who you are— friends, colleagues, and students of Barbara's, who have been so instrumental, thank you. And a special shout out to *Undecided*'s loudest cheerleaders: Silvia, Page, Lotta, Lauren, Leslie, Marisa, Alison, Jobabe, Sue, Tamara, Aly, Bebe and Hill, Valerie and Randy, Kathy and Bill, Roger and Dan, Mark and Barb, Ani, Clean Jean, Tweety, Joy, Nancy, Katie, Sam, Jenny, Hollee, Gail, Harriett, Alice, Andy, Whitney, Heather, Marjorie, Megan, Dana and Dayna, Mary, Trishia, Laura, and Marcus, and everyone who has followed and contributed to our blog.

Also, Shannon wants to thank her dog, Rose, who made her laugh when she just wanted to cry. (Barbara thinks she flunks the sniff test.)

ABOUT THE AUTHORS

BARBARA KELLEY teaches journalism and directs the journalism emphasis at Santa Clara University. As an award-winning freelance journalist, she has written for daily newspapers and their Sunday magazine sections, as well as a variety of national and regional magazines. Among them: the *Christian Science Monitor, San Francisco Chronicle, San Jose Mercury News, Los Angeles Times, Salon, California* magazine, *San Francisco* magazine, *Utne Reader, Health* magazine, *Parenting* magazine, *Redbook, Bay Area Parent,* and *Pacific News Service.*

SHANNON KELLEY is a columnist at the *Santa Barbara Independent,* a freelance writer and photographer, and a corporate consultant. Her work has appeared in the *Christian Science Monitor, Woman's Day,* the *Arizona Republic,* and *Santa Barbara* magazine, and her essay "Something Worth Saving," from the 2008 anthology *Submerged: Tales from the Basin,* was nominated for a Pushcart Prize.

SELECTED TITLES FROM SEAL PRESS

For more than thirty years, Seal Press has published
groundbreaking books. By women. For women.

The Choice Effect: Love and Commitment in an Age of Too Many Options, by
Amalia McGibbon, Lara Vogel, and Claire A. Williams. $16.95, 978-1-58005-
293-1. Three young, successful, and ambitious women provide insight into the
quarterlife angst that surrounds dating and relationships and examine why
more options equals less commitment for today's twentysomethings.

Wanderlust: A Love Affair with Five Continents, by Elisabeth Eaves. $16.95,
978-1-58005-311-2. Documents Elisabeth Eaves's insatiable hunger for the
rush of the unfamiliar and the experience of encountering new people and
cultures as a young woman traveling the world.

*Just Don't Call Me Ma'am: How I Ditched the South for the Big City, Forgot
My Manners, and Managed to Survive My Twenties with (Most of) My Dignity
Still Intact,* by Anna Mitchael. $15.95, 978-1-58005-316-7. In this disarmingly
funny tale about the choices that add up to be her twentysomething life, Anna
Mitchael offers young women comic relief—with the reality check that there's
no possible way to hit all of their desired benchmarks on the way to thirty.

*The Anti 9-to-5 Guide: Practical Career Advice for Women Who Think Out-
side the Cube,* by Michelle Goodman. $14.95, 978-1-58005-186-6. Escape the
wage-slave trap of your cubicle with Goodman's hip career advice on creating
your dream job and navigating the work world without compromising your
aspirations.

*The Boss of You: Everything a Woman Needs to Know to Start, Run, and Maintain
Her Own Business,* by Emira Mears & Lauren Bacon. $15.95, 978-1-58005-
236-8. Provides women entrepreneurs the advice, guidance, and straightfor-
ward how-to's they need to start, run, and maintain a business.

Two Is Enough: A Couple's Guide to Living Childless by Choice, by Laura S.
Scott. $16.95, 978-1-58005-263-4. Childless by Choice Project founder Laura
S. Scott explores the assumptions surrounding childrearing and the reasons
many couples are choosing to forgo this experience.

FIND SEAL PRESS ONLINE
www.SealPress.com
www.Facebook.com/SealPress
Twitter: @SealPress